AN ANTHOLOGY OF VERSE

AN ANTHOLOGY OF VERSE

Edited by
Roberta A. Charlesworth
& Dennis Lee

TORONTO OXFORD UNIVERSITY PRESS

The editors are grateful to DONNA LEE *for much assistance in the preparation of this book, and for her illumination of a number of difficulties that were encountered on the way.*

9 10 11 12 13 — 6 5 4 3 2

Printed in Canada by
THE BRYANT PRESS LIMITED

Contents

Preface

This anthology is more than a collection of poems to be studied by senior students. It is a reading anthology designed to excite the imagination and interest of the student so that he will be drawn to read the poems for their own sake, and in doing so come to his own understanding of poetry.

The selection of poems provides a careful balance of British, American, and Canadian authors, from the early periods of literature to the present day. All the major periods of literary history have been represented. The most generous single selection is from the twentieth century – in part because many of the best North American poets wrote within the last sixty years, in part because the best cure for the awe and mistrust with which many readers approach modern poetry is to present, with explanation, a cross-section of the more imaginative and engaging modern poems.

As well as the poems found in many of the standard anthologies, there are passages of poetic prose, long poems and groups of very short ones, humorous poems and denunciatory poems, light verse and difficult poems, all of which provide a wide range of subject matter and refreshing changes of pace and intensity. Many different groups of readers have been kept in mind, and a sufficiently large number of poems has been provided for each.

The basic pattern of the book owes its inspiration to the structure used with such effect in the *Sheldon Books of Verse,* compiled by P. G. Smith and J. F. Wilkins. This pattern is not purely thematic; rather, the arrangement of the selections draws the reader by a natural thread of association from poem to poem. For example, a poem dealing with a particular theme may be followed by another which echoes the theme in a contrasting poetic form, and which is in turn followed by a poem related in mood. A number of serious poems may be contrasted with a nonsense poem; a pure lyric may be followed by a tragic poem or witty invective; love poetry may be set off by a satire. A series of poems may rely on related techniques, or may be by one author who uses a distinctive style. The poems are indexed by subject and form, period, author, title, and first line, permitting chronological or biographical study, or the study of various poetic forms.

The annotations and biographical notes provide essential information; they seek to avoid those ready-made judgements which might limit the reader's response. Each natural transition in the pattern of the poems is marked by the appearance in the notes of a number of questions which can be used to illuminate a group of poems or one or more poems within the group. The notes on the techniques of poetry and on the kinds of poetry have been expanded beyond mere identification, since the intent of the anthology is to provide a basis for intelligent appreciation. It is hoped that the two well-known essays on poetry, 'How Does A Poem Mean?' by John Ciardi and 'Modern Poetry and the Plain Reader's Rights' by Robert Graves, will complement the discussion and analysis of some of the techniques of modern poetry, and will be of value in the study of poetry in high school.

Acknowledgements

The publishers and editors are grateful for permission to reproduce the copyright poems by the following authors.

MILTON ACORN: 'The Fights'. Reprinted from *The Brain's the Target* by Milton Acorn, by permission of The Ryerson Press, Toronto.

MARTIN ARMSTRONG: 'Mrs Reece Laughs' by permission of the author.

W. H. AUDEN: 'Look Stranger', 'The Average', 'The Unknown Citizen', 'True Love'. Faber & Faber Ltd.

MARGARET AVISON: 'The Swimmer's Moment' from *Winter Sun*. Routledge & Kegan Paul Ltd.

PATRICK BARRINGTON: 'I had a Duck-Billed Platypus'. © *Punch*, London.

HILAIRE BELLOC: 'On His Books'. By permission of Mr A. D. Peters.

JOHN BETJEMAN: 'A Subaltern's Love Song' from *Collected Poems*. John Murray.

EARLE BIRNEY: 'Dusk on English Bay' by permission of the author.

ROBERT BRIDGES: 'I Love All Beauteous Things' from *The Shorter Poems of Robert Bridges,* by permission of the Clarendon Press, Oxford.

RUPERT BROOKE: 'Fishes' Heaven', 'The Hill'. McClelland & Stewart Ltd.

ROY CAMPBELL: 'Song of the Horseman' from *Lorca: An Appreciation of His Poetry*. Bowes & Bowes.

BLISS CARMAN: 'Low Tide on Grand Pré' from *The Selected Poems of Bliss Carman*. McClelland & Stewart Ltd.

JOHN CIARDI: *The Inferno, Canto III*. Copyright 1954 by John Ciardi. Reprinted by permission of the author.

LEONARD COHEN: 'Go by Brooks' from *The Spice-Box of Earth*. McClelland & Stewart Ltd.

FRANCES CORNFORD: 'To a Fat Lady Seen from the Train' from *Collected Poems*. The Cresset Press.

E. E. CUMMINGS: 'anyone lived in a pretty how town'. Copyright, 1940, by E. E. Cummings. Reprinted from his volume *Poems 1923-1954* by permission of Harcourt, Brace & World, Inc.

WALTER DE LA MARE: 'All That's Past', 'Echo', 'The Song of the Mad Prince'. The Literary Trustees of Walter de la Mare and the Society of Authors as their representative.

EMILY DICKINSON: 'Apparently with No Surprise', 'I Taste a Liquor Never Brewed', 'The Last Night that She Lived'. Reprinted by permission of the publishers and the Trustees of Amherst College from *The Poems of Emily Dickinson* edited by Thomas H. Johnson; Cambridge, Mass.: The Belknap Press of Harvard University Press; copyright 1951, 1955 by The President & Fellows of Harvard College.

EMILY DICKINSON: 'A Route of Evanescence', 'Within My Garden Rides a Bird, from *The Complete Poems of Emily Dickinson* by permission of Little, Brown and Co. 'Within My Garden Rides a Bird' copyright 1929, © 1957 by Mary L. Hampson.

AUSTIN DOBSON: 'A Kiss' from *The Poetical Works of Austin Dobson* by permission of A. T. A. Dobson and Oxford University Press.

T. S. ELIOT: Chorus from *Murder in the Cathedral,* 'The Hollow Men', 'The Love Song of J. Alfred Prufrock'. Faber & Faber Ltd.

JAMES ELROY FLECKER: 'To a Poet a Thousand Years Hence'. J. M. Dent & Sons Ltd.

ROBERT FROST: 'Death of the Hired Man', 'Departmental', 'Stopping by Woods on a Snowy Evening' from *Complete Poems of Robert Frost*. Copyright 1923, 1930, 1939 by Holt, Rinehart and Winston, Inc. Copyright 1936 by Robert Frost. Copyright renewed 1951 by Robert Frost. Reprinted by permission of Holt, Rinehart and Winston, Inc., New York.

THOM GUNN: 'On the Move'. Faber & Faber Ltd.

THOMAS HARDY: 'Great Things', 'In Time of "The Breaking of Nations" ', 'The Darkling Thrush'. Reprinted from *Collected Poems of Thomas Hardy* by permission of Macmillan & Co. Ltd., and The Macmillan Company of Canada Limited.

HAROLD HENDERSON: 'In Exile', 'The Apprentice Priestling' from *An Introduction to Haiku* by Harold G. Henderson. Copyright © 1958 by Harold G. Henderson. Reprinted by permission of Doubleday & Company, Inc.

PAUL HIEBERT: 'Hymn to Rover' from *Sarah Binks*. Oxford University Press (Canadian Branch).

RALPH HODGSON: 'Reason has Moons' reprinted from *Collected Poems* by Ralph Hodgson by permission of Macmillan & Co. Ltd., and The Macmillan Company of Canada Limited.

GERARD MANLEY HOPKINS: 'Hurrahing in Harvest' from *Poems of Gerard Manley Hopkins* by permission of Oxford University Press.

A. E. HOUSMAN: 'Eight O'Clock', 'Fancy's Knell', 'Her Strong

Enchantments Failing', 'On Wenlock Edge' from *The Collected Poems of A. E. Housman*. The Executors of the A. E. Housman Estate and Jonathan Cape Ltd.

LANGSTON HUGHES: 'Little Green Tree', 'Snail'. Reprinted from *Selected Poems* by Langston Hughes, by permission of Alfred A. Knopf, Inc. 'Little Green Tree' copyright 1948 by Alfred A. Knopf, Inc. 'Snail' copyright 1947 by Langston Hughes.

TED HUGHES: 'Hawk Roosting'. Faber & Faber Ltd.

RANDALL JARRELL: 'The Truth' from *Seven-League Crutches* by Randall Jarrell. Copyright, 1951, by Harcourt, Brace & World, Inc. and reprinted with their permission.

GEORGE JOHNSTON: 'War on the Periphery' by permission of the author and *The New Yorker*. Copyright © 1951 The New Yorker Magazine, Inc.

JAMES JOYCE: 'I Hear an Army Charging upon the Land' from *Chamber Music*. The Executors of the James Joyce Estate and Jonathan Cape.

JAMES JOYCE: Lines from *Finnegan's Wake* by James Joyce. Copyright 1939 by James Joyce. Reprinted by permission of The Viking Press, Inc.

RUDYARD KIPLING: 'Cities and Thrones and Powers' reprinted from *Puck of Pooks Hill* by Rudyard Kipling by permission of Mrs George Bambridge and The Macmillan Company of Canada Limited.

ABRAHAM KLEIN: 'Autobiographical'. Copyright, 1951 by A. M. Klein. Reprinted from *The Second Scroll* by permission of Alfred A. Knopf, Inc.

PHILIP LARKIN: 'Church Going'. Reprinted from *The Less Deceived* by permission of The Marvell Press, Hessle, Yorkshire.

RICHMOND LATTIMORE: Lines from *The Iliad, Book IV.* The University of Chicago Press. Copyright 1951 by the University of Chicago.

D. H. LAWRENCE: 'Giorno Dei Morti', 'Snake'. Laurence Pollinger Limited and the Estate of the late Mrs Frieda Lawrence.

IRVING LAYTON: 'The Birth of Tragedy', 'The Cold Green Element' from *A Red Carpet for the Sun.* McClelland and Stewart Ltd.

ROBERT LOWELL: 'Home after Three Months Away' reprinted from *Life Studies* by Robert Lowell, by permission of Farrar, Straus & Company, Inc. Copyright © 1956, 1959 by Robert Lowell.

MALCOLM LOWRY: 'Kingfishers in British Columbia' by permission of Earle Birney.

LOUIS MACKAY: Lines reprinted from *The Ill-Tempered Lover* by Louis Mackay, by permission of The Ryerson Press, Toronto.

ARCHIBALD MACLEISH: 'Epistle to be Left in the Earth' from *Collected Poems: 1917-1952.* Houghton Mifflin Company.

LOUIS MACNEICE: 'Snow' from *Collected Poems.* Faber & Faber Ltd.

JAY MACPHERSON: 'Cold Stone' from *The Boatman.* Oxford University Press (Canadian Branch).

DON MARQUIS: 'Cheerio my Deario' from *Archy and Mehitabel* by Don Marquis. Copyright 1927 by Doubleday & Company, Inc. Reprinted by permission of the publisher.

PHYLLIS MCGINLEY: 'Girl's-Eye View of Relatives' from *Times Three* by Phyllis McGinley. Copyright 1959 by Phyllis McGinley. First published in *The New Yorker.* Reprinted by permission of The Viking Press, Inc.

MARIANNE MOORE: 'Silence'. Reprinted with permission of The Macmillan Company from *Selected Poems* by Marianne Moore. Copyright 1935 by Marianne Moore, renewed 1963 by Marianne Moore and T. S. Eliot.

EDNA ST VINCENT MILLAY: 'Dirge without Music' from *Collected Poems,* Harper & Row. Copyright 1928, 1955 by Edna St Vincent Millay and Norma Millay Ellis.

J. B. MORTON: 'The Dancing Cabman' by permission of the author.

OGDEN NASH: 'No Doctors Today, Thank You', 'Reflections on Ice-Breaking' from *Verses from 1929 on* by Ogden Nash, by permission of Little, Brown and Co. 'No Doctors Today, Thank You' copyright 1942 by Ogden Nash, originally appeared in *The New Yorker.* 'Reflections on Ice-Breaking' copyright 1930, © 1958 by Odgen Nash, originally appeared in *The New Yorker.*

WILFRED OWEN: 'Anthem for Doomed Youth', 'Strange Meeting' from *Poems.* Chatto & Windus, Ltd.

MERVYN PEAKE: 'The Cocky Walkers' from *Shapes and Sounds.* Chatto & Windus, Ltd.

MARJORIE PICKTHALL: 'St Yves' Poor' from *The Selected Poems of Marjorie Pickthall.* McClelland & Stewart Ltd.

EZRA POUND: Lines from *The Cantos of Ezra Pound,* 'In a Station of the Metro', 'Salutation', 'The River Merchant's Wife: A Letter' reprinted by permission of New Directions, Publishers. Lines from *The Cantos of Ezra Pound* copyright 1948 by Ezra Pound. 'In a Station of the Metro' and 'The River Merchant's Wife: A Letter' copyright 1926, 1954, by Ezra Pound. 'Salutation' from *Personae: The Collected Poems of Ezra Pound,* copyright 1926, 1954 by Ezra Pound.

E. J. PRATT: 'Erosion', 'The Iceberg' from *The Titanic,* 'The Prize Cat' reprinted from *Collected Poems* by E. J. Pratt by permission of The Macmillan Company of Canada Limited.

WALTER RALEIGH: 'Wishes of an Elderly Man at a Garden Party'. Constable & Co., Ltd.

JAMES REANEY: Lines from *A Suit of Nettles* by permission of Sybil Hutchinson.

CHARLES G. D. ROBERTS: 'In the Wide Awe and Wisdom of the Night', 'The Mowing', 'The Unsleeping'. Reprinted from *Selected Poems of Charles G. D. Roberts* by permission of The Ryerson Press, Toronto.

EDWIN ARLINGTON ROBINSON: 'Richard Cory'. Reprinted with the permission of Charles Scribner's Sons from *The Children of the Night* by Edwin Arlington Robinson (1897).

THEODORE ROETHKE: 'A Field of Light'. Copyright 1948 by Theodore Roethke from *Lost Son and Other Poems.* Reprinted by permission of Doubleday & Company, Inc.

V. SACKVILLE-WEST: Lines from 'The Land' by permission of Sir Harold Nicolson.

CARL SANDBURG: 'Night Bells'. Copyright, 1950, by Carl Sandburg. Reprinted from his volume *Complete Poems* by permission of Harcourt, Brace & World, Inc.

EDITH SITWELL: 'Green Flows the River of Lethe–O' from *Collected Poems.* David Higham Associates, Ltd.

A. J. M. SMITH: Lines from 'The Lonely Land' from *Collected Poems.* Oxford University Press (Canadian Branch).

RAYMOND SOUSTER: 'Top Hat' by permission of the author.

STEPHEN SPENDER: 'I Think Continually'. Faber & Faber Ltd.

JAMES STEPHENS: 'A Glass of Beer', 'What the Devil Said'. Reprinted from *Collected Poems* by James Stephens by permission of Mrs Iris Wise, Macmillan & Co. Ltd., London, and The Macmillan Company of Canada Limited.

WALLACE STEVENS: 'Domination of Black'. Reprinted from *The Collected Poems of Wallace Stevens* by permission of Alfred A. Knopf, Inc. Copyright, 1923, 1951 by Wallace Stevens.

J. M. SYNGE: 'An Old Woman's Lamentations' from *Villon.* George Allen & Unwin Ltd.

A. S. J. TESSIMOND: 'Cats' by permission of Hubert Nicholson.

DYLAN THOMAS: 'And Death Shall Have no Dominion', 'Fern Hill', lines from *Under Milk Wood.* J. M. Dent & Sons Ltd.

R. S. THOMAS: 'A Peasant'. Rupert Hart-Davis, Ltd.

GAEL TURNBULL: 'An Irish Monk on Lindisfarne, about 650 A.D.', by permission of the author.

ARTHUR WALEY: 'Plucking the Rushes' from *A Hundred and Seventy Chinese Poems.* Constable & Co., Ltd.

ANNE WILKINSON: 'Carol'. The Anne C. Wilkinson Estate.

WILLIAM CARLOS WILLIAMS: 'Raleigh was Right'. Reprinted by permission of New Directions, Publishers. Copyright 1944, 1963 by William Carlos Williams.

W. B. YEATS: Lines from 'A Dialogue of Self and Soul', 'A Drunken Man's Praise of Sobriety', 'Death', 'The Fisherman'. Reprinted from *Collected Poems of W. B. Yeats* by permission of Mrs W. B. Yeats and The Macmillan Company of Canada Limited and Macmillan & Co. Ltd.

YEVGENY YEVTUSHENKO: 'Birthday' from *Selected Poems of Yevtushenko* translated by Robin Milner-Gulland and Peter Levi. Penguin Books Ltd.

'Jesse James' is taken from *The American Songbag,* compiled by Carl Sandburg and published by Harcourt, Brace & World, Inc.

'Good Mornin' Blues'. New words and new music arranged by Huddie Ledbetter. Edited with new additional material by Alan Lomax. © Copyright 1959 Folkways Music Publishers, Inc., New York, N.Y. Used by permission.

A List of the Poems

IN NUMERICAL ORDER

1

Fern Hill

Now as I was young and easy under the apple boughs
About the lilting house and happy as the grass was green,
The night above the dingle starry,
Time let me hail and climb
Golden in the heydays of his eyes,
And honoured among wagons I was prince of the apple
towns
And once below a time I lordly had the trees and leaves
Trail with daisies and barley
Down the rivers of the windfall light. 9

And as I was green and carefree, famous among the barns
About the happy yard and singing as the farm was home,
In the sun that is young once only,
Time let me play and be
Golden in the mercy of his means,
And green and golden I was huntsman and herdsman, the
calves
Sang to my horn, the foxes on the hills barked clear and
cold,
And the sabbath rang slowly
In the pebbles of the holy streams.

All the sun long it was running, it was lovely, the hay
Fields high as the house, the tunes from the chimneys, it
was air 20
And playing, lovely and watery
And fire green as grass.
And nightly under the simple stars

As I rode to sleep the owls were bearing the farm away,
All the moon long I heard, blessed among stables, the
    nightjars
  Flying with the ricks, and the horses
    Flashing into the dark.

And then to awake, and the farm, like a wanderer white
With the dew, come back, the cock on his shoulder: it
    was all
  Shining, it was Adam and maiden, 30
    The sky gathered again
  And the sun grew round that very day.
So it must have been after the birth of the simple light
In the first, spinning place, the spellbound horses walking
    warm
  Out of the whinnying green stable
    On to the fields of praise.

And honoured among foxes and pheasants by the gay house
Under the new made clouds and happy as the heart was
    long,
  In the sun born over and over,
    I ran my heedless ways, 40
  My wishes raced through the house high hay
And nothing I cared, at my sky blue trades, that time allows
In all his tuneful turning so few and such morning songs
  Before the children green and golden
    Follow him out of grace,

Nothing I cared, in the lamb white days, that time would
    take me
Up to the swallow thronged loft by the shadow of my hand,
  In the moon that is always rising,

Nor that riding to sleep
I should hear him fly with the high fields 50
And wake to the farm forever fled from the childless land.
Oh as I was young and easy in the mercy of his means,
Time held me green and dying
Though I sang in my chains like the sea.

DYLAN THOMAS

2

Look, Stranger

Look, stranger, at this island now
The leaping light for your delight discovers,
Stand stable here
And silent be,
That through the channels of the ear
May wander like a river
The swaying sound of the sea.

Here at the small field's ending pause
Where the chalk wall falls to the foam, and its tall ledges
Oppose the pluck
And knock of the tide,
And the shingle scrambles after the sucking surf, and the
gull lodges
A moment on its sheer side.

Far off like floating seeds the ships
Diverge on urgent voluntary errands;
And the full view
Indeed may enter
And move in memory as now these clouds do,
That pass the harbour mirror
And all the summer through the water saunter.

W. H. AUDEN

3

There Was a Boy

FROM *The Prelude*

There was a Boy: ye knew him well, ye cliffs
And islands of Winander! – many a time
At evening, when the earliest stars began
To move along the edges of the hills,
Rising or setting, would he stand alone
Beneath the trees or by the glimmering lake,
And there, with fingers interwoven, both hands
Pressed closely palm to palm, and to his mouth
Uplifted, he, as through an instrument,
Blew mimic hootings to the silent owls, 10
That they might answer him; and they would shout
Across the watery vale, and shout again,
Responsive to his call, with quivering peals,
And long halloos and screams, and echoes loud,
Redoubled and redoubled, concourse wild
Of jocund din; and, when a lengthened pause
Of silence came and baffled his best skill,
Then sometimes, in that silence while he hung
Listening, a gentle shock of mild surprise
Has carried far into his heart the voice 20
Of mountain torrents; or the visible scene
Would enter unawares into his mind,
With all its solemn imagery, its rocks,
Its woods, and that uncertain heaven, received
Into the bosom of the steady lake.

WILLIAM WORDSWORTH

4

Sonnet

The World is too much with us; late and soon,
Getting and spending, we lay waste our powers;
Little we see in Nature that is ours;
We have given our hearts away, a sordid boon!
This Sea that bares her bosom to the moon,
The winds that will be howling at all hours
And are up-gather'd now like sleeping flowers,
For this, for everything, we are out of tune;
It moves us not. – Great God! I'd rather be
A Pagan suckled in a creed outworn, –
So might I, standing on this pleasant lea,
Have glimpses that would make me less forlorn;
Have sight of Proteus rising from the sea;
Or hear old Triton blow his wreathèd horn.

WILLIAM WORDSWORTH

5

To a Fat Lady Seen from the Train

O why do you walk through the fields in gloves,
   Missing so much and so much?
O fat white woman whom nobody loves,
Why do you walk through the fields in gloves,
When the grass is soft as the breast of doves
   And shivering-sweet to the touch?
O why do you walk through the fields in gloves,
   Missing so much and so much?

FRANCES CORNFORD

6

Autobiographical

Out of the ghetto streets where a Jewboy
Dreamed pavement into pleasant Bible-land,
Out of the Yiddish slums where childhood met
The friendly beard, the loutish Sabbath-goy,
Or followed, proud, the Torah-escorting band,
Out of the jargoning city I regret,
Rise memories, like sparrows rising from
The gutter-scattered oats,
Like sadness sweet of synagogal hum,
Like Hebrew violins 10
Sobbing delight upon their Eastern notes.

Again they ring their little bells, those doors
Deemed by the tender-year'd, magnificent:
Old Ashkenazi's cellar, sharp with spice;
The widows' double-parloured candy-stores
And nuggets sweet bought for one sweaty cent;
The warm fresh-smelling bakery, its pies,
Its cakes, its navel'd bellies of black bread;
The lintels candy-poled
Of barber-shop, bright-bottled, green, blue, red; 20
And fruit-stall piled, exotic,
And the big synagogue door, with letters of gold.

Again my kindergarten home is full –
Saturday night – with kin and compatriot:
My brothers playing Russian card-games; my
Mirroring sisters looking beautiful,
Humming the evening's imminent fox-trot;
My uncle Mayer, of blessed memory,

Still murmuring maariv, counting holy words;
And the two strangers, come 30
Fiery from Volhynia's murderous hordes –
The cards and humming stop.
And I too swear revenge for that pogrom.

Occasions dear: the four-legged aleph named
And angel pennies dropping on my book;
The rabbi patting a coming scholar-head;
My mother, blessing candles, Sabbath-flamed,
Queenly in her Warsovian perruque;
My father pickabacking me to bed
To tell tall tales about the Baal Shem Tov – 40
Letting me curl his beard.
Oh memory of unsurpassing love,
Love leading a brave child
Through childhood's ogred corridors, unfear'd!

The week in the country at my brother's – (May
He own fat cattle in the fields of heaven!)
Its picking of strawberries from grassy ditch,
Its odour of dogrose and of yellowing hay –
Dusty, adventurous, sunny days, all seven! –
Still follow me, still warm me, still are rich 50
With the cow-tinkling peace of pastureland.
The meadow'd memory
Is sodded with its clover, and is spanned
By that same pillow'd sky
A boy on his back one day watched enviously.

And paved again the street: the shouting boys,
Oblivious of mothers on the stoops,
Playing the robust robbers and police,

The corncob battle – all high-spirited noise
Competitive among the lot-drawn groups. 60
Another day, of shaken apple trees
In the rich suburbs, and a furious dog,
And guilty boys in flight;
Hazlenut games, and games in the synagogue –
The burrs, the Haman rattle,
The Torah dance on Simchas Torah night.

Immortal days of the picture calendar
Dear to me always with the virgin joy
Of the first flowering of senses five,
Discovering birds, or textures, or a star, 70
Or tastes sweet, sour, acid, those that cloy;
And perfumes. Never was I more alive.
All days thereafter are a dying off,
A wandering away
From home and the familiar. The years doff
Their innocence.
No other day is ever like that day.

I am no old man fatuously intent
On memoirs, but in memory I seek
The strength and vividness of nonage days, 80
Not tranquil recollection of event.
It is a fabled city that I seek;
It stands in Space's vapours and Time's haze;
Thence comes my sadness in remembered joy
Constrictive of the throat;
Thence do I hear, as heard by a Jewboy,
The Hebrew violins,
Delighting in the sobbed Oriental note.

ABRAHAM KLEIN

7

Home Thoughts from Abroad

Oh, to be in England
Now that April's there,
And whoever wakes in England
Sees, some morning, unaware,
That the lowest boughs and the brushwood sheaf
Round the elm-tree bole are in tiny leaf,
While the chaffinch sings on the orchard bough
In England – now!
And after April, when May follows,
And the whitethroat builds, and all the swallows!
Hark, where my blossomed pear-tree in the hedge
Leans to the field and scatters on the clover
Blossoms and dewdrops – at the bent spray's edge –
That's the wise thrush; he sings each song twice over,
Lest you should think he never could recapture
The first fine careless rapture!
And though the fields look rough with hoary dew,
All will be gay when noontide wakes anew
The buttercups, the little children's dower
– Far brighter than this gaudy melon-flower.

ROBERT BROWNING

8

Snake

A snake came to my water-trough
On a hot, hot day, and I in pyjamas for the heat,
To drink there.

In the deep, strange-scented shade of the great dark
carob-tree
I came down the steps with my pitcher
And must wait, must stand and wait, for there he was at the
trough before me.

He reached down from a fissure in the earth-wall in the
gloom
And trailed his yellow-brown slackness soft-bellied down,
over the edge of the stone trough
And rested his throat upon the stone bottom,
And where the water had dripped from the tap, in a small
clearness, 10
He sipped with his straight mouth,
Softly drank through his straight gums, into his slack long
body,
Silently.

Someone was before me at my water-trough,
And I, like a second-comer, waiting.

He lifted his head from his drinking, as cattle do,
And looked at me vaguely, as drinking cattle do,
And flickered his two-forked tongue from his lips, and
mused a moment,

And stooped and drank a little more,
Being earth-brown, earth-golden from the burning bowels of
    the earth   20
On the day of Sicilian July, with Etna smoking.

The voice of my education said to me
He must be killed,
For in Sicily the black, black snakes are innocent, the gold
    are venomous.

And voices in me said, If you were a man
You would take a stick and break him now, and finish him
    off.

But must I confess how I liked him,
How glad I was he had come like a guest in quiet, to drink
    at my water-trough
And depart peaceful, pacified, and thankless,
Into the burning bowels of this earth?   30

Was it cowardice, that I dared not kill him?
Was it perversity, that I longed to talk to him?
Was it humility, to feel honoured?
I felt so honoured.

And yet those voices:
If you were not afraid, you would kill him!

And truly I was afraid, I was most afraid,
But even so, honoured still more
That he should seek my hospitality
From out the dark door of the secret earth.   40

He drank enough
And lifted his head, dreamily, as one who has drunken,
And flickered his tongue like a forked night on the air,
so black,
Seeming to lick his lips,
And looked around like a god, unseeing, into the air,
And slowly turned his head,
And slowly, very slowly, as if thrice adream,
Proceeded to draw his slow length curving round
And climb again the broken bank of my wall-face.

And as he put his head into that dreadful hole, 50
And as he slowly drew up, snake-easing his shoulders, and
entered farther,
A sort of horror, a sort of protest against his withdrawing
into that horrid black hole,
Deliberately going into the blackness, and slowly drawing
himself after,
Overcame me now his back was turned.

I looked round, I put down my pitcher,
I picked up a clumsy log
And threw it at the water-trough with a clatter.

I think it did not hit him,
But suddenly that part of him that was left behind
convulsed in undignified haste,
Writhed like lightning, and was gone 60
Into the black hole, the earth-lipped fissure in the
wall-front,
At which, in the intense still noon, I stared with fascination.

And immediately I regretted it.
I thought how paltry, how vulgar, what a mean act!
I despised myself and the voices of my accursèd human
    education.

And I thought of the albatross,
And I wished he would come back, my snake.

For he seemed to me again like a king,
Like a king in exile, uncrowned in the underworld,
Now due to be crowned again. 70

And so, I missed my chance with one of the lords
Of life.
And I have something to expiate;
A pettiness.

D. H. LAWRENCE

9

A Field of Light

1

Came to lakes; came to dead water,
Ponds with moss and leaves floating,
Planks sunk in the sand.

A log turned at the touch of a foot;
A long weed floated upward;
An eye tilted.

Small winds made
A chilly noise;
The softest cove
Cried for sound. 10

Reached for a grape
And the leaves changed;
A stone's shape
Became a clam.

A fine rain fell
On fat leaves;
I was there alone
In a watery drowse.

2

Angel within me, I asked,
Did I ever curse the sun? 20
Speak and abide.

Under, under the sheaves,
Under the blackened leaves,
Behind the green viscid trellis,
In the deep grass at the edge of a field,
Along the low ground dry only in August, —

Was it dust I was kissing?
A sigh came far.
Alone, I kissed the skin of a stone;
Marrow-soft, danced in the sand. 30

3

The dirt left my hand, visitor.
I could feel the mare's nose.
A path went walking.
The sun glittered on a small rapids.
Some morning thing came, beating its wings.
The great elm filled with birds.

Listen, love,
The fat lark sang in the field;
I touched the ground, the ground warmed by the
killdeer,
The salt laughed and the stones; 40
The ferns had their ways, and the pulsing lizards,
And the new plants, still awkward in their soil,
The lovely diminutives.

I could watch! I could watch!
I saw the separateness of all things!
My heart lifted up with the great grasses;
The weeds believed me, and the nesting birds.
There were clouds making a rout of shapes crossing a
windbreak of cedars,

And a bee shaking drops from a rain-soaked honeysuckle.
The worms were delighted as wrens. 50
And I walked, I walked through the light air;
I moved with the morning.

THEODORE ROETHKE

10

The Lonely Land

Cedar and jagged fir
uplift sharp barbs
against the gray
and cloud-piled sky;
and in the bay
blown spume and windrift
and thin, bitter spray
snap
at the whirling sky;
and the pine trees 10
lean one way.

A wild duck calls
to her mate,
and the ragged
and passionate tones
stagger and fall,
and recover,
and stagger and fall,
on these stones —
are lost 20
in the lapping of water
on smooth, flat stones.

This is a beauty
of dissonance,
this resonance
of stony strand,
this smoky cry
curled over a black pine
like a broken
and wind-battered branch 30

when the wind
bends the tops of the pines
and curdles the sky
from the north.

This is the beauty
of strength
broken by strength
and still strong.

A. J. M. SMITH

11

Shepherds and Stars

FROM

The Land

Shepherds and stars are quiet with the hills,
There is a bond between the men who go
From youth about the business of the earth,
And the earth they serve, their cradle and their grave;
Stars with the seasons alter; only he
Who wakeful follows the pricked revolving sky,
Turns concordant with the earth while others sleep;
To him the dawn is punctual; to him
The quarters of the year no empty name.
A loutish life, but in the midst of dark
Cut to a gash of beauty, as when the hawk
Bears upwards in its talons the striking snake,
High, and yet higher, till those two hang close,
Sculptural on the blue, together twined,
Exalted, deathly, silent, and alone.

V. SACKVILLE-WEST

12

The Shepherd To His Love

Come live with me and be my Love,
And we will all the pleasures prove
That hills and valleys, dale and field,
And all the craggy mountains yield.

There will we sit upon the rocks
And see the shepherds feed their flocks,
By shallow rivers, to whose falls
Melodious birds sing madrigals.

There will I make thee beds of roses
And a thousand fragrant posies,
A cap of flowers, and a kirtle
Embroidered all with leaves of myrtle.

A gown made of the finest wool,
Which from our pretty lambs we pull,
Fair lined slippers for the cold,
With buckles of the purest gold.

A belt of straw and ivy buds
With coral clasps and amber studs:
And if these pleasures may thee move,
Come live with me and be my Love.

Thy silver dishes for thy meat
As precious as the gods do eat

Shall on an ivory table be
Prepared each day for thee and me.

The shepherd swains shall dance and sing
For thy delight each May-morning:
If these delights thy mind may move,
Then live with me and be my Love.

CHRISTOPHER MARLOWE

13

The Nymph's Reply

If all the world and love were young,
And truth in every shepherd's tongue,
These pretty pleasures might me move
To live with thee, and be thy Love.

But Time drives flocks from field to fold,
When rivers rage and rocks grow cold;
And Philomel becometh dumb;
The rest complain of cares to come.

The flowers do fade, and wanton fields
To wayward Winter reckoning yields:
A honey tongue, a heart of gall,
Is fancy's spring, but sorrow's fall.

Thy gowns, thy shoes, thy beds of roses,
Thy cap, thy kirtle, and thy posies,
Soon break, soon wither, – soon forgotten,
In folly ripe, in reason rotten.

Thy belt of straw and ivy-buds,
Thy coral clasps and amber studs, –
All these in me no means can move
To come to thee and be thy Love.

But could youth last, and love still breed,
Had joys no date, nor age no need,
Then these delights my mind might move
To live with thee and be thy Love.

SIR WALTER RALEGH

14

Raleigh Was Right

We cannot go to the country
for the country will bring us no peace.
What can the small violets tell us
that grow on furry stems in
the long grass among lance shaped leaves?

Though you praise us
and call to mind the poets
who sung of our loveliness
it was long ago!
long ago! when country people
would plough and sow with
flowering minds and pockets at ease —
if ever this were true.

Not now. Love itself a flower
with roots in a parched ground.
Empty pockets make empty heads.
Cure it if you can but
do not believe that we can live
today in the country
for the country will bring us no peace.

WILLIAM CARLOS WILLIAMS

15

The Village Master

FROM

The Deserted Village

Beside yon straggling fence that skirts the way,
With blossom'd furze unprofitably gay,
There, in his noisy mansion, skill'd to rule,
The village master taught his little school.
A man severe he was, and stern to view;
I knew him well, and every truant knew;
Well had the boding tremblers learn'd to trace
The day's disasters in his morning face;
Full well they laugh'd with counterfeited glee
At all his jokes, for many a joke had he; 10
Full well the busy whisper circling round
Convey'd the dismal tidings when he frown'd.
Yet he was kind, or, if severe in aught,
The love he bore to learning was in fault;
The village all declar'd how much he knew;
'Twas certain he could write and cypher too:
Lands he could measure, terms and tides presage,
And even the story ran that he could gauge:
In arguing, too, the parson own'd his skill,
For, even though vanquish'd, he could argue still; 20
While words of learned length and thundering sound
Amazed the gazing rustics rang'd around;
And still they gaz'd, and still the wonder grew,
That one small head could carry all he knew.
But past is all his fame. The very spot
Where many a time he triumph'd is forgot.

OLIVER GOLDSMITH

16

Ode to the West Wind

I

O wild West Wind, thou breath of Autumn's being,
  Thou, from whose unseen presence the leaves dead
Are driven, like ghosts from an enchanter fleeing,

Yellow, and black, and pale, and hectic red,
  Pestilence-stricken multitudes: O thou
Who chariotest to their dark wintry bed

The wingèd seeds, where they lie cold and low,
  Each like a corpse within its grave, until
Thine azure sister of the Spring shall blow

Her clarion o'er the dreaming earth, and fill 10
  (Driving sweet buds like flocks to feed in air)
With living hues and odours plain and hill:

Wild Spirit, which art moving everywhere;
Destroyer and Preserver; hear, oh, hear!

II

Thou on whose stream, mid the steep sky's commotion,
  Loose clouds like earth's decaying leaves are shed,
Shook from the tangled boughs of Heaven and Ocean,

Angels of rain and lightning: there are spread
  On the blue surface of thine airy surge,
Like the bright hair uplifted from the head 20

Of some fierce Maenad, even from the dim verge
  Of the horizon to the zenith's height,
The locks of the approaching storm. Thou dirge

Of the dying year, to which this closing night
  Will be the dome of a vast sepulchre,
Vaulted with all thy congregated might

Of vapours, from whose solid atmosphere
Black rain, and fire, and hail, will burst: oh, hear!

III

Thou who didst waken from his summer dreams
  The blue Mediterranean, where he lay, 30
Lull'd by the coil of his crystalline streams,

Beside a pumice isle in Baiae's bay,
  And saw in sleep old palaces and towers
Quivering within the wave's intenser day,

All overgrown with azure moss and flowers
  So sweet, the sense faints picturing them! Thou
For whose path the Atlantic's level powers

Cleave themselves into chasms, while far below
  The sea-blooms and the oozy woods which wear
The sapless foliage of the ocean, know 40

Thy voice, and suddenly grow grey with fear,
And tremble and despoil themselves: oh, hear!

IV

If I were a dead leaf thou mightest bear;
  If I were a swift cloud to fly with thee;
A wave to pant beneath thy power, and share

The impulse of thy strength, only less free
  Than thou, O uncontrollable! If even
I were as in my boyhood, and could be

The comrade of thy wanderings over Heaven,
  As then, when to outstrip thy skyey speed 50
Scarce seemed a vision, I would ne'er have striven

As thus with thee in prayer in my sore need.
  Oh, lift me as a wave, a leaf, a cloud!
I fall upon the thorns of life! I bleed!

A heavy weight of hours has chained and bowed
One too like thee: tameless, and swift, and proud.

V

Make me thy lyre, even as the forest is:
  What if my leaves are falling like its own!
The tumult of thy mighty harmonies

Will take from both a deep, autumnal tone, 60
  Sweet though in sadness. Be thou, Spirit fierce,
My spirit! Be thou me, impetuous one!

Drive my dead thoughts over the universe
  Like withered leaves to quicken a new birth!
And, by the incantation of this verse,

Scatter, as from an unextinguished hearth
  Ashes and sparks, my words among mankind!
Be through my lips to unawakened earth

The trumpet of a prophecy! O Wind,
If Winter comes, can Spring be far behind?

PERCY BYSSHE SHELLEY

17

Fall, Leaves, Fall

Fall, leaves, fall; die, flowers, away;
Lengthen night and shorten day;
Every leaf speaks bliss to me
Fluttering from the autumn tree.

I shall smile when wreaths of snow
Blossom where the rose should grow;
I shall sing when night's decay
Ushers in a drearier day.

EMILY BRONTË

18

I Hear an Army Charging Upon the Land

I hear an army charging upon the land
  And the thunder of horses plunging, foam about their
    knees.
Arrogant, in black armour, behind them stand,
  Disdaining the reins, with fluttering whips, the
    charioteers.

They cry unto the night their battlename:
  I moan in sleep when I hear afar their whirling laughter.
They cleave the gloom of dreams, a blinding flame,
  Clanging, clanging upon the heart as upon an anvil.

They come shaking in triumph their long green hair:
  They come out of the sea and run shouting by the shore.
My heart, have you no wisdom thus to despair?
  My love, my love, my love, why have you left me alone?

JAMES JOYCE

19

The Hitherandthithering Waters of

FROM

Finnegan's Wake

Can't hear with the waters of. The chittering waters of. Flittering bats, fieldmice bawk talk. Ho! Are you not gone ahome? What Thom Malone? Can't hear with bawk of bats, all thim liffeying waters of. Ho, talk save us! My foos won't moos. I feel as old as yonder elm. A tale told of Shaun or Shem? All Livia's daughtersons. Dark hawks hear us. Night! Night! My ho head halls. I feel as heavy as yonder stone. Tell me of John or Shaun? Who were Shem and Shaun the living sons or daughters of? Night now! Tell me, tell me, tell me, elm! Night night! Telmetale of stem or stone. Beside the rivering waters of, hitherandthithering waters of. Night!

JAMES JOYCE

20

Little Green Tree

It looks like to me
My good-time days done past.
Nothin' in this world
Is due to last.

I used to play
And I played so dog-gone hard.
Now old age has
Dealt my bad-luck card.

I look down the road
And I see a little tree.
A little piece down the road.
I see a little tree.

Them cool green leaves
Is waitin' to shelter me.

O, little tree!

LANGSTON HUGHES

21

Lines

FROM

'The Garden of Proserpine'

We are not sure of sorrow,
  And joy was never sure;
To-day will die to-morrow;
  Time stoops to no man's lure;
And love, grown faint and fretful,
With lips but half regretful
Sighs, and with eyes forgetful
  Weeps that no loves endure.

From too much love of living,
  From hope and fear set free,
We thank with brief thanksgiving
  Whatever gods may be
That no life lives for ever;
That dead men rise up never;
That even the weariest river
  Winds somewhere safe to sea.

Then star nor sun shall waken,
  Nor any change of light:
Nor sound of waters shaken,
  Nor any sound or sight:
Nor wintry leaves nor vernal,
Nor days nor things diurnal;
Only the sleep eternal
  In an eternal night.

ALGERNON CHARLES SWINBURNE

22

Giorno dei Morti

Along the avenue of cypresses,
All in their scarlet cloaks, and surplices
Of linen, go the chanting choristers,
The priests in gold and black, the villagers . . .

And all along the path to the cemetery
The round dark heads of men crowd silently,
And black-scarved faces of women-folk, wistfully
Watch at the banner of death, and the mystery.

And at the foot of a grave a father stands
With sunken head, and forgotten, folded hands;
And at the foot of a grave a mother kneels
With pale shut face, and neither hears nor feels

The coming of the chanting choristers
Between the avenue of cypresses,
The silence of the many villagers,
The candle-flames beside the surplices.

D. H. LAWRENCE

23

Self Portrait

How pleasant to know Mr Lear!
  Who has written such volumes of stuff!
Some think him ill-tempered and queer,
  But a few think him pleasant enough.

His mind is concrete and fastidious,
  His nose is remarkably big;
His visage is more or less hideous,
  His beard it resembles a wig.

He has ears, and two eyes, and ten fingers,
  Leastways, if you reckon two thumbs;
Long ago he was one of the singers,
  But now he is one of the dumbs.

He sits in a beautiful parlour,
  With hundreds of books on the wall;
He drinks a great deal of Marsala,
  But never gets tipsy at all.

He has many friends, laymen and clerical;
  Old Foss is the name of his cat;
His body is perfectly spherical,
  He weareth a runcible hat.

When he walks in a waterproof white,
  The children run after him so!
Calling out, 'He's come out in his night-
  Gown, that crazy old Englishman, oh!'

He weeps by the side of the ocean,
He weeps on the top of the hill;
He purchases pancakes and lotion,
And chocolate shrimps from the mill.

He reads but he cannot speak Spanish,
He cannot abide ginger-beer:
Ere the days of his pilgrimage vanish,
How pleasant to know Mr Lear!

EDWARD LEAR

24

Richard Cory

Whenever Richard Cory went down town,
  We people on the pavement looked at him:
He was a gentleman from sole to crown,
  Clean favoured, and imperially slim.

And he was always quietly arrayed,
  And he was always human when he talked;
But still he fluttered pulses when he said,
  'Good-morning,' and he glittered when he walked.

And he was rich – yes, richer than a king –
  And admirably schooled in every grace:
In fine, we thought that he was everything
  To make us wish that we were in his place.

So on we worked, and waited for the light,
  And went without the meat, and cursed the bread;
And Richard Cory, one calm summer night,
  Went home and put a bullet through his head.

EDWIN ARLINGTON ROBINSON

25

A Peasant

Iago Prytherch his name, though, be it allowed,
Just an ordinary man of the bald Welsh hills,
Who pens a few sheep in a gap of cloud.
Docking mangels, chipping the green skin
From the yellow bones with a half-witted grin
Of satisfaction, or churning the crude earth
To a stiff sea of clods that glint in the wind –
So are his days spent, his spittled mirth
Rarer than the sun that cracks the cheeks
Of the gaunt sky perhaps once in a week.
And then at night see him fixed in his chair
Motionless, except when he leans to gob in the fire.
There is something frightening in the vacancy of his
mind.
His clothes, sour with years of sweat
And animal contact, shock the refined,
But affected, sense with their stark naturalness.
Yet this is your prototype, who, season by season
Against siege of rain and the wind's attrition,
Preserves his stock, an impregnable fortress
Not to be stormed even in death's confusion.
Remember him then, for he, too, is a winner of wars,
Enduring like a tree under the curious stars.

R. S. THOMAS

26

The Average

His peasant parents killed themselves with toil
To let their darling leave a stingy soil
For any of those smart professions which
Encourage shallow breathing, and grow rich.

The pressure of their fond ambition made
Their shy and country-loving child afraid
No sensible career was good enough,
Only a hero could deserve such love.

So here he was without maps or supplies,
A hundred miles from any decent town;
The desert glared into his blood-shot eyes;

The silence roared displeasure: looking down,
He saw the shadow of an Average Man
Attempting the exceptional, and ran.

W. H. AUDEN

27

The Unknown Citizen

TO

JS/07/M/378

THIS MARBLE MONUMENT

IS ERECTED BY THE STATE

He was found by the Bureau of Statistics to be
One against whom there was no official complaint,
And all the reports on his conduct agree
That, in the modern sense of an old-fashioned word, he was
    a saint,
For in everything he did he served the Greater Community.
Except for the War till the day he retired
He worked in a factory and never got fired,
But satisfied his employers, Fudge Motors Inc.
Yet he wasn't a scab or odd in his views,
For his Union reports that he paid his dues, 10
(Our report on his Union shows it was sound)
And our Social Psychology workers found
That he was popular with his mates and liked a drink.
The Press are convinced that he bought a paper every day
And that his reactions to advertisements were normal in
    every way.
Policies taken out in his name prove that he was fully
    insured,
And his Health-card shows he was once in hospital but left
    it cured.
Both Producers Research and High-Grade Living declare
He was fully sensible to the advantages of the Instalment
    Plan

And had everything necessary to the Modern Man, 20
A phonograph, a radio, a car and a frigidaire.
Our researchers into Public Opinion are content
That he held the proper opinions for the time of year;
When there was peace, he was for peace; when there was
war, he went.
He was married and added five children to the population,
Which our Eugenist says was the right number for a parent
of his generation.
And our teachers report that he never interfered with their
education.
Was he free? Was he happy? The question is absurd:
Had anything been wrong, we should certainly have heard.

W. H. AUDEN

28

Departmental

THE END OF MY ANT JERRY

An ant on the table cloth
Ran into a dormant moth
Of many times his size.
He showed not the least surprise.
His business wasn't with such.
He gave it scarcely a touch,
And was off on his duty run.
Yet if he encountered one
Of the hive's enquiry squad
Whose work is to find out God 10
And the nature of time and space,
He would put him onto the case.
Ants are a curious race;
One crossing with hurried tread
The body of one of their dead
Isn't given a moment's arrest—
Seems not even impressed.
But he no doubt reports to any
With whom he crosses antennae,
And they no doubt report 20
To the higher up at court.
Then word goes forth in Formic:
'Death's come to Jerry McCormic,
Our selfless forager Jerry.
Will the special Janizary
Whose office it is to bury
The dead of the commissary

Go bring him home to his people.
Lay him in state on a sepal.
Wrap him for shroud in a petal. 30
Embalm him with ichor of nettle.
This is the word of your Queen.'
And presently on the scene
Appears a solemn mortician;
And taking formal position
With feelers calmly atwiddle,
Seizes the dead by the middle,
And heaving him high in air,
Carries him out of there.
No one stands round to stare. 40
It is nobody else's affair.

It couldn't be called ungentle.
But how thoroughly departmental.

ROBERT FROST

29

The Newspaper

I sing of News, and all those vapid sheets
The rattling hawker vends through gaping streets;
Whate'er their name, whate'er the time they fly,
Damp from the press, to charm the reader's eye:
For, soon as morning dawns with roseate hue,
The Herald of the morn arises too;
Post after Post succeeds, and, all day long,
Gazettes and Ledgers swarm, a noisy throng.
When evening comes, she comes with all her train
Of Ledgers, Chronicles, and Posts again – 10
Like bats, appearing, when the sun goes down,
From holes obscure and corners of the town.

We, who for longer fame with labour strive,
Are pain'd to keep our sickly works alive;
Studious we toil, with patient care refine,
Nor let our love protect one languid line.
Severe ourselves, at last our works appear,
When, ah! we find our readers more severe;
For after all our care and pains, how few
Acquire applause, or keep it if they do! – 20
Not so these sheets, ordain'd to happier fate,
Praised through their day, and but that day their date;
Their careless authors only strive to join
As many words as make an even line;
As many lines as fill a row complete;
As many rows as furnish up a sheet:
From side to side, with ready types they run,
The measure's ended, and the work is done;

Oh, born with ease, how envied and how blest!
Your fate to-day and your to-morrow's rest. 30
To you all readers turn, and they can look
Pleased on a paper, who abhor a book;
Those, who ne'er deign'd their Bible to peruse,
Would think it hard to be denied their news;
Sinners and saints, the wisest with the weak,
Here mingle tastes, and one amusement seek;
This, like the public inn, provides a treat,
Where each promiscuous guest sits down to eat;
And such this mental food, as we may call
Something to all men, and to some men all. 40

A master passion is the love of news,
Not music so commands, nor so the Muse:
Give poets claret, they grow idle soon;
Feed the musician, and he's out of tune;
But the sick mind, of this disease possess'd,
Flies from all cure, and sickens when at rest.

Now sing, my Muse, what various parts compose
These rival sheets of politics and prose.
First, from each brother's hoard a part they draw,
A mutual theft that never fear'd a law; 50
Whate'er they gain, to each man's portion fall,
And read it once, you read it through them all:
For this their runners rumble day and night,
To drag each lurking deed to open light;
For daily bread the dirty trade they ply,
Coin their fresh tales, and live upon the lie:
Like bees for honey, forth for news they spring, —
Industrious creatures! ever on the wing;
Home to their several cells they bear the store,
Cull'd of all kinds, then roam abroad for more. 60

No anxious virgin flies to 'fair Tweed-side';
No injured husband mourns his faithless bride;
No duel dooms the fiery youth to bleed,
But through the town transpires each vent'rous deed.

Should some fair frail-one drive her prancing pair,
Where rival peers contend to please the fair;
When, with new force, she aids her conquering eyes,
And beauty decks with all that beauty buys –
Quickly we learn whose heart her influence feels,
Whose acres melt before her glowing wheels. 70
To these a thousand idle themes succeed,
Deeds of all kinds, and comments to each deed.
Here stocks, the state-barometers, we view,
That rise or fall, by causes known to few;
Promotion's ladder who goes up or down;
Who wed, or who seduced, amuse the town;
What new-born heir has made his father blest;
What heir exults, his father now at rest;
That ample list the Tyburn-herald gives,
And each known knave, who still for Tyburn lives.

GEORGE CRABBE

30

An Old Woman's Lamentations

The man I had a love for – a great rascal would kick me in the gutter – is dead thirty years and over it, and it is I am left behind, grey and aged. When I do be minding the good days I had, minding what I was one time, and what it is I'm come to, and when I do look on my own self, poor and dry, and pinched together, it wouldn't be much would set me raging in the streets.

Where is the round forehead I had, and the fine hair, and the two eyebrows, and the eyes with a big gay look out of them would bring folly from a great scholar? Where is my straight shapely nose, and two ears, and my chin with a valley in it, and my lips were red and open?

Where are the pointed shoulders were on me, and the long arms and nice hands to them? Where is my bosom was as white as any, or my straight rounded sides?

It's the way I am this day – my forehead is gone away into furrows, the hair of my head is grey and whitish, my eyebrows are tumbled from me, and my two eyes have died out within my head – those eyes that would be laughing to the men, – my nose has a hook on it, my ears are hanging down, and my lips are sharp and skinny.

That's what's left over from the beauty of a right woman – a bag of bones, and legs the like of two shrivelled sausages going beneath it.

It's of the like of that we old hags do be thinking, of the good times are gone away from us, and we crouching on our hunkers by a little fire of twigs, soon kindled and soon spent, we that were the pick of many.

J. M. SYNGE
after FRANÇOIS VILLON

31

The Love Song of J. Alfred Prufrock

S'io credesse che mia risposta fosse
A persona che mai tornasse al mondo,
Questa fiamma staria senza piu scosse.
Ma perciocche giammai di questo fondo
Non torno vivo alcun, s'i'odo il vero,
Senza tema d'infamia ti rispondo.

Let us go then, you and I,
When the evening is spread out against the sky
Like a patient etherised upon a table;
Let us go, through certain half-deserted streets,
The muttering retreats
Of restless nights in one-night cheap hotels
And sawdust restaurants with oyster-shells:
Streets that follow like a tedious argument
Of insidious intent
To lead you to an overwhelming question . . . 10
Oh, do not ask, 'What is it?'
Let us go and make our visit.

In the room the women come and go
Talking of Michelangelo.

The yellow fog that rubs its back upon the window-panes,
The yellow smoke that rubs its muzzle on the window-panes
Licked its tongue into the corners of the evening,
Lingered upon the pools that stand in drains,
Let fall upon its back the soot that falls from chimneys,
Slipped by the terrace, made a sudden leap, 20

And seeing that it was a soft October night,
Curled once about the house, and fell asleep.

And indeed there will be time
For the yellow smoke that slides along the street
Rubbing its back upon the window-panes;
There will be time, there will be time
To prepare a face to meet the faces that you meet;
There will be time to murder and create,
And time for all the works and days of hands
That lift and drop a question on your plate; 30
Time for you and time for me,
And time yet for a hundred indecisions,
And for a hundred visions and revisions,
Before the taking of a toast and tea.

In the room the women come and go
Talking of Michelangelo.

And indeed there will be time
To wonder, 'Do I dare?' and, 'Do I dare?'
Time to turn back and descend the stair,
With a bald spot in the middle of my hair – 40
[They will say: 'How his hair is growing thin!']
My morning coat, my collar mounting firmly to the chin,
My necktie rich and modest, but asserted by a simple pin –
[They will say: 'But how his arms and legs are thin!']
Do I dare
Disturb the universe?
In a minute there is time
For decisions and revisions which a minute will reverse.

For I have known them all already, known them all –

Have known the evenings, mornings, afternoons, 50
I have measured out my life with coffee spoons;
I know the voices dying with a dying fall
Beneath the music from a farther room.
  So how should I presume?

And I have known the eyes already, known them all—
The eyes that fix you in a formulated phrase,
And when I am formulated, sprawling on a pin,
When I am pinned and wriggling on the wall,
Then how should I begin
To spit out all the butt-ends of my days and ways? 60
  And how should I presume?

And I have known the arms already, known them all—
Arms that are braceleted and white and bare
[But in the lamplight, downed with light brown hair!]
Is it perfume from a dress
That makes me so digress?
Arms that lie along a table, or wrap about a shawl.
  And should I then presume?
  And how should I begin?

. . . . . .

Shall I say, I have gone at dusk through narrow streets 70
And watched the smoke that rises from the pipes
Of lonely men in shirt-sleeves, leaning out of windows? . . .

I should have been a pair of ragged claws
Scuttling across the floors of silent seas.

. . . . . .

And the afternoon, the evening, sleeps so peacefully!
Smoothed by long fingers,
Asleep . . . tired . . . or it malingers,

Stretched on the floor, here beside you and me.
Should I, after tea and cakes and ices,
Have the strength to force the moment to its crisis? 80
But though I have wept and fasted, wept and prayed,
Though I have seen my head [grown slightly bald]
brought in upon a platter,
I am no prophet — and here's no great matter;
I have seen the moment of my greatness flicker,
And I have seen the eternal Footman hold my coat, and
snicker,
And in short, I was afraid.

And would it have been worth it, after all,
After the cups, the marmalade, the tea,
Among the porcelain, among some talk of you and me,
Would it have been worth while, 90
To have bitten off the matter with a smile,
To have squeezed the universe into a ball
To roll it toward some overwhelming question,
To say: 'I am Lazarus, come from the dead,
Come back to tell you all, I shall tell you all' —
If one, settling a pillow by her head,
Should say: 'That is not what I meant at all.
That is not it, at all.'

And would it have been worth it, after all,
Would it have been worth while, 100
After the sunsets and the dooryards and the sprinkled
streets,
After the novels, after the teacups, after the skirts that
trail along the floor —
And this, and so much more? —
It is impossible to say just what I mean!

But as if a magic lantern threw the nerves in patterns on a
    screen:
Would it have been worth while
If one, settling a pillow or throwing off a shawl,
And turning toward the window, should say:
  'That is not it at all,
  That is not what I meant, at all.' 110

. . . . . .

No! I am not Prince Hamlet, nor was meant to be;
Am an attendant lord, one that will do
To swell a progress, start a scene or two,
Advise the prince; no doubt, an easy tool,
Deferential, glad to be of use,
Politic, cautious, and meticulous;
Full of high sentence, but a bit obtuse;
At times, indeed, almost ridiculous –
Almost, at times, the Fool.

I grow old . . . I grow old . . . 120
I shall wear the bottoms of my trousers rolled.

Shall I part my hair behind? Do I dare to eat a peach?
I shall wear white flannel trousers, and walk upon the
    beach.
I have heard the mermaids singing, each to each.

I do not think that they will sing to me.

I have seen them riding seaward on the waves
Combing the white hair of the waves blown back
When the wind blows the water white and black.

We have lingered in the chambers of the sea
By sea-girls wreathed with seaweed red and brown 130
Till human voices wake us, and we drown.

T. S. ELIOT

32

A Kiss

Rose kissed me to-day.
  Will she kiss me to-morrow?
Let it be as it may,
Rose kissed me to-day.
But the pleasure gives way
  To a savour of sorrow; –
Rose kissed me to-day, –
  Will she kiss me to-morrow?

AUSTIN DOBSON

33

Sonnet XVIII

Shall I compare thee to a summer's day?
Thou art more lovely and more temperate.
Rough winds do shake the darling buds of May,
And summer's lease hath all too short a date:
Sometime too hot the eye of heaven shines,
And often is his gold complexion dimm'd;
And every fair from fair some time declines,
By chance, or nature's changing course, untrimm'd;
But thy eternal summer shall not fade
Nor lose possession of that fair thou ow'st;
Nor shall Death brag thou wand'rest in his shade,
When in eternal lines to time thou grow'st.
  So long as men can breathe or eyes can see,
  So long lives this, and this gives life to thee.

WILLIAM SHAKESPEARE

34

Sonnet

Bright Star! would I were steadfast as thou art –
Not in lone splendour hung aloft the night,
And watching, with eternal lids apart,
Like Nature's patient sleepless Eremite,
The moving waters at their priestlike task
Of pure ablution around earth's human shores,
Or gazing on the new soft-fallen mask
Of snow upon the mountains and the moors: –
No – yet still steadfast, still unchangeable,
Pillow'd upon my fair love's ripening breast,
To feel for ever its soft fall and swell,
Awake for ever in a sweet unrest,
  Still, still to hear her tender-taken breath,
  And so live ever, – or else swoon to death.

JOHN KEATS

35

The Hill

Breathless, we flung us on the windy hill,
Laughed in the sun, and kissed the lovely grass.
You said, 'Through glory and ecstasy we pass;
Wind, sun, and earth remain, the birds sing still,
When we are old, are old. . . .' 'And when we die
All's over that is ours; and life burns on
Through other lovers, other lips,' said I,
'Heart of my heart, our heaven is now, is won!'
'We are Earth's best, that learnt her lesson here.
Life is our cry. We have kept the faith!' we said;
'We shall go down with unreluctant tread
Rose-crowned into the darkness! . . .' Proud we were,
And laughed, that had such brave true things to say.
And then you suddenly cried, and turned away.

RUPERT BROOKE

36

The Ill-Tempered Lover

I wish my tongue were a quiver the size of a huge cask
Packed and crammed with long black venomous rankling
darts.
I'd fling you more full of them, and joy in the task,
Than ever Sebastian was, or Caesar, with thirty-three swords
in his heart.

I'd make a porcupine out of you, or a pin-cushion, say;
The shafts should stand so thick you'd look like a headless
hen
Hung up by the heels, with the long bare red neck
stretching, curving, and dripping away
From the soiled floppy ball of ruffled feathers standing on
end.

You should bristle like those cylindrical brushes they use to
scrub out bottles,
Not even to reach the kindly earth with the soles of your
prickled feet.
And I would stand by and watch you wriggle and writhe,
gurgling through the barbs in your throttle
Like a woolly caterpillar pinned on its back – man, that
would be sweet!

LOUIS MACKAY

37

Thomas the Rhymer

True Thomas lay on Huntlie bank;
  A ferlie° he spied wi' his e'e; — marvel
And there he saw a ladye bright
  Come riding down by the Eildon Tree.

Her skirt was o' the grass-green silk,
  Her mantle o' the velvet fyne;
At ilka tett° o' her horse's mane, — every lock
  Hung fifty siller bells and nine.

True Thomas he pu'd aff his cap,
  And louted° low down on his knee: 10 — bowed
'Hail to thee, Mary, Queen of Heaven!
  For thy peer on earth could never be.'

'O no, O no, Thomas,' she said,
  'That name does not belang to me;
I'm but the Queen o' fair Elfland,
  That am hither come to visit thee.

'Harp and carp, Thomas,' she said;
  'Harp and carp along wi' me;
And if ye dare to kiss my lips,
  Sure of your bodie I will be.' 20

'Betide me weal, betide me woe,
  That weird° shall never daunten me.' — doom
Syne° he has kiss'd her rosy lips, — since then
  All underneath the Eildon Tree.

'Now ye maun go wi' me,' she said,
  'True Thomas, ye maun go wi' me;
And ye maun serve me seven years,
  Thro' weal or woe as may chance to be.'

She's mounted on her milk-white steed,
  She's ta'en true Thomas up behind; 30
And aye, whene'er her bridle rang,
  The steed gaed swifter than the wind;

O they rade on, and farther on,
  The steed gaed swifter than the wind;
Until they reach'd a desert wide,
  And living land was left behind.

'Light down, light down now, true Thomas,
  And lean your head upon my knee;
Abide ye there a little space,
  And I will show you ferlies three. 40

'O see ye not yon narrow road,
  So thick beset wi' thorns and briers?
That is the Path of Righteousness,
  Though after it but few inquires.

'And see ye not yon braid°, braid road, broad
  That lies across the lily leven°? lawn
That is the Path of Wickedness,
  Though some call it the Road to Heaven.

'And see ye not yon bonny road
  That winds about the fernie brae°? 50 hillside

That is the Road to fair Elfland,
  Where thou and I this night maun gae.

'But, Thomas, ye sall haud your tongue,
  Whatever ye may hear or see;
For speak ye word in Elfyn-land,
  Ye'll ne'er win back to your ain countrie.'

O they rade on, and farther on,
  And they waded rivers abune the knee;
And they saw neither sun nor moon,
  But they heard the roaring of the sea. 60

It was mirk°, mirk night, there was nae starlight, murky
  They waded thro' red blude to the knee;
For a' the blude that's shed on the earth
  Rins through the springs o' that countrie.

Syne they came to a garden green,
  And she pu'd an apple frae a tree:
'Take this for thy wages, true Thomas;
  It will give thee the tongue that can never lee.'

'My tongue is my ain,' true Thomas he said;
  'A gudely gift ye wad gie to me! 70
I neither dought° to buy or sell could
  At fair or tryst where I might be.

'I dought neither speak to prince or peer,
  Nor ask of grace from fair ladye!' –
'Now haud thy peace, Thomas,' she said,
  'For as I say, so must it be.'

He has gotten a coat of the even° cloth, smooth
  And a pair o' shoon of the velvet green,
And till seven years were gane and past,
  True Thomas on earth was never seen.

ANONYMOUS

38

The Song of the Mad Prince

Who said, 'Peacock Pie'?
The old King to the sparrow:
Who said, 'Crops are ripe'?
Rust to the harrow:
Who said, 'Where sleeps she now?
Where rests she now her head,
Bathed in eve's loveliness'? –
That's what I said.

Who said, 'Ay, mum's the word'?
Sexton to willow:
Who said, 'Green dusk for dreams,
Moss for a pillow'?
Who said, 'All Time's delight
Hath she for narrow bed;
Life's troubled bubble broken'?
That's what I said.

WALTER DE LA MARE

39

Tom O' Bedlam's Song

From the hag and hungry goblin
That into rags would rend ye
And the spirit that stan' by the naked man
In the Book of Moons defend ye!
That of your five sound senses
You never be forsaken
Nor travel from yourselves with Tom
Abroad to beg your bacon.

Nor never sing 'Any food, any feeding,
Money, drink or clothing':
Come dame or maid, be not afraid,
Poor Tom will injure nothing.

Of thirty bare years have I
Twice twenty been enragéd
And of forty bin three times fifteen
In durance soundly cagéd
In the lordly lofts of Bedlam
On stubble soft and dainty,
Brave bracelets strong, sweet whips ding dong,
With wholesome hunger plenty.

And now I sing 'Any food, any feeding,
Money, drink or clothing':
Come dame or maid, be not afraid,
Poor Tom will injure nothing.

ANONYMOUS

40

Song for Saint Cecilia's Day, 1687

From Harmony, from heavenly Harmony
        This universal frame began:
    When Nature underneath a heap
        Of jarring atoms lay
    And could not heave her head,
The tuneful voice was heard from high
        Arise, ye more than dead!
Then cold, and hot, and moist, and dry
In order to their stations leap,
        And Music's power obey. 10
From harmony, from heavenly harmony
        This universal frame began:
        From harmony to harmony
Through all the compass of the notes it ran,
The diapason closing full in Man.

What passion cannot Music raise and quell?
        When Jubal struck the chorded shell
    His listening brethren stood around,
        And, wondering, on their faces fell
    To worship that celestial sound. 20
Less than a god they thought there could not
      dwell
        Within the hollow of that shell
        That spoke so sweetly and so well.
What passion cannot Music raise and quell?

The trumpet's loud clangor
Excites us to arms,
With shrill notes of anger
And mortal alarms.
The double double double beat
Of the thundering drum 30
Cries 'Hark! the foes come;
Charge, charge, 'tis too late to retreat!'

The soft complaining flute
In dying notes discovers
The woes of hopeless lovers,
Whose dirge is whisper'd by the warbling lute.

Sharp violins proclaim
Their jealous pangs and desperation,
Fury, frantic indignation,
Depth of pains, and height of passion 40
For the fair disdainful dame.

But oh! what art can teach,
What human voice can reach
The sacred organ's praise?
Notes inspiring holy love,
Notes that wing their heavenly ways
To mend the choirs above.

Orpheus could lead the savage race,
And trees unrooted left their place
Sequacious of the lyre: 50
But bright Cecilia raised the wonder higher:
When to her Organ vocal breath was given,
An Angel heard, and straight appear'd –
Mistaking Earth for Heaven!

Grand Chorus

As from the power of sacred lays
 The spheres began to move,
And sung the great Creator's praise
 To all the blest above;

So when the last and dreadful hour
This crumbling pageant shall devour 60
The trumpet shall be heard on high,
The dead shall live, the living die,
And Music shall untune the sky.

JOHN DRYDEN

41

Sonnet

It is not to be thought of that the Flood
Of British freedom, which, to the open sea
Of the world's praise, from dark antiquity
Hath flowed, 'with pomp of waters, unwithstood,'
Roused though it be full often to a mood
Which spurns the check of salutary bands,
That this most famous Stream in bogs and sands
Should perish; and to evil and to good
Be lost for ever. In our halls is hung
Armoury of the invincible Knights of old:
We must be free or die, who speak the tongue
That Shakespeare spake; the faith and morals hold
Which Milton held. – In every thing we are sprung
Of Earth's first blood, have titles manifold.

WILLIAM WORDSWORTH

42

Anthem for Doomed Youth

What passing-bells for these who die as cattle?
Only the monstrous anger of the guns.
Only the stuttering rifles' rapid rattle
Can patter out their hasty orisons.
No mockeries for them; no prayers nor bells,
Nor any voice of mourning save the choirs, –
The shrill, demented choirs of wailing shells;
And bugles calling for them from sad shires.
What candles may be held to speed them all?
Not in the hands of boys, but in their eyes
Shall shine the holy glimmers of good-byes.
The pallor of girls' brows shall be their pall;
Their flowers the tenderness of patient minds,
And each slow dusk a drawing-down of blinds.

WILFRED OWEN

43

Strange Meeting

It seemed that out of the battle I escaped
Down some profound dull tunnel, long since scooped
Through granites which Titanic wars had groined.
Yet also there encumbered sleepers groaned,
Too fast in thought or death to be bestirred.
Then, as I probed them, one sprang up, and stared
With piteous recognition in fixed eyes,
Lifting distressful hands as if to bless.
And by his smile, I knew that sullen hall,
By his dead smile I knew we stood in Hell. 10
With a thousand pains that vision's face was grained;
Yet no blood reached there from the upper ground,
And no guns thumped, or down the flues made moan.
'Strange friend,' I said, 'here is no cause to mourn.'
'None,' said the other, 'save the undone years,
The hopelessness. Whatever hope is yours,
Was my life also; I went hunting wild
After the wildest beauty in the world,
Which lies not calm in eyes, or braided hair,
But mocks the steady running of the hour, 20
And if it grieves, grieves richlier than here.
For by my glee might many men have laughed,
And of my weeping something had been left,
Which must die now. I mean the truth untold,
The pity of war, the pity war distilled.
Now men will go content with what we spoiled.
Or, discontent, boil bloody, and be spilled.
They will be swift with swiftness of the tigress,
None will break ranks, though nations trek from progress.

Courage was mine, and I had mystery, 30
Wisdom was mine, and I had mastery;
To miss the march of this retreating world
Into vain citadels that are not walled.
Then, when much blood had clogged their chariot-wheels
I would go up and wash them from sweet wells,
Even with truths that lie too deep for taint.
I would have poured my spirit without stint
But not through wounds; not on the cess of war.
Foreheads of men have bled where no wounds were.
I am the enemy you killed, my friend. 40
I knew you in this death: for so you frowned
Yesterday through me as you jabbed and killed.
I parried; but my hands were loath and cold.
Let us sleep now.' . . .

WILFRED OWEN

44

The Truth

When I was four my father went to Scotland.
They *said* he went to Scotland.

When I woke up I think I thought that I was dreaming –
I was so little then that I thought dreams
Are in the room with you, like the cinema.
That's why you don't dream when it's still light –
They pull the shades down when it is, so you can sleep.
I thought that then, but that's not right.
Really it's in your head.

And it was light then – light at *night*. 10
I heard Stalky bark outside.
But really it was Mother crying –
She coughed so hard she cried.
She kept shaking Sister,
She shook her and shook her.
I thought Sister had had her nightmare.
But he wasn't barking, he had died.
There was dirt all over Sister.
It was all streaks, like mud. I cried.
She didn't but she was older. 20
I thought she didn't
Because she was older, I thought Stalky had just gone.
I got *everything* wrong.
I didn't get one single thing right.
It seems to me that I'd have thought
It didn't happen, like a dream,
Except that it was light. At night.

They burnt our house down, they burnt down London.
Next day my mother cried all day, and after that
She said to me when she would come to see me: 30
'Your father has gone away to Scotland.
He will be back after the war.'

The war then was different from the war now.
The war now is *nothing*.

I used to live in London till they burnt it.
What was it like? It was just like here.
No, that's the truth.
My mother would come here, some, but she would cry.
She said to Miss Elise, 'He's not himself';
She said, 'Don't you love me any more at all?' 40
I was *my*self.
Finally she wouldn't come at all.
She never said one thing my father said, or Sister.
Sometimes she did,
Sometimes she was the same, but that was when I dreamed
it.
I could tell I was dreaming, she was just the same.

That Christmas she bought me a toy dog.

I asked her what was its name, and when she didn't know
I asked her over, and when she didn't know
I said, 'You're not my mother, you're not my mother. 50
She *hasn't* gone to Scotland, she is dead!'
And she said, 'Yes, he's dead, he's dead!'
And cried and cried; she *was* my mother,
She put her arms around me and we cried.

RANDALL JARRELL

45

War on the Periphery

Around the battlements go by
Soldier men against the sky,
Violent lovers, husbands, sons,
Guarding my peaceful life with guns.

My pleasures, how discreet they are!
A little booze, a little car,
Two little children and a wife
Living a small suburban life.

My little children eat my heart;
At seven o'clock we kiss and part,
At seven o'clock we meet again;
They eat my heart and grow to men.

I watch their tenderness with fear
While on the battlements I hear
The violent, obedient ones
Guarding my family with guns.

GEORGE JOHNSTON

46

Dusk on English Bay

The lighting rooms perfect a chequerboard
Across apartment boxes. Through the popcorn
Reek, hotdogs and chips, the air lets fall
A rain of quiet coolness on the flesh. The calling
Bathers trot the footpocked sand on legs
Unsexed by distance, waving arms severed
With twilight. From the whitening ribs of the raft divers
Flash cream arcs across the expiring
Sunset, and are quenched. Beyond the bay the files
Of regimented lamps are pulsing evenly 10
On the long tamed whale of Point Grey. The evening
Star detaches and floats into the chartreuse heavens,
An arrested rocket. The moon, behind a row
Of moons along the promenade, contracts and yellows
Upward. Night's dissolvent eats into the west,
Browning the stippled mauve, the copper sulphate,
Paling and paling the opal, melting the latest
Speck of robin's eggshell into the Gulf of Georgia,
And ever over the Pacific pursuing tomorrow's
Sun. But tomorrow's sun is clean escaped 20
And rushes down through Asian skies, garish
With burst of shell and unarrested rocket,
And burns on Libyan sands, by bombs
Cratered and red with libations poured to the guns.
Past Narvik's blanching hulks the morrowing sun
Is flying, over the Mediterranean's smudged
Embattled sharks, and the sailors quenched, and climbing
To stricken dawn in England, widening his light

On limbs unsexed and severed, and the rain of iron
Cooling the flesh, and the stench of the flesh cooled, 30
While the flame untamed probes the tenement ruins.
Speeding and soaring he comes, the Atlantic sighting,
And there is no Joshua can brake his flight, nor
Any clutch of ours can hold this precious night.

EARLE BIRNEY

47

I Think Continually

I think continually of those who were truly great.
Who, from the womb, remembered the soul's history
Through corridors of light where the hours are suns,
Endless and singing. Whose lovely ambition
Was that their lips, still touched with fire,
Should tell of the Spirit clothed from head to foot in song.
And who hoarded from the Spring branches
The desires falling across their bodies like blossoms.

What is precious is never to forget
The essential delight of the blood drawn from ageless
    springs 10
Breaking through rocks in worlds before our earth;
Never to deny its pleasure in the simple morning light,
Nor its grave evening demand for love;
Never to allow gradually the traffic to smother
With noise and fog the flowering of the spirit.

Near the snow, near the sun, in the highest fields
See how these names are feted by the wavering grass,
And by the streamers of white cloud,
And whispers of wind in the listening sky;
The names of those who in their lives fought for life, 20
Who wore at their hearts the fire's centre.
Born of the sun they travelled a short while towards the
    sun,
And left the vivid air signed with their honour.

STEPHEN SPENDER

48
Sonnet xxx

When to the sessions of sweet silent thought
I summon up remembrance of things past,
I sigh the lack of many a thing I sought,
And with old woes new wail my dear time's waste.
Then can I drown an eye, unus'd to flow,
For precious friends hid in death's dateless night,
And weep afresh love's long-since-cancell'd woe,
And moan th'expense of many a vanish'd sight.
Then can I grieve at grievances foregone,
And heavily from woe to woe tell o'er
The sad account of fore-bemoaned moan,
Which I new pay as if not paid before.
  But if the while I think on thee, dear friend,
  All losses are restor'd, and sorrows end.

WILLIAM SHAKESPEARE

49

Sonnet LX

Like as the waves make towards the pebbled shore,
So do our minutes hasten to their end;
Each changing place with that which goes before,
In sequent toil all forwards do contend.
Nativity, once in the main of light,
Crawls to maturity, wherewith being crown'd,
Crooked eclipses 'gainst his glory fight,
And Time that gave doth now his gift confound.
Time doth transfix the flourish set on youth,
And delves the parallels in beauty's brow;
Feeds on the rarities of Nature's truth,
And nothing stands but for his scythe to mow:
  And yet to times in hope my verse shall stand,
  Praising thy worth, despite his cruel hand.

WILLIAM SHAKESPEARE

50

Heraclitus

They told me, Heraclitus, they told me you were dead,
They brought me bitter news to hear and bitter tears to
shed.
I wept as I remember'd how often you and I
Had tired the sun with talking and sent him down the sky.

And now that thou art lying, my dear old Carian guest,
A handful of grey ashes, long, long ago at rest,
Still are thy pleasant voices, thy nightingales, awake;
For Death, he taketh all away, but them he cannot take.

WILLIAM CORY

51

Eight O'Clock

He stood, and heard the steeple
  Sprinkle the quarters on the morning town.
One, two, three, four, to market-place and people
  It tossed them down.

Strapped, noosed, nighing his hour,
  He stood and counted them and cursed his luck;
And then the clock collected in the tower
  Its strength, and struck.

A. E. HOUSMAN

52

What the Devil Said

It was night time! God, the Father Good,
Weary of praises, on a sudden stood
From His great Throne, and leaned upon the sky:
For He had heard a sound; a little cry,
Thin as a whisper, climbing up the Steep.

And so He looked to where the Earth, asleep,
Rocked with the moon: He saw the whirling sea
Swing round the world in surgent energy,
Tangling the moonlight in its netted foam:
And, nearer, saw the white and fretted dome 10
Of the ice-capped pole spin back again a ray
To whistling stars, bright as a wizard's day.

But these He passed, with eyes intently wide,
Till, closer still, the mountains He espied
Squatting tremendous on the broad-backed Earth.
Each nursing twenty rivers at a birth!
And then, minutely, sought He for the cry
That had climbed the slant of space so hugely high.

He found it in a ditch outside a town:
A tattered hungry woman, crouching down 20
By a dead babe – So there was nought to do,
For what is done is done! And sad He drew
Back to His Heaven of ivory and gold:
And, as He sat, all suddenly there rolled,
From where the woman wept upon the sod,
Satan's deep voice – *O thou unhappy God!*

JAMES STEPHENS

53

St Yves' Poor

Jeffik was there, and Matthieu, and brown Bran,
Warped in old wars and babbling of the sword,
And Jannedik, a white rose pinched and paled
With the world's frosts, and many more beside,
Lamed, rheumed and palsied, aged, impotent
Of all but hunger and blind lifted hands.
I set the doors wide at the given hour,
Took the great basket piled with bread, the fish
Yet silvered of the sea, the curds of milk,
And called them Brethren, brake, and blest, and gave. 10

For O, my Lord, the house dove knows her nest
Above my window builded from the rain;
In the brown mere the heron finds her rest,
But these shall seek in vain.
And O, my Lord, the thrush may fold her wing,
The curlew seek the long lift of the seas,
The wild swan sleep amid his journeying, –
There is no rest for these.

Thy dead are sheltered; housed and warmed they wait
Under the golden fern, the falling foam; 20
But these, Thy living, wander desolate
And have not any home.

I called them Brethren, brake, and blest, and gave.
Old Jeffik had her withered hand to show,
Young Jannedik had dreamed of death, and Bran
Would tell me wonders wrought on fields of war,

When Michael and his warriors rode the storm,
And all the heavens were thrilled with clanging spears, –
Ah, God, my poor, my poor. – Till there came one
Wrapped in foul rags, who caught me by the robe, 30
And pleaded, 'Bread, my father.'

In his hand
I laid the last loaf of the daily dole,
Saw on the palm a red wound like a star,
And bade him, 'Let me bind it.'
'These my wounds,'
He answered softly, 'daily dost thou bind.'
And I, 'My son, I have not seen thy face.
But thy bruised feet have trodden on my heart.
I will get water for thee.'
'These my hurts,'
Again he answered, 'daily dost thou wash.'
And I once more, 'My son, I know thee not. 40
But the bleak wind blows bitter from the sea,
And even the gorse is perished. Rest thee here.'
And he again, 'My rest is in thy heart.
I take from thee as I have given to thee.
Dost thou not know Me, Breton?'
I, – 'My Lord!' –

A scent of lilies on the cold sea-wind,
A thin, white blaze of wings, a face of flame
Over the gateway, and the vision passed,
And there were only Matthieu and brown Bran,
And the young girl, the foam-white Jannedik, 50
Wondering to see their father rapt from them,
And Jeffik weeping o'er her withered hand.

MARJORIE PICKTHALL

54

The Tyger

An Early Draft

1 Tyger Tyger burning bright
In the forests of the night
What immortal hand & eye
or
Could frame thy fearful symmetry
Dare

2 In what distant deeps or skies
Burnt in
Burnt the fire of thine eyes
The cruel
On what wings dare he aspire
What the hand dare sieze the fire

3 And what shoulder & what art
Could twist the sinews of thy heart
And when thy heart began to beat
What dread hand & what dread feet

Could fetch it from the furnace deep
And in thy horrid ribs dare steep
In the well of sanguine woe
In what clay & in what mould
Were thy eyes of fury rolld

What the hammer what the chain
Where where
In what furnace was thy brain

What the anvil What the arm
arm
grasp
clasp
dread grasp
Could its deadly terrors clasp
Dare grasp
clasp

6 Tyger Tyger burning bright
In the forests of the night
What immortal hand & eye
Dare form thy fearful symmetry
frame

2 Burnt in distant deeps or skies
The cruel fire of thine eyes
Could heart descend or wings aspire
What the hand dare sieze the fire

5 And did he laugh his work to see
dare he smile
laugh
What the shoulder what the knee
ankle
Did he who made the lamb make thee
Dare
When the stars threw down their spears
And waterd heaven with their tears

WILLIAM BLAKE

55

The Tyger

Tyger! Tyger! burning bright
In the forests of the night,
What immortal hand or eye
Could frame thy fearful symmetry?

In what distant deeps or skies
Burnt the fire of thine eyes?
On what wings dare he aspire?
What the hand dare seize the fire?

And what shoulder, and what art,
Could twist the sinews of thy heart?
And when thy heart began to beat,
What dread hand? and what dread feet?

What the hammer? what the chain?
In what furnace was thy brain?
What the anvil? what dread grasp
Dare its deadly terrors clasp?

When the stars threw down their spears,
And water'd heaven with their tears,
Did he smile his work to see?
Did he who made the Lamb make thee?

Tyger! Tyger! burning bright
In the forests of the night,
What immortal hand or eye,
Dare frame thy fearful symmetry?

WILLIAM BLAKE

56

Then the Lord Answered Job Out of the Whirlwind

Then the Lord answered Job out of the whirlwind and said,
Who is this that darkeneth counsel by words without knowledge?
Gird up now thy loins like a man; for I will demand of thee, and answer thou me.
Where wast thou when I laid the foundations of the earth? declare, if thou hast understanding.
Who hath laid the measures thereof, if thou knowest? or who hath stretched the line upon it? 10
Whereupon are the foundations thereof fastened? or who laid the corner-stone thereof;
When the morning stars sang together, and all the sons of God shouted for joy?
Or who shut up the sea with doors, when it brake forth, as if it had issued out of the womb?
When I made the cloud the garment thereof, and thick darkness a swaddling band for it,
And brake up for it my decreed place, and set bars and doors, 20
And said, Hitherto shalt thou come, but no further: and here shall thy proud waves be stayed?

Canst thou bind the sweet influences of Pleiades, or loose the bands of Orion?

Canst thou bring forth Mazzaroth in his season? or canst thou guide Arcturus with his sons?

Knowest thou the ordinances of heaven? canst thou set the dominion thereof in the earth?

Canst thou lift up thy voice to the clouds, that abundance of waters may cover thee? 30

Canst thou send lightnings, that they may go, and say unto thee, Here we are?

JOB 38: 1-11, 31-35

57

Apparently with No Surprise

Apparently with no surprise
To any happy flower,
The frost beheads it at its play
In accidental power.

The blond assassin passes on,
The sun proceeds unmoved
To measure off another day
For an approving God.

EMILY DICKINSON

58

The Last Night That She Lived

The last night that she lived,
It was a common night,
Except the dying; this to us
Made nature different.

We noticed smallest things, –
Things overlooked before,
By this great light upon our minds
Italicized, as 'twere.

That others could exist
While she must finish quite,
A jealousy for her arose
So nearly infinite.

We waited while she passed;
It was a narrow time,
Too jostled were our souls to speak,
At length the notice came.

She mentioned, and forgot;
Then lightly as a reed
Bent to the water, shivered scarce,
Consented, and was dead.

And we, we placed the hair,
And drew the head erect;
And then an awful leisure was,
Our faith to regulate.

EMILY DICKINSON

59

Within My Garden Rides a Bird

Within my garden rides a bird
Upon a single wheel,
Whose spokes a dizzy music make
As 'twere a traveling mill.

He never stops, but slackens
Above the ripest rose,
Partakes without alighting,
And praises as he goes;

Till every spice is tasted,
And then his fairy gig
Reels in remoter atmospheres,
And I rejoin my dog.

And he and I perplex us
If positive 'twere we –
Or bore the garden in the brain
This curiosity?

But he, the best logician,
Refers my duller eye
To just vibrating blossoms –
An exquisite reply!

EMILY DICKINSON

60

A Route of Evanescence

A route of evanescence
With a revolving wheel;
A resonance of emerald,
A rush of cochineal;
And every blossom on the bush
Adjusts its tumbled head –
The mail from Tunis, probably,
An easy morning's ride.

EMILY DICKINSON

61

I Taste a Liquor Never Brewed

I taste a liquor never brewed,
From tankards scooped in pearl;
Not all the vats upon the Rhine
Yield such an alcohol!

Inebriate of air am I,
And debauchee of dew,
Reeling, through endless summer days,
From inns of molten blue.

When landlords turn the drunken bee
Out of the foxglove's door,
When butterflies renounce their drams,
I shall but drink the more!

Till seraphs swing their snowy hats,
And saints to windows run,
To see the little tippler
Leaning against the sun!

EMILY DICKINSON

62

Drinking

The thirsty earth soaks up the rain,
And drinks and gapes for drink again;
The plants suck in the earth, and are
With constant drinking fresh and fair;
The sea itself (which one would think
Should have but little need of drink)
Drinks twice ten thousand rivers up,
So fill'd that they o'erflow the cup.
The busy Sun (and one would guess
By's drunken fiery face no less)
Drinks up the sea, and when he's done,
The Moon and Stars drink up the Sun:
They drink, and dance by their own light,
They drink and revel all the night:
Nothing in Nature's sober found,
But an eternal health goes round.
Fill up the bowl, then, fill it high,
Fill all the glasses there – for why
Should every creature drink but I?
Why, man of morals, tell me why?

ABRAHAM COWLEY

63

A Drunken Man's Praise of Sobriety

Come swish around, my pretty punk,
And keep me dancing still
That I may stay a sober man
Although I drink my fill.
Sobriety is a jewel
That I do much adore;
And therefore keep me dancing
Though drunkards lie and snore.
O mind your feet, O mind your feet,
Keep dancing like a wave,
And under every dancer
A dead man in his grave.
No ups and downs, my pretty,
A mermaid, not a punk;
A drunkard is a dead man,
And all dead men are drunk.

WILLIAM BUTLER YEATS

64

A Glass of Beer

The lanky hank of a she in the inn over there
Nearly killed me for asking the loan of a glass of beer;
May the devil grip the whey-faced slut by the hair,
And beat bad manners out of her skin for a year.

That parboiled ape, with the toughest jaw you will see
On virtue's path, and a voice that would rasp the dead,
Came roaring and raging the minute she looked at me,
And threw me out of the house on the back of my head!

If I asked her master he'd give me a cask a day;
But she, with the beer at hand, not a gill would arrange!
May she marry a ghost and bear him a kitten, and may
The High King of Glory permit her to get the mange.

JAMES STEPHENS

65

Reflections on Ice-breaking

Candy
Is dandy
But liquor
Is quicker.

OGDEN NASH

66

The Dancing Cabman

Alone on the lawn
  The cabman dances;
In the dew of dawn
  He kicks and prances.
His bowler is set
  On his bullet head,
For his boots are wet,
  And his aunt is dead.
There on the lawn
  As the light advances, 10
On the tide of the dawn,
  The cabman dances.

Swift and strong
  As a garden roller,
He dances along
  In his little bowler,
Skimming the lawn
  With royal grace,
The dew of the dawn
  On his great red face. 20
To fairy flutes,
  As the light advances,
In square black boots
  The cabman dances.

J. B. MORTON

67

Epigram

(Engraved on the
Collar of a dog which
I gave to His Royal Highness)

I am His Highness' dog at Kew;
Pray tell me, sir, whose dog are you?

ALEXANDER POPE

68

Zimri

FROM

Absalom and Achitophel

In the first rank of these did Zimri stand,
A man so various that he seemed to be
Not one, but all mankind's epitome:
Stiff in opinions, always in the wrong,
Was everything by starts and nothing long;
But in the course of one revolving moon
Was chymist, fiddler, statesman, and buffoon;
Then all for women, painting, rhyming, drinking,
Besides ten thousand freaks that died in thinking.
Blest madman, who could every hour employ
With something new to wish or to enjoy!
Railing and praising were his usual themes,
And both, to show his judgment, in extremes:
So over violent or over civil
That every man with him was God or Devil.
In squandering wealth was his peculiar art;
Nothing went unrewarded but desert.
Beggared by fools whom still he found too late,
He had his jest, and they had his estate.

JOHN DRYDEN

69

The Rape of the Lock

CANTO THIRD

Close by those meads, for ever crown'd with flow'rs,
Where Thames with pride surveys his rising tow'rs,
There stands a structure of majestic frame,
Which from the neighb'ring Hampton takes its name.
Here Britain's statesmen oft the fall foredoom
Of foreign tyrants, and of nymphs at home;
Here thou, great ANNA! whom three realms obey,
Dost sometimes counsel take – and sometimes tea.
Hither the heroes and the nymphs resort,
To taste a while the pleasures of a court; 10
In various talk th' instructive hours they pass'd,
Who gave the ball, or paid the visit last;
One speaks the glory of the British Queen,
And one describes a charming Indian screen;
A third interprets motions, looks, and eyes;
At every word a reputation dies.
Snuff, or the fan, supply each pause of chat,
With singing, laughing, ogling, and all that.
Meanwhile, declining from the noon of day,
The sun obliquely shoots his burning ray; 20
The hungry judges soon the sentence sign,
And wretches hang that jurymen may dine;
The merchant from th' Exchange returns in peace,
And the long labours of the toilet cease.
Belinda now, whom thirst of fame invites,
Burns to encounter two advent'rous knights,

At ombre singly to decide their doom;
And swells her breast with conquests yet to come.
Straight the three bands prepare in arms to join,
Each band the number of the sacred nine. 30
Soon as she spreads her hand, th' aërial guard
Descend, and sit on each important card:
First Ariel perch'd upon a Matadore,
Then each according to the rank they bore;
For sylphs, yet mindful of their ancient race,
Are, as when women, wondrous fond of place.
  Behold, four kings, in majesty revered,
With hoary whiskers and a forky beard;
And four fair queens whose hands sustain a flow'r,
The expressive emblem of their softer pow'r; 40
Four knaves in garbs succinct, a trusty band,
Caps on their heads, and halberts in their hand;
And parti-colour'd troops, a shining train,
Draw forth to combat on the velvet plain.
  The skilful nymph reviews her force with care;
Let spades be trumps! she said, and trumps they were.
  Now move to war her sable Matadores,
In show like leaders of the swarthy Moors.
Spadillio first, unconquerable lord!
Led off two captive trumps, and swept the board. 50
As many more Manillio forced to yield,
And march'd a victor from the verdant field.
Him Basto follow'd, but his fate more hard
Gain'd but one trump and one plebeian card.
With his broad sabre next, a chief in years,
The hoary majesty of Spades appears,
Puts forth one manly leg, to sight revealed,
The rest, his many-colour'd robe concealed.
The rebel knave, who dares his prince engage,

Proves the just victim of his royal rage. 60
Ev'n mighty Pam, that kings and queens o'erthrew,
And mow'd down armies in the fights of Loo,
Sad chance of war! now destitute of aid,
Falls undistinguish'd by the victor spade!
  Thus far both armies to Belinda yield;
Now to the Baron fate inclines the field.
His warlike Amazon her host invades,
Th' imperial consort of the crown of Spades.
The Club's black tyrant first her victim died,
Spite of his haughty mien and barb'rous pride: 70
What boots the regal circle on his head,
His giant limbs, in state unwieldy spread;
That long behind he trails his pompous robe,
And, of all monarchs, only grasps the globe?
  The Baron now his Diamonds pours apace;
Th' embroider'd King who shews but half his face,
And his refulgent Queen, with pow'rs combined,
Of broken troops an easy conquest find.
Clubs, Diamonds, Hearts, in wild disorder seen,
With throngs promiscuous strew the level green. 80
Thus when dispersed a routed army runs,
Of Asia's troops, and Afric's sable sons,
With like confusion different nations fly,
Of various habit, and of various dye;
The pierc'd battalions disunited fall,
In heaps on heaps; one fate o'erwhelms them all.
  The Knave of Diamonds tries his wily arts,
And wins (oh shameful chance!) the Queen of Hearts.
At this, the blood the virgin's cheek forsook,
A livid paleness spreads o'er all her look; 90
She sees, and trembles at th' approaching ill,
Just in the jaws of ruin, and codille.

And now (as oft in some distemper'd state)
On one nice trick depends the general fate:
An Ace of Hearts steps forth: the King, unseen,
Lurk'd in her hand, and mourn'd his captive Queen:
He springs to vengeance with an eager pace,
And falls like thunder on the prostrate Ace.
The nymph exulting fills with shouts the sky;
The walls, the woods, and long canals reply. 100
Oh thoughtless mortals! ever blind to fate,
Too soon dejected, and too soon elate.
Sudden these honours shall be snatch'd away,
And curs'd for ever this victorious day.
For lo! the board with cups and spoons is crown'd,
The berries crackle, and the mill turns round;
On shining altars of Japan they raise
The silver lamp; the fiery spirits blaze:
From silver spouts the grateful liquors glide,
While China's earth receives the smoking tide: 110
At once they gratify their scent and taste,
And frequent cups prolong the rich repast.
Straight hover round the fair her airy band;
Some, as she sipp'd, the fuming liquor fanned,
Some o'er her lap their careful plumes displayed,
Trembling, and conscious of the rich brocade.
Coffee (which makes the politician wise,
And see through all things with his half-shut eyes)
Sent up in vapours to the Baron's brain
New stratagems, the radiant lock to gain. 120
Ah cease, rash youth! desist ere 'tis too late,
Fear the just gods, and think of Scylla's fate!
Changed to a bird, and sent to flit in air,
She dearly pays for Nisus' injur'd hair!
But when to mischief mortals bend their will,

How soon they find fit instruments of ill!
Just then Clarissa drew, with tempting grace,
A two-edg'd weapon from her shining case:
So ladies in romance assist their knight,
Present the spear, and arm him for the fight. 130
He takes the gift with rev'rence, and extends
The little engine on his fingers' ends;
This just behind Belinda's neck he spread,
As o'er the fragrant steams she bends her head.
Swift to the lock a thousand sprites repair,
A thousand wings, by turns, blow back the hair;
And thrice they twitch'd the diamond in her ear;
Thrice she look'd back, and thrice the foe drew near.
Just in that instant anxious Ariel sought
The close recesses of the virgin's thought: 140
As on the nosegay in her breast reclin'd,
He watch'd th' ideas rising in her mind,
Sudden he view'd, in spite of all her art,
An earthly lover lurking at her heart.
Amaz'd, confus'd, he found his power expired,
Resign'd to fate, and with a sigh retired.
The peer now spreads the glitt'ring forfex wide,
T' enclose the lock; now joins it, to divide.
Even then, before the fatal engine closed,
A wretched sylph too fondly interposed; 150
Fate urged the shears, and cut the sylph in twain,
(But airy substance soon unites again)
The meeting points the sacred hair dissever
From the fair head, for ever, and for ever!
Then flash'd the living lightning from her eyes,
And screams of horror rend the affrighted skies;
Not louder shrieks to pitying Heav'n are cast,
When husbands, or when lapdogs, breathe their last;

Or when rich China vessels fallen from high,
In glitt'ring dust, and painted fragments lie! 160
  Let wreaths of triumph now my temples twine,
(The victor cried) the glorious prize is mine!
While fish in streams, or birds delight in air,
Or in a coach-and-six the British fair,
As long as Atalantis shall be read,
Or the small pillow grace a lady's bed,
While visits shall be paid on solemn days,
When num'rous wax-lights in bright order blaze,
While nymphs take treats, or assignations give,
So long my honour, name, and praise shall live! 170
What time would spare, from steel receives its date,
And monuments, like men, submit to fate!
Steel could the labour of the gods destroy,
And strike to dust th' imperial towers of Troy;
Steel could the works of mortal pride confound,
And hew triumphal arches to the ground.
What wonder then, fair nymph! thy hairs should feel
The conqu'ring force of unresisted steel?

ALEXANDER POPE

70

The Wif of Bathe

FROM THE
PROLOGUE
TO THE
Canterbury Tales

A good wif was ther of bisidè Bathe,
But she was som-del° deef, and that was scathe.° — somewhat — a pity
Of clooth-makyng she haddè swich an haunt° — such a skill
She passèd hem° of Ypres and of Gaunt. — surpassed them
In al the parisshe wif ne was ther noon
That to the offrynge bifore hire sholde goon;° — go
And if ther dide, certeyn so wrooth was she,
That she was out of allè charitee.
Hir coverchiefs° ful fyne weren of ground,° — — head-coverings — texture
I dorstè° swere they weyèden ten pound, — — would dare
That on a Sonday weren upon hir heed.
Hir hosen° weren of fyn scarlet° reed, — leggings — cloth
Ful streite y-teyd,° and shoes ful moyste and
newe. — tightly tied
Boold was hir face, and fair, and reed of hewe.
She was a worthy womman al hir lyve. 15
Housbondes at chirchè dore she haddè fyve,
Withouten° oother compaignye in youthe, — — Not to mention
But ther-of nedeth nat to speke as nowthe.° — now
And thries hadde she been at Jerusalem;
She haddè passèd many a straungè° strem; — foreign
At Rome she haddè been, and at Boloigne,
In Galice at Seint Jame, and at Coloigne,
She koude° muchel of wandrynge by the weye. — knew

Gat-tothèd was she, soothly° for to seye. — truly
Upon an amblere esily she sat, 25
Y-wympled wel, and on hir heed an hat
As brood as is a bokeler° or a targe;° — buckler shield
A foot-mantel° aboute hir hipès large, — outer skirt
And on hire feet a paire of sporès° sharpe. — spurs
In felaweship wel koude she laughe and
carpe;° — talk
Of remedies of love she knew perchaunce,
For she koude° of that art the oldè daunce! — knew

GEOFFREY CHAUCER

71

Mrs Reece Laughs

Laughter, with us, is no great undertaking,
A sudden wave that breaks and dies in breaking.
Laughter with Mrs Reece is much less simple:
It germinates, it spreads, dimple by dimple,
From small beginnings, things of easy girth,
To formidable redundancies of mirth.

Clusters of subterranean chuckles rise
And presently the circles of her eyes
Close into slits and all the woman heaves
As a great elm with all its mounds of leaves
Wallows before the storm. From hidden sources
A mustering of blind volcanic forces
Takes her and shakes her till she sobs and gapes.
Then all that load of bottled mirth escapes
In one wild crow, a lifting of huge hands,
And creaking stays, a visage that expands
In scarlet ridge and furrow. Thence collapse,
A hanging head, a feeble hand that flaps
An apron-end to stir an air and waft
A steaming face. And Mrs Reece has laughed.

MARTIN ARMSTRONG

72

Silence

My father used to say,
'Superior people never make long visits,
have to be shown Longfellow's grave
or the glass flowers at Harvard.
Self-reliant like the cat –
that takes its prey to privacy,
the mouse's limp tail hanging like a shoelace from its
    mouth –
they sometimes enjoy solitude,
and can be robbed of speech
by speech which has delighted them.
The deepest feeling always shows itself in silence;
not in silence, but restraint.'
Nor was he insincere in saying, 'Make my house your inn.
Inns are not residences.

MARIANNE MOORE

73

Great Things

Sweet cyder is a great thing,
  A great thing to me,
Spinning down to Weymouth town
  By Ridgway thirstily,
And maid and mistress summoning
  Who tend the hostelry:
O cyder is a great thing,
  A great thing to me!

The dance is a great thing,
  A great thing to me, 10
With candles lit and partners fit
  For night-long revelry;
And going home when day-dawning
  Peeps pale upon the lea:
O dancing is a great thing,
  A great thing to me!

Love is, yea, a great thing,
  A great thing to me,
When, having drawn across the lawn
  In darkness silently, 20
A figure flits like one a-wing
  Out from the nearest tree:
O love is, yes, a great thing,
  A great thing to me!

Will these be always great things,
  Great things to me? . . . .

Let it befall that One will call,
'Soul, I have need of thee';
What then? Joy-jaunts, impassioned flings,
Love, and its ecstasy, 30
Will always have been great things,
Great things to me!

THOMAS HARDY

74
Song of Myself

SELECTIONS

[1]

I celebrate myself, and sing myself,
And what I assume you shall assume,
For every atom belonging to me as good belongs to you.

I loafe and invite my soul,
I lean and loafe at my ease observing a spear of summer grass.

My tongue, every atom of my blood, form'd from this soil, this air,
Born here of parents born here from parents the same, and their parents the same,
I, now thirty-seven years old in perfect health begin,
Hoping to cease not till death.

Creeds and schools in abeyance,
Retiring back a while sufficed at what they are, but never
forgotten,
I harbor for good or bad, I permit to speak at every hazard,
Nature without check with original energy.

[*From* 6]
. . .

A child said *What is the grass?* fetching it to me with full
hands;

How could I answer the child? I do not know what it is
any more than he.

I guess it must be the flag of my disposition, out of hopeful
green stuff woven.

Or I guess it is the handkerchief of the Lord,
A scented gift and remembrancer designedly dropt,
Bearing the owner's name someway in the corners, that we
may see and remark, and say *Whose?*

Or I guess the grass is itself a child, the produced babe of
the vegetation.

Or I guess it is a uniform hieroglyphic,
And it means, Sprouting alike in broad zones and narrow
zones,
Growing among black folks as among white,
Kanuck, Tuckahoe, Congressman, Cuff, I give them the
same, I receive them the same.

And now it seems to me the beautiful uncut hair of graves.

. . .

[*From* 33]

. . .

I am the man, I suffer'd, I was there.

The disdain and calmness of martyrs,
The mother of old, condemn'd for a witch, burnt with dry
wood, her children gazing on,
The hounded slave that flags in the race, leans by the
fence, blowing, cover'd with sweat,
The twinges that sting like needles his legs and neck, the
murderous buckshot and the bullets,
All these I feel or am.

I am the hounded slave, I wince at the bite of the dogs,
Hell and despair are upon me, crack and again crack the
marksmen,
I clutch the rails of the fence, my gore dribs, thinn'd with
the ooze of my skin,
I fall on the weeds and stones,
The riders spur their unwilling horses, haul close,
Taunt my dizzy ears and beat me violently over the head
with whip-stocks.

Agonies are one of my changes of garments,
I do not ask the wounded person how he feels, I myself
become the wounded person,
My hurts turn livid upon me as I lean on a cane and
observe.

I am the mash'd fireman with breast-bone broken,
Tumbling walls buried me in their debris,
Heat and smoke I inspired, I heard the yelling shouts of
my comrades,
I heard the distant click of their picks and shovels,
They have clear'd the beams away, they tenderly lift me
forth.

I lie in the night air in my red shirt, the pervading hush is
for my sake,
Painless after all I lie exhausted but not so unhappy,
White and beautiful are the faces around me, the heads
are bared of their fire-caps,
The kneeling crowd fades with the light of the torches.

Distant and dead resuscitate,
They show as the dial or move as the hands of me, I am
the clock myself.
. . .

[52]

The spotted hawk swoops by and accuses me, he complains
of my gab and my loitering.

I too am not a bit tamed, I too am untranslatable,
I sound my barbaric yawp over the roofs of the world.

The last scud of day holds back for me,
It flings my likeness after the rest and true as any on the
shadow'd wilds,
It coaxes me to the vapor and the dusk.

I depart as air, I shake my white locks at the runaway
    sun,
I effuse my flesh in eddies, and drift it in lacy jags.

I bequeath myself to the dirt to grow from the grass I
    love,
If you want me again look for me under your boot-soles.

You will hardly know who I am or what I mean,
But I shall be good health to you nevertheless,
And filter and fibre your blood.

Failing to fetch me at first keep encouraged,
Missing me one place search another,
I stop somewhere waiting for you.

WALT WHITMAN

75
Sonnet

When I have fears that I may cease to be
  Before my pen has glean'd my teeming brain,
Before high-pilèd books, in charact'ry,
  Hold like rich garners the full ripen'd grain;
When I behold, upon the night's starr'd face,
  Huge cloudy symbols of a high romance,
And feel that I may never live to trace
  Their shadows, with the magic hand of chance;
And when I feel, fair creature of an hour!
  That I shall never look upon thee more,
Never have relish in the faery power
  Of unreflecting love; – then on the shore
Of the wide world I stand alone, and think,
Till Love and Fame to nothingness do sink.

JOHN KEATS

76

The Birth of Tragedy

And me happiest when I compose poems.
    Love, power, the huzza of battle
    are something, are much;
yet a poem includes them like a pool
    water and reflection.
In me, nature's divided things –
    tree, mould on tree –
    have their fruition;
I am their core. Let them swap,
bandy, like a flame swerve   10
I am their mouth; as a mouth I serve.

And I observe how the sensual moths
    big with odour and sunshine
    dart into the perilous shrubbery;
or drop their visiting shadows
    upon the garden I one year made
of flowering stone to be a footstool
    for the perfect gods:
    who, friends to the ascending orders,
sustain all passionate meditations   20
and call down pardons
for the insurgent blood.

A quiet madman, never far from tears,
    I lie like a slain thing
    under the green air the trees
inhabit, or rest upon a chair
    towards which the inflammable air
tumbles on many robins' wings;
    noting how seasonably
    leaf and blossom uncurl 30
and living things arrange their death,
while someone from afar off
blows birthday candles for the world.

IRVING LAYTON

77

Sonnet LV

Not marble, nor the gilded monuments
Of princes, shall outlive this powerful rhyme;
But you shall shine more bright in these contents
Than unswept stone, besmeared with sluttish time.
When wasteful war shall statues overturn,
And broils root out the work of masonry,
Nor Mars his sword nor war's quick fire shall burn
The living record of your memory.
'Gainst death and all-oblivious enmity
Shall you pace forth; your praise shall still find room
Even in the eyes of all posterity
That wear this world out to the ending doom.
So, till the judgment that yourself arise,
You live in this, and dwell in lovers' eyes.

WILLIAM SHAKESPEARE

78

On His Books

When I am dead, I hope it may be said:
His sins were scarlet, but his books were read.

HILAIRE BELLOC

79

To a Poet a Thousand Years Hence

I who am dead a thousand years,
  And wrote this sweet archaic song,
Send you my words for messengers
  The way I shall not pass along.

I care not if you bridge the seas,
  Or ride secure the cruel sky,
Or build consummate palaces
  Of metal or of masonry.

But have you wine and music still,
  And statues and a bright-eyed love,
And foolish thoughts of good and ill,
  And prayers to them who sit above?

How shall we conquer? Like a wind
  That falls at eve our fancies blow,
And old Maeonides the blind
  Said it three thousand years ago.

O friend unseen, unborn, unknown,
  Student of our sweet English tongue,
Read out my words at night, alone:
  I was a poet, I was young.

Since I can never see your face,
  And never shake you by the hand,
I send my soul through time and space
  To greet you. You will understand.

JAMES ELROY FLECKER

80

Jesse James

It was on a Wednesday night, the moon was shining bright,
  They robbed the Glendale train.
And the people they did say, for many miles away,
  'Twas the outlaws Frank and Jesse James.

Jesse had a wife to mourn all her life,
  The children they are brave.
'Twas a dirty little coward shot Mister Howard,
  And laid Jesse James in his grave.

It was Robert Ford, the dirty little coward,
  I wonder how he does feel,
For he ate of Jesse's bread and he slept in Jesse's bed,
  Then he laid Jesse James in his grave.

It was his brother Frank that robbed the Gallatin bank,
  And carried the money from the town.
It was in this very place that they had a little race,
  For they shot Captain Sheets to the ground.

They went to the crossing not very far from there,
  And there they did the same;
And the agent on his knees he delivered up the keys
  To the outlaws Frank and Jesse James.

It was on a Saturday night, Jesse was at home
  Talking to his family brave,
When the thief and the coward, little Robert Ford,
  Laid Jesse James in his grave.

How people held their breath when they heard of Jesse's
    death,
  And wondered how he ever came to die.
'Twas one of the gang, dirty Robert Ford,
  That shot Jesse James on the sly.

Jesse went to his rest with his hand on his breast.
  The devil will be upon his knee.
He was born one day in the county of Clay,
  And came from a solitary race.

ANONYMOUS

81

John Henry

John Henry was a lil baby,
Sittin' on his mama's knee,
Said: 'De Big Bend Tunnel on de C. & O. road
Gonna cause de death of me,
Lawd, Lawd, gonna cause de death of me.'

Cap'n says to John Henry,
'Gonna bring me a steam drill 'round,
Gonna take dat steam drill out on de job,
Gonna whop dat steel on down,
Lawd, Lawd, gonna whop dat steel on down.' 10

John Henry tol' his cap'n,
Lightnin' was in his eye:
'Cap'n, bet yo' las' red cent on me,
Fo' I'll beat it to de bottom or I'll die,
Lawd, Lawd, I'll beat it to de bottom or I'll die.'

Sun shine hot an' burnin',
Wer'n't no breeze a-tall,
Sweat ran down like water down a hill,
Dat day John Henry let his hammer fall,
Lawd, Lawd, dat day John Henry let his hammer fall. 20

John Henry went to de tunnel,
An' dey put him in de lead to drive,
De rock so tall an' John Henry so small,
Dat he lied down his hammer an' he cried,
Lawd, Lawd, dat he lied down his hammer an' he cried.

John Henry started on de right hand,
De steam drill started on de lef' –
'Before I'd let dis steam drill beat me down,
I'd hammer my fool self to death,
Lawd, Lawd, I'd hammer my fool self to death.' 30

White man tol' John Henry,
'Nigger, damn yo' soul,
You might beat dis steam an' drill of mine,
When de rocks in dis mountain turn to gol',
Lawd, Lawd, when de rocks in dis mountain turn to gol'.'

John Henry said to his shaker,
'Nigger, why don' you sing?
I'm throwin' twelve poun's from my hips on down,
Jes' listen to de col' steel ring,
Lawd, Lawd, jes' listen to de col' steel ring.' 40

Oh, de captain said to John Henry,
'I b'lieve this mountain's sinkin' in.'
John Henry said to his captain, oh my!
'Ain' nothin' but my hammer suckin' win',
Lawd, Lawd, ain' nothin' but my hammer suckin' win'.'

John Henry tol' his shaker,
'Shaker, you better pray,
For, if I miss dis six-foot steel,
Tomorrow'll be yo' buryin' day,
Lawd, Lawd, tomorrow'll be yo' buryin' day.' 50

John Henry tol' his captain,
'Look yonder what I see –
Yo' drill's done broke an' yo' hole's done choke,

An' you cain' drive steel like me,
Lawd, Lawd, an' you cain' drive steel like me.'

De man dat invented de steam drill,
Thought he was mighty fine.
John Henry drove his fifteen feet,
An' de steam drill only made nine,
Lawd, Lawd, an' de steam drill only made nine. 60

De hammer dat John Henry swung,
It weighed over nine pound;
He broke a rib in his lef'-han' side,
An' his intrels fell on de groun',
Lawd, Lawd, an' his intrels fell on de groun'.

All de womens in de Wes',
When dey heared of John Henry's death,
Stood in de rain, flagged de eas'-boun' train,
Goin' where John Henry fell dead,
Lawd, Lawd, goin' where John Henry fell dead. 70

John Henry's lil mother,
She was all dressed in red,
She jumped in bed, covered up her head,
Said she didn't know her son was dead,
Lawd, Lawd, didn' know her son was dead.

Dey took John Henry to de graveyard,
An' dey buried him in de san',
An' every locomotive come roarin' by,
Says, 'Dere lays a steel-drivin' man,
Lawd, Lawd, dere lays a steel-drivin' man.'

ANONYMOUS

82

The Iceberg

FROM

The Titanic

Calved from a glacier near Godhaven coast,
It left the fiord for the sea – a host
Of white flotillas gathering in its wake,
And joined by fragments from a Behring floe,
Had circumnavigated it to make
It centre of an archipelago.
Its lateral motion on the Davis Strait
Was casual and indeterminate,
And each advance to southward was as blind
As each recession to the north. No smoke 10
Of steamships nor the hoist of mainsails broke
The polar wastes – no sounds except the grind
Of ice, the cry of curlews and the lore
Of winds from mesas of eternal snow;
Until, caught by the western undertow,
It struck the current of the Labrador
Which swung it to its definite southern stride.
Pressure and glacial time had stratified
The berg to the consistency of flint,
And kept inviolate, through clash of tide 20
And gale, façade and columns with their hint
Of inward altars and of steepled bells
Ringing the passage of the parallels.
But when with months of voyaging it came
To where both streams – the Gulf and Polar – met,
The sun which left its crystal peaks aflame

In the sub-Arctic noons, began to fret
The arches, flute the spires and deform
The features, till the batteries of storm,
Playing above the slow-eroding base, 30
Demolished the last temple touch of grace.
Another month, and nothing but the brute
And palaeolithic outline of a face
Fronted the transatlantic shipping route.
A sloping spur that tapered to a claw
And lying twenty feet below had made
It lurch and shamble like a plantigrade;
But with an impulse governed by the raw
Mechanics of its birth, it drifted where
Ambushed, fog-gray, it stumbled on its lair, 40
North forty-one degrees and forty-four,
Fifty and fourteen west the longitude,
Waiting a world-memorial hour, its rude
Corundum form stripped to its Greenland core.

E. J. PRATT

83

Erosion

It took the sea a thousand years,
A thousand years to trace
The granite features of this cliff,
In crag and scarp and base.

It took the sea an hour one night,
An hour of storm to place
The sculpture of these granite seams
Upon a woman's face.

E. J. PRATT

84

In a Station of the Metro

The apparition of these faces in the crowd;
Petals on a wet, black bough.

EZRA POUND

85

Epistle To Be Left in the Earth

. . . It is colder now
there are many stars
we are drifting
North by the Great Bear
the leaves are falling
The water is stone in the scooped rocks
to southward
Red sun gray air
the crows are
Slow on their crooked wings 10
the jays have left us
Long since we passed the flares of Orion
Each man believes in his heart he will die
Many have written last thoughts and last letters
None know if our deaths are now or forever
None know if this wandering earth will be found

We lie down and the snow covers our garments
I pray you
you (if any open this writing)
Make in your mouths the words that were our names 20
I will tell you all we have learned
I will tell you everything
The earth is round
there are springs under the orchards
The loam cuts with a blunt knife
beware of

Elms in thunder
                    the lights in the sky are stars
We think they do not see
                    we think also   30
The trees do not know nor the leaves of the grasses
                    hear us
The birds too are ignorant
                    Do not listen
Do not stand at dark in the open windows
We before you have heard this
                    they are voices
They are not words at all but the wind rising
Also none among us has seen God
(. . . We have thought often   40
The flaws of sun in the late and driving weather
Pointed to one tree but it was not so)
As for the nights I warn you the nights are dangerous
The wind changes at night and the dreams come

It is very cold
                    there are strange stars near Arcturus

Voices are crying an unknown name in the sky

ARCHIBALD MACLEISH

86

Domination of Black

At night, by the fire,
The colors of the bushes
And of the fallen leaves,
Repeating themselves,
Turned in the room,
Like the leaves themselves
Turning in the wind.
Yes: but the color of the heavy hemlocks
Came striding.
And I remembered the cry of the peacocks. 10

The colors of their tails
Were like the leaves themselves
Turning in the wind,
In the twilight wind.
They swept over the room,
Just as they flew from the boughs of the hemlocks
Down to the ground.
I heard them cry – the peacocks:
Was it a cry against the twilight
Or against the leaves themselves 20
Turning in the wind,
Turning as the flames
Turned in the fire,
Turning as the tails of the peacocks
Turned in the loud fire,
Loud as the hemlocks
Full of the cry of the peacocks?

Or was it a cry against the hemlocks?
Out of the window,
I saw how the planets gathered 30
Like the leaves themselves
Turning in the wind.
I saw how the night came,
Came striding like the color of the heavy hemlocks.
I felt afraid.
And I remembered the cry of the peacocks.

WALLACE STEVENS

87

Carol

I was a lover of turkey and holly
But my true love was the Christmas tree
We hung our hearts from a green green bough
And merry swung the mistletoe

He decked the tree with a silver apple
And a golden pear,
A partridge and a cockle shell
And a fair maiden

No rose can tell the fumes of myrrh
That filled the forest of our day
Till fruit and shell and maid fell down
And the partridge flew away

Now I swing from a brittle twig
For the green bough of my true love hid
A laily worm. Around my neck
The hangman ties the holly.

ANNE WILKINSON

88

The Hollow Men

'Mistah Kurtz – he dead.

A penny for the Old Guy.

I

We are the hollow men
We are the stuffed men
Leaning together
Headpiece filled with straw. Alas!
Our dried voices, when
We whisper together
Are quiet and meaningless
As wind in dried grass
Or rats' feet over broken glass
In our dry cellar. 10

Shape without form, shade without colour,
Paralysed force, gesture without motion;
Those who have crossed
With direct eyes, to death's other Kingdom
Remember us – if at all – not as lost
Violent souls, but only
As the hollow men
The stuffed men.

II

Eyes I dare not meet in dreams
In death's dream kingdom 20
These do not appear:

There, the eyes are
Sunlight on a broken column
There, is a tree swinging
And voices are
In the wind's singing
More distant and more solemn
Than a fading star.
Let me be no nearer
In death's dream kingdom 30
Let me also wear
Such deliberate disguises
Rat's coat, crowskin, crossed staves
In a field
Behaving as the wind behaves
No nearer –

Not that final meeting
In the twilight kingdom.

III

This is the dead land
This is cactus land 40
Here the stone images
Are raised, here they receive
The supplication of a dead man's hand
Under the twinkle of a fading star.

Is it like this
In death's other kingdom
Waking alone
At the hour when we are
Trembling with tenderness
Lips that would kiss 50
Form prayers to broken stone.

IV

The eyes are not here
There are no eyes here
In this valley of dying stars
In this hollow valley
This broken jaw of our lost kingdoms.

In this last of meeting places
We grope together
And avoid speech
Gathered on this beach of the tumid river. 60

Sightless, unless
The eyes reappear
And the perpetual star
Multifoliate rose
Of death's twilight kingdom
The hope only
Of empty men.

V

Here we go round the prickly pear
Prickly pear prickly pear
Here we go round the prickly pear 70
At five o'clock in the morning.

Between the idea
And the reality
Between the emotion
And the act
Falls the Shadow
For Thine is the Kingdom

Between the conception
And the creation
Between the emotion 80
And the response
Falls the Shadow
Life is very long

Between the desire
And the spasm
Between the potency
And the existence
Between the essence
And the descent
Falls the Shadow 90
For Thine is the Kingdom

For Thine is
Life is
For Thine is the

This is the way the world ends
This is the way the world ends
This is the way the world ends
Not with a bang but a whimper.

T. S. ELIOT

89

The Inferno

CANTO THIRD

I AM THE WAY INTO THE CITY OF WOE.
I AM THE WAY TO A FORSAKEN PEOPLE.
I AM THE WAY INTO ETERNAL SORROW.

SACRED JUSTICE MOVED MY ARCHITECT.
I WAS RAISED HERE BY DIVINE OMNIPOTENCE,
PRIMORDIAL LOVE AND ULTIMATE INTELLECT.

ONLY THOSE ELEMENTS TIME CANNOT WEAR
WERE MADE BEFORE ME, AND BEYOND TIME I STAND.
ABANDON ALL HOPE YE WHO ENTER HERE.

These mysteries I read cut into stone 10
above a gate. And turning I said: 'Master,
what is the meaning of this harsh inscription?'

And he then as initiate to novice:
'Here must you put by all division of spirit
and gather your soul against all cowardice.

This is the place I told you to expect.
Here you shall pass among the fallen people,
souls who have lost the good of intellect.'

So saying, he put forth his hand to me,
and with a gentle and encouraging smile 20
he led me through the gate of mystery.

Here sighs and cries and wails coiled and recoiled
on the starless air, spilling my soul to tears.
A confusion of tongues and monstrous accents toiled

in pain and anger. Voices hoarse and shrill
and sounds of blows, all intermingled, raised
tumult and pandemonium that still

whirls on the air forever dirty with it
as if a whirlwind sucked at sand. And I,
holding my head in horror, cried: 'Sweet Spirit, 30

what souls are these who run through this black haze?'
And he to me: 'These are the nearly soulless
whose lives concluded neither blame nor praise.

They are mixed here with that despicable corps
of angels who were neither for God nor Satan,
but only for themselves. The High Creator

scourged them from Heaven for its perfect beauty,
and Hell will not receive them since the wicked
might feel some glory over them.' And I:

'Master, what gnaws at them so hideously 40
their lamentation stuns the very air?'
'They have no hope of death,' he answered me,

'and in their blind and unattaining state
their miserable lives have sunk so low
that they must envy every other fate.

No word of them survives their living season.
Mercy and Justice deny them even a name.
Let us not speak of them: look, and pass on.'

I saw a banner there upon the mist.
Circling and circling, it seemed to scorn all pause. 50
So it ran on, and still behind it pressed

a never-ending rout of souls in pain.
I had not thought death had undone so many
as passed before me in that mournful train.

And some I knew among them; last of all
I recognized the shadow of that soul
who, in his cowardice, made the Great Denial.

At once I understood for certain: these
were of that retrograde and faithless crew
hateful to God and to His enemies. 60

These wretches never born and never dead
ran naked in a swarm of wasps and hornets
that goaded them the more the more they fled,

and made their faces stream with bloody gouts
of pus and tears that dribbled to their feet
to be swallowed there by loathsome worms and maggots.

Then looking onward I made out a throng
assembled on the beach of a wide river,
whereupon I turned to him: 'Master, I long

to know what souls these are, and what strange usage 70
makes them as eager to cross as they seem to be
in this infected light.' At which the Sage:

'All this shall be made known to you when we stand
on the joyless beach of Acheron.' And I
cast down my eyes, sensing a reprimand

in what he said, and so walked at his side
in silence and ashamed until we came
through the dead cavern to that sunless tide.

There, steering toward us in an ancient ferry
came an old man with a white bush of hair, 80
bellowing: 'Woe to you depraved souls! Bury

here and forever all hope of Paradise:
I come to lead you to the other shore,
into eternal dark, into fire and ice.

And you who are living yet, I say begone
from these who are dead.' But when he saw me stand
against his violence he began again:

'By other windings and by other steerage
shall you cross to that other shore. Not here! Not here!
A lighter craft than mine must give you passage.' 90

And my Guide to him: 'Charon, bite back your spleen:
this has been willed where what is willed must be,
and is not yours to ask what it may mean.'

The steersman of that marsh of ruined souls,
who wore a wheel of flame around each eye,
stifled the rage that shook his woolly jowls.

But those unmanned and naked spirits there
turned pale with fear and their teeth began to chatter
at sound of his crude bellow. In despair

they blasphemed God, their parents, their time
on earth, 100
the race of Adam, and the day and the hour
and the place and the seed and the womb that gave
them birth.

But all together they drew to that grim shore
where all must come who lose the fear of God.
Weeping and cursing they come for evermore,

and demon Charon with eyes like burning coals
herds them in, and with a whistling oar
flails on the stragglers to his wake of souls.

As leaves in autumn loosen and stream down
until the branch stands bare above its tatters 110
spread on the rustling ground, so one by one

the evil seed of Adam in its Fall
cast themselves, at his signal, from the shore
and streamed away like birds who hear their call.

So they are gone over that shadowy water,
and always before they reach the other shore
a new noise stirs on this, and new throngs gather.

'My son,' the courteous Master said to me,
  'all who die in the shadow of God's wrath
  converge to this from every clime and country. 120

And all pass over eagerly, for here
  Divine Justice transforms and spurs them so
  their dread turns wish: they yearn for what they fear.

No soul in Grace comes ever to this crossing;
  therefore if Charon rages at your presence
  you will understand the reason for his cursing.'

When he had spoken, all the twilight country
  shook so violently, the terror of it
  bathes me with sweat even in memory:

the tear-soaked ground gave out a sigh of wind 130
  that spewed itself in flame on a red sky,
  and all my shattered senses left me. Blind,

like one whom sleep comes over in a swoon,
I stumbled into darkness and went down.

DANTE

Translated by JOHN CIARDI

90

Ulysses

It little profits that an idle king,
By this still hearth, among these barren crags,
Match'd with an aged wife, I mete and dole
Unequal laws unto a savage race,
That hoard, and sleep, and feed, and know not me.
I cannot rest from travel: I will drink
Life to the lees: all times I have enjoy'd
Greatly, have suffer'd greatly, both with those
That loved me, and alone; on shore, and when
Thro' scudding drifts the rainy Hyades 10
Vext the dim sea: I am become a name;
For always roaming with a hungry heart
Much have I seen and known; cities of men
And manners, climates, councils, governments,
Myself not least, but honour'd of them all;
And drunk delight of battle with my peers,
Far on the ringing plains of windy Troy.
I am a part of all that I have met;
Yet all experience is an arch wherethro'
Gleams that untravell'd world, whose margin fades 20
For ever and for ever when I move.
How dull it is to pause, to make an end,
To rust unburnish'd, not to shine in use!
As tho' to breathe were life. Life piled on life
Were all too little, and of one to me
Little remains: but every hour is saved
From that eternal silence, something more,
A bringer of new things; and vile it were
For some three suns to store and hoard myself,

And this grey spirit yearning in desire 30
To follow knowledge, like a sinking star,
Beyond the utmost bound of human thought.
  This is my son, mine own Telemachus,
To whom I leave the sceptre and the isle –
Well-loved of me, discerning to fulfil
This labour, by slow prudence to make mild
A rugged people, and thro' soft degrees
Subdue them to the useful and the good.
Most blameless is he, centred in the sphere
Of common duties, decent not to fail 40
In offices of tenderness, and pay
Meet adoration to my household gods,
When I am gone. He works his work, I mine.
  There lies the port; the vessel puffs her sail:
There gloom the dark broad seas. My mariners,
Souls that have toil'd, and wrought, and thought with me –
That ever with a frolic welcome took
The thunder and the sunshine, and opposed
Free hearts, free foreheads – you and I are old;
Old age hath yet his honour and his toil; 50
Death closes all: but something ere the end,
Some work of noble note, may yet be done,
Not unbecoming men that strove with Gods.
The lights begin to twinkle from the rocks:
The long day wanes: the slow moon climbs: the deep
Moans round with many voices. Come, my friends,
'Tis not too late to seek a newer world.
Push off, and sitting well in order smite
The sounding furrows; for my purpose holds
To sail beyond the sunset, and the baths 60
Of all the western stars, until I die.
It may be that the gulfs will wash us down:

It may be we shall touch the Happy Isles,
And see the great Achilles, whom we knew.
Tho' much is taken, much abides; and tho'
We are not now that strength which in old days
Moved earth and heaven; that which we are, we are;
One equal temper of heroic hearts,
Made weak by time and fate, but strong in will
To strive, to seek, to find, and not to yield.

ALFRED LORD TENNYSON

91

The Death of the Hired Man

Mary sat musing on the lamp-flame at the table
Waiting for Warren. When she heard his step,
She ran on tip-toe down the darkened passage
To meet him in the doorway with the news
And put him on his guard. 'Silas is back.'
She pushed him outward with her through the door
And shut it after her. 'Be kind,' she said.
She took the market things from Warren's arms
And set them on the porch, then drew him down
To sit beside her on the wooden steps. 10

'When was I ever anything but kind to him?
But I'll not have the fellow back,' he said.
'I told him so last haying, didn't I?
"If he left then," I said, "that ended it."
What good is he? Who else will harbour him
At his age for the little he can do?
What help he is there's no depending on.
Off he goes always when I need him most.

"He thinks he ought to earn a little pay,
Enough at least to buy tobacco with, 20
So he won't have to beg and be beholden."
"All right," I say, "I can't afford to pay
Any fixed wages, though I wish I could."
"Someone else can." "Then someone else will have to."
I shouldn't mind his bettering himself
If that was what it was. You can be certain,
When he begins like that, there's someone at him
Trying to coax him off with pocket-money, –
In haying time, when any help is scarce.
In winter he comes back to us. I'm done.' 30

'Sh! not so loud: he'll hear you,' Mary said.

'I want him to: he'll have to soon or late.'

'He's worn out. He's asleep beside the stove.
When I came up from Rowe's I found him here,
Huddled against the barn-door fast asleep,
A miserable sight, and frightening, too –
You needn't smile – I didn't recognize him –
I wasn't looking for him – and he's changed.
Wait till you see.'

'Where did you say he'd been?'

'He didn't say. I dragged him to the house, 40
And gave him tea and tried to make him smoke.
I tried to make him talk about his travels.
Nothing would do: he just kept nodding off.'

'What did he say? Did he say anything?'

'But little.'

'Anything? Mary, confess
He said he'd come to ditch the meadow for me.'

'Warren!'

'But did he? I just want to know.'

'Of course he did. What would you have him say?
Surely you wouldn't grudge the poor old man
Some humble way to save his self-respect. 50
He added, if you really care to know,
He meant to clear the upper pasture, too.
That sounds like something you have heard before?
Warren, I wish you could have heard the way
He jumbled everything. I stopped to look
Two or three times – he made me feel so queer –
To see if he was talking in his sleep.
He ran on Harold Wilson – you remember –
The boy you had in haying four years since.
He's finished school, and teaching in his college. 60
Silas declares you'll have to get him back.
He says they two will make a team for work:

Between them they will lay this farm as smooth!
The way he mixed that in with other things.
He thinks young Wilson a likely lad, though daft
On education – you know how they fought
All through July under the blazing sun,
Silas up on the cart to build the load,
Harold along beside to pitch it on.'

'Yes, I took care to keep well out of earshot.' 70

'Well, those days trouble Silas like a dream.
You wouldn't think they would. How some things linger!
Harold's young college boy's assurance piqued him.
After so many years he still keeps finding
Good arguments he sees he might have used.
I sympathise. I know just how it feels
To think of the right thing to say too late.
Harold's associated in his mind with Latin.
He asked me what I thought of Harold's saying
He studied Latin like the violin 80
Because he liked it – that an argument!
He said he couldn't make the boy believe
He could find water with a hazel prong –
Which showed how much good school had ever done him.
He wanted to go over that. But most of all
He thinks if he could have another chance
To teach him how to build a load of hay –'

'I know, that's Silas' one accomplishment.
He bundles every forkful in its place,
And tags and numbers it for future reference, 90
So he can find and easily dislodge it
In the unloading. Silas does that well.

He takes it out in bunches like big birds' nests.
You never see him standing on the hay
He's trying to lift, straining to lift himself.'

'He thinks if he could teach him that, he'd be
Some good perhaps to someone in the world.
He hates to see a boy the fool of books.
Poor Silas, so concerned for other folk,
And nothing to look backward to with pride, 100
And nothing to look forward to with hope,
So now and never any different.'

Part of a moon was falling down the west,
Dragging the whole sky with it to the hills.
Its light poured softly in her lap. She saw it
And spread her apron to it. She put out her hand
Among the harp-like morning-glory strings,
Taut with the dew from garden bed to eaves,
As if she played unheard some tenderness
That wrought on him beside her in the night. 110
'Warren,' she said, 'he has come home to die:
You needn't be afraid he'll leave you this time.'

'Home,' he mocked gently.

'Yes, what else but home?
It all depends on what you mean by home.
Of course he's nothing to us, any more
Than was the hound that came a stranger to us
Out of the woods, worn out upon the trail.'

'Home is the place where, when you have to go there,
They have to take you in.'

'I should have called it
Something you somehow haven't to deserve.' 120

Warren leaned out and took a step or two,
Picked up a little stick, and brought it back
And broke it in his hand and tossed it by.
'Silas has better claim on us you think
Than on his brother? Thirteen little miles
As the road winds would bring him to his door.
Silas has walked that far no doubt to-day.
Why didn't he go there? His brother's rich,
A somebody – director in the bank.'

'He never told us that.'

'We know it though.' 130

'I think his brother ought to help, of course.
I'll see to that if there is need. He ought of right
To take him in, and might be willing to –
He may be better than appearances.
But have some pity on Silas. Do you think
If he had any pride in claiming kin
Or anything he looked for from his brother,
He'd keep so still about him all this time?'

'I wonder what's between them.'

'I can tell you.
Silas is what he is – we wouldn't mind him – 140
But just the kind that kinsfolk can't abide.
He never did a thing so very bad.
He don't know why he isn't quite as good

As anybody. Worthless though he is,
He won't be made ashamed to please his brother.'

'*I* can't think Si ever hurt anyone.'

'No, but he hurt my heart the way he lay
And rolled his old head on that sharp-edged chairback.
He wouldn't let me put him on the lounge.
You must go in and see what you can do. 150
I made the bed up for him there to-night.
You'll be surprised at him – how much he's broken.
His working days are done; I'm sure of it.'

'I'd not be in a hurry to say that.'

'I haven't been. Go, look, see for yourself.
But, Warren, please remember how it is:
He's come to help you ditch the meadow.
He has a plan. You mustn't laugh at him.
He may not speak of it, and then he may.
I'll sit and see if that small sailing cloud 160
Will hit or miss the moon.'

It hit the moon.
Then there were three there, making a dim row,
The moon, the little silver cloud, and she.
Warren returned – too soon, it seemed to her,
Slipped to her side, caught up her hand and waited.

'Warren?' she questioned.

'Dead,' was all he answered.

ROBERT FROST

92

Stopping by Woods on a Snowy Evening

Whose woods these are I think I know.
His house is in the village though;
He will not see me stopping here
To watch his woods fill up with snow.

My little horse must think it queer
To stop without a farmhouse near
Between the woods and frozen lake
The darkest evening of the year.

He gives his harness bells a shake
To ask if there is some mistake.
The only other sound's the sweep
Of easy wind and downy flake.

The woods are lovely, dark and deep.
But I have promises to keep,
And miles to go before I sleep,
And miles to go before I sleep.

ROBERT FROST

93

Snow

The room was suddenly rich and the great bay-
    window was
Spawning snow and pink roses against it
Soundlessly collateral and incompatible:
World is suddener than we fancy it.

World is crazier and more of-it than we think,
Incorrigibly plural. I peel and portion
A tangerine and spit the pips and feel
The drunkenness of things being various.

And the fire flames with a bubbling sound for world
Is more spiteful and gay than one supposes –
On the tongue on the eyes on the ears in the palms
    of one's hands –
There is more than glass between the snow and the
    huge roses.

LOUIS MACNEICE

94

In November

The hills and leafless forests slowly yield
To the thick-driving snow. A little while
And night shall darken down. In shouting file
The woodmen's carts go by me homeward-wheeled,
Past the thin fading stubbles, half concealed,
Now golden-grey, sowed softly through with snow,
Where the last ploughman follows still his row,
Turning black furrows through the whitening field.
Far off the village lamps begin to gleam,
Fast drives the snow, and no man comes this way;
The hills grow wintry white, and bleak winds moan
About the naked uplands. I alone
Am neither sad, nor shelterless, nor grey,
Wrapped round with thought, content to watch and dream.

ARCHIBALD LAMPMAN

95

Low Tide on Grand Pré

The sun goes down, and over all
  These barren reaches by the tide
Such unelusive glories fall,
  I almost dream they yet will bide
  Until the coming of the tide.

And yet I know that not for us,
  By any ecstasy of dream,
He lingers to keep luminous
  A little while the grievous stream,
  Which frets, uncomforted of dream – 10

A grievous stream, that to and fro
  Athrough the fields of Acadie
Goes wandering, as if to know
  Why one beloved face should be
  So long from home and Acadie.

Was it a year or lives ago
  We took the grasses in our hands,
And caught the summer flying low
  Over the waving meadow lands,
  And held it there between our hands? 20

The while the river at our feet –
  A drowsy inland meadow stream –
At set of sun the after-heat
  Made running gold, and in the gleam
  We freed our birch upon the stream.

There down along the elms at dusk
  We lifted dripping blade to drift,
Through twilight scented fine like musk,
  Where night and gloom awhile uplift,
  Nor sunder soul and soul adrift. 30

And that we took into our hands
  Spirit of life or subtler thing –
Breathed on us there, and loosed the bands
  Of death, and taught us, whispering,
  The secret of some wonder-thing.

Then all your face grew light, and seemed
  To hold the shadow of the sun;
The evening faltered, and I deemed
  That time was ripe, and years had done
  Their wheeling underneath the sun. 40

So all desire and all regret,
  And fear and memory, were naught;
One to remember or forget
  The keen delight our hands had caught;
  Morrow and yesterday were naught.

The night has fallen, and the tide . . .
  Now and again comes drifting home,
Across these aching barrens wide,
  A sigh like driven wind or foam:
In grief the flood is bursting home.

BLISS CARMAN

96

Lines

COMPOSED A FEW MILES
ABOVE TINTERN ABBEY, ON
REVISITING THE BANKS OF THE
WYE DURING A TOUR. JULY 13, 1798

Five years have past; five summers, with the length
Of five long winters! and again I hear
These waters, rolling from their mountain-springs
With a soft inland murmur. – Once again
Do I behold these steep and lofty cliffs,
That on a wild secluded scene impress
Thoughts of more deep seclusion; and connect
The landscape with the quiet of the sky.
The day is come when I again repose
Here, under this dark sycamore, and view 10
These plots of cottage-ground, these orchard-tufts,
Which at this season, with their unripe fruits,
Are clad in one green hue, and lose themselves
'Mid groves and copses. Once again I see
These hedge-rows, hardly hedge-rows, little lines
Of sportive wood run wild: these pastoral farms,
Green to the very door; and wreaths of smoke
Sent up, in silence, from among the trees!
With some uncertain notice, as might seem
Of vagrant dwellers in the houseless woods, 20
Or of some Hermit's cave, where by his fire
The Hermit sits alone.
These beauteous forms,
Through a long absence, have not been to me
As is a landscape to a blind man's eye:

But oft, in lonely rooms, and 'mid the din
Of towns and cities, I have owed to them,
In hours of weariness, sensations sweet,
Felt in the blood, and felt along the heart;
And passing even into my purer mind,
With tranquil restoration: – feelings too 30
Of unremembered pleasure: such, perhaps,
As have no slight or trivial influence
On that best portion of a good man's life,
His little, nameless, unremembered, acts
Of kindness and of love. Nor less, I trust,
To them I may have owed another gift,
Of aspect more sublime; that blessed mood,
In which the burthen of the mystery,
In which the heavy and the weary weight
Of all this unintelligible world, 40
Is lightened: – that serene and blessed mood,
In which the affections gently lead us on, –
Until, the breath of this corporeal frame
And even the motion of our human blood
Almost suspended, we are laid asleep
In body, and become a living soul:
While with an eye made quiet by the power
Of harmony, and the deep power of joy,
We see into the life of things.

If this
Be but a vain belief, yet, oh! how oft – 50
In darkness and amid the many shapes
Of joyless daylight; when the fretful stir
Unprofitable, and the fever of the world,
Have hung upon the beatings of my heart –
How oft, in spirit, have I turned to thee,
O sylvan Wye! thou wanderer thro' the woods,

How often has my spirit turned to thee!

And now, with gleams of half-extinguished thought,
With many recognitions dim and faint,
And somewhat of a sad perplexity, 60
The picture of the mind revives again:
While here I stand, not only with the sense
Of present pleasure, but with pleasing thoughts
That in this moment there is life and food
For future years. And so I dare to hope,
Though changed, no doubt, from what I was when first
I came among these hills; when like a roe
I bounded o'er the mountains, by the sides
Of the deep rivers, and the lonely streams,
Wherever nature led: more like a man 70
Flying from something that he dreads than one
Who sought the thing he loved. For nature then
(The coarser pleasures of my boyish days,
And their glad animal movements all gone by)
To me was all in all. – I cannot paint
What then I was. The sounding cataract
Haunted me like a passion: the tall rock,
The mountain, and the deep and gloomy wood,
Their colours and their forms, were then to me
An appetite; a feeling and a love, 80
That had no need of a remoter charm,
By thought supplied, nor any interest
Unborrowed from the eye. – That time is past,
And all its aching joys are now no more,
And all its dizzy raptures. Not for this
Faint I, nor mourn nor murmur; other gifts
Have followed; for such loss, I would believe,
Abundant recompense. For I have learned

To look on nature, not as in the hour
Of thoughtless youth; but hearing oftentimes 90
The still, sad music of humanity,
Nor harsh nor grating, though of ample power
To chasten and subdue. And I have felt
A presence that disturbs me with the joy
Of elevated thoughts; a sense sublime
Of something far more deeply interfused,
Whose dwelling is the light of setting suns,
And the round ocean and the living air,
And the blue sky, and in the mind of man:
A motion and a spirit, that impels 100
All thinking things, all objects of all thought,
And rolls through all things. Therefore am I still
A lover of the meadows and the woods,
And mountains; and of all that we behold
From this green earth; of all the mighty world
Of eye, and ear, – both what they half create,
And what perceive; well pleased to recognise
In nature and the language of the sense
The anchor of my purest thoughts, the nurse,
The guide, the guardian of my heart, and soul 110
Of all my moral being.

Nor perchance,
If I were not thus taught, should I the more
Suffer my genial spirits to decay:
For thou art with me here upon the banks
Of this fair river; thou my dearest Friend,
My dear, dear Friend; and in thy voice I catch
The language of my former heart, and read
My former pleasures in the shooting lights
Of thy wild eyes. Oh! yet a little while
May I behold in thee what I was once, 120

My dear, dear Sister! and this prayer I make,
Knowing that Nature never did betray
The heart that loved her; 'tis her privilege,
Through all the years of this our life, to lead
From joy to joy: for she can so inform
The mind that is within us, so impress
With quietness and beauty, and so feed
With lofty thoughts, that neither evil tongues,
Rash judgments, nor the sneers of selfish men,
Nor greetings where no kindness is, nor all 130
The dreary intercourse of daily life,
Shall e'er prevail against us, or disturb
Our cheerful faith, that all which we behold
Is full of blessings. Therefore let the moon
Shine on thee in thy solitary walk;
And let the misty mountain-winds be free
To blow against thee: and, in after years,
When these wild ecstasies shall be matured
Into a sober pleasure; when thy mind
Shall be a mansion for all lovely forms, 140
Thy memory be as a dwelling-place
For all sweet sounds and harmonies; oh! then,
If solitude, or fear, or pain, or grief,
Should be thy portion, with what healing thoughts
Of tender joy wilt thou remember me,
And these my exhortations! Nor, perchance –
If I should be where I no more can hear
Thy voice, nor catch from thy wild eyes these gleams
Of past existence – wilt thou then forget
That on the banks of this delightful stream 150
We stood together; and that I, so long
A worshipper of Nature, hither came
Unwearied in that service: rather say

With warmer love – oh! with far deeper zeal
Of holier love. Nor wilt thou then forget
That after many wanderings, many years
Of absence, these steep woods and lofty cliffs,
And this green pastoral landscape, were to me
More dear, both for themselves and for thy sake!

WILLIAM WORDSWORTH

97
In Exile

In my old home, still
  my parents live. – The insect-cries
    are shrill. . .

An anonymous Japanese poem
translated by HAROLD HENDERSON

98

Hurrahing in Harvest

Summer ends now; now, barbarous in beauty, the stooks
arise
Around: up above, what wind-walks! what lovely
behaviour
Of silk-sack clouds! has wilder, wilful-wavier
Meal-drift moulded ever and melted across skies?

I walk, I lift up, I lift up heart, eyes,
Down all that glory in the heavens to glean our Saviour;
And éyes, heárt, what looks, what lips yet gave you a
Rapturous love's greeting of realer, of rounder replies?

And the azurous hung hills are his world-wielding shoulder
Majestic – as a stallion stalwart, very-violet-sweet! –
These things, these things were here and but the beholder
Wanting; which two when they once meet,
The heart rears wings bold and bolder
And hurls for him, O half hurls earth for him off under
his feet.

GERARD MANLEY HOPKINS

99

The Mowing

This is the voice of high midsummer's heat.
  The rasping vibrant clamour soars and shrills
  O'er all the meadowy range of shadeless hills,
As if a host of giant cicadae beat
The cymbals of their wings with tireless feet,
  Or brazen grasshoppers with triumphing note
  From the long swath proclaimed the fate that smote
The clover and timothy-tops and meadowsweet.

The crying knives glide on; the green swath lies.
  And all noon long the sun, with chemic ray,
  Seals up each cordial essence in its cell,
That in the dusky stalls, some winter's day,
  The spirit of June, here prisoned by his spell,
  May cheer the herds with pasture memories.

SIR CHARLES G. D. ROBERTS

100

The Shepheardes Lament

FROM

The Shepheardes Calender

DECEMBER

Thus is my sommer worne away and wasted,
Thus is my haruest hastened all to rathe°: too soon
The eare° that budded faire, is burnt and blasted, ear of corn
And all my hoped gaine is turned to scathe°. loss
  Of all the seede, that in my youth was sowne,
  Was nought but brakes° and brambles to be mowne. bracken

And thus of all my haruest hope I haue
Nought reaped but a weedye crop of care:
Which, when I thought haue thresht in swelling sheaue,
Cockel° for corne, and chaffe for barley bare. a weed
  Soone as the chaffe should in the fan be fynd,
  All was blowne away of the wauering wynd.

So now my yeare drawes to his latter terme,
My spring is spent, my sommer burnt vp quite:
My haruest hasts to stirre vp winter sterne,
And bids him clayme with rigorous rage hys right.
  So nowe he stormes with many a sturdy stoure°, turmoil
  So now his blustring blast eche coste° doth scoure. direction

The carefull cold hath nypt my rugged rynde°, skin
And in my face deepe furrowes eld° hath pight°: old age set
My head besprent° with hoary frost I fynd, besprinkled
And by myne eie the Crow his clawe dooth wright.
  Delight is layd abedde, and pleasure past,
  No sonne now shines, cloudes han all ouercast.

Now leaue ye shepheards boyes your merry glee,
My Muse is hoarse and weary of thys stounde:
Here will I hang my pype vpon this tree,
Was neuer pype of reede did better sounde.
  Winter is come, that blowes the bitter blaste,
  And after Winter dreerie death does hast.

Gather ye together my little flocke,
My little flock, that was to me so liefe°: dear
Let me, ah lette me in your folds ye lock,
Ere the breme° Winter breede you greater griefe. bitter
  Winter is come, that blowes the balefull breath,
  And after Winter commeth timely death.

EDMUND SPENSER

101

Branwell's Lament

FROM

A Suit of Nettles

JUNE

  I am like a hollow tree
Where the owl & weasel hide
  I am like a hollow tree
Dead in the forest of his brothers.

  My feet are sensitive as brains
Put hats upon them
  My feet are sensitive as brains
All the ground is grassed with knives.

  These fingers that once played
Nimbly the harp   10
  These fingers that once played
Are soft & suck as leeches.

  My throat where once a song
Flew out like a golden bird
  My throat where once a song
Is a woodpecker's bitten door.

  My eyes are the entrances
To the kingfishers' nests
  My eyes are the entrances
Tunnels of clay lined with fish bones.   20

I see the red sun sink
For the last time this far north.
The full moon rises: my thoughts fly forth.
Leap forth, oh bird of prey & turncoat ermine,
Nebula out of my mind
That swampy fair
Where the bittern pumps from its cistern of despair.

JAMES REANEY

102

Tears, Idle Tears

Tears, idle tears, I know not what they mean,
Tears from the depth of some divine despair
Rise in the heart, and gather to the eyes,
In looking on the happy Autumn-fields,
And thinking of the days that are no more.

Fresh as the first beam glittering on a sail,
That brings our friends up from the underworld,
Sad as the last which reddens over one
That sinks with all we love below the verge;
So sad, so fresh, the days that are no more.

Ah, sad and strange as in dark summer dawns
The earliest pipe of half-awaken'd birds
To dying ears, when unto dying eyes
The casement slowly grows a glimmering square;
So sad, so strange, the days that are no more.

Dear as remember'd kisses after death,
And sweet as those by hopeless fancy feign'd
On lips that are for others; deep as love,
Deep as first love, and wild with all regret;
O Death in Life, the days that are no more.

ALFRED LORD TENNYSON

103

In Memoriam

SELECTIONS

VII

Dark house, by which once more I stand
   Here in the long unlovely street,
   Doors, where my heart was used to beat
So quickly, waiting for a hand,

A hand that can be clasp'd no more –
   Behold me, for I cannot sleep,
   And like a guilty thing I creep
At earliest morning to the door.

He is not here; but far away
   The noise of life begins again,
   And ghastly thro' the drizzling rain
On the bald street breaks the blank day.

LIV

Oh yet we trust that somehow good
   Will be the final goal of ill,
   To pangs of nature, sins of will,
Defects of doubt, and taints of blood;

That nothing walks with aimless feet;
   That not one life shall be destroy'd,
   Or cast as rubbish to the void,
When God hath made the pile complete;

That not a worm is cloven in vain;
  That not a moth with vain desire
  Is shrivell'd in a fruitless fire,
Or but subserves another's gain.

Behold, we know not anything;
  I can but trust that good shall fall
  At last – far off – at last, to all,
And every winter change to spring.

So runs my dream: but what am I?
  An infant crying in the night:
  An infant crying for the light:
And with no language but a cry.

CXV

Now fades the last long streak of snow,
  Now burgeons every maze of quick
  About the flowering squares, and thick
By ashen roots the violets blow.

Now rings the woodland loud and long,
  The distance takes a lovelier hue,
  And drown'd in yonder living blue
The lark becomes a sightless song.

Now dance the lights on lawn and lea,
  The flocks are whiter down the vale,
  And milkier every milky sail
On winding stream or distant sea;

Where now the seamew pipes, or dives
   In yonder greening gleam, and fly
   The happy birds, that change their sky
To build and brood; that live their lives

From land to land; and in my breast
   Spring wakens too; and my regret
   Becomes an April violet,
And buds and blossoms like the rest.

CXVIII

Contemplate all this work of Time,
   The giant labouring in his youth;
   Nor dream of human love and truth,
As dying Nature's earth and lime;

But trust that those we call the dead
   Are breathers of an ampler day
   For ever nobler ends. They say
The solid earth whereon we tread

In tracts of fluent heat began,
   And grew to seeming-random forms,
   The seeming prey of cyclic storms,
Till at the last arose the man;

Who throve and branch'd from clime to clime,
   The herald of a higher race,
   And of himself in higher place,
If so he type this work of time

Within himself, from more to more;
Or, crown'd with attributes of woe
Like glories, move his course, and show
That life is not as idle ore,

But iron dug from central gloom,
And heated hot with burning fears,
And dipt in baths of hissing tears,
And batter'd with the shocks of doom

To shape and use. Arise and fly
The reeling Faun, the sensual feast;
Move upward, working out the beast,
And let the ape and tiger die.

CXXIII

There rolls the deep where grew the tree.
O earth, what changes hast thou seen!
There where the long street roars, hath been
The stillness of the central sea.

The hills are shadows, and they flow
From form to form, and nothing stands;
They melt like mist, the solid lands,
Like clouds they shape themselves and go.

But in my spirit will I dwell,
And dream my dream, and hold it true;
For tho' my lips may breathe adieu,
I cannot think the thing farewell.

ALFRED LORD TENNYSON

104

Cold Stone

I lay my cheek against cold stone
And feel my self returned to me
As soft my flesh and firm my bone
By it declare their quality.
I hear my distant blood drive still
Its obscure purpose with clear will.

The stone's unordered rigour stands
Remote and heavy as a star.
My returned self in cheek and hands
Regards as yet not very far
The leap from shape to living form;
For where I rested, the stone is warm.

JAY MACPHERSON

105

Brahma

If the red slayer think he slays,
  Or if the slain think he is slain,
They know not well the subtle ways
  I keep, and pass, and turn again.

Far or forgot to me is near;
  Shadow and sunlight are the same;
The vanished gods to me appear;
  And one to me are shame and fame.

They reckon ill who leave me out;
  When me they fly, I am the wings;
I am the doubter and the doubt,
  And I the hymn the Brahmin sings.

The strong gods pine for my abode,
  And pine in vain the sacred Seven;
But thou, meek lover of the good!
  Find me, and turn thy back on heaven.

RALPH WALDO EMERSON

106

The Triumph of Bacchus

From CANTO II

Acoetes describes his conversion to the rites of Bacchus, god of wine and physical ecstasy. Years before, Acoetes had been one of a crew of sailors who kidnapped a boy at Scios, having agreed to carry him to Naxos.[1] *Acoetes protested, sensing something divine in the lad, but was overruled. When the ship was well out at sea the boy revealed himself as Bacchus, summoned into being his attendant panthers and lynxes, and turned all the sailors but Acoetes to dolphins.*

The ship landed in Scios,
  men wanting spring-water,
And by the rock-pool a young boy loggy with vine-must,
  'To Naxos? Yes, we'll take you to Naxos,
Cum' along lad.' 'Not that way!'
'Aye, that way is Naxos.'
  And I said: 'It's a straight ship.'
And an ex-convict out of Italy
  knocked me into the fore-stays,
(He was wanted for manslaughter in Tuscany) 10
  And the whole twenty against me,
Mad for a little slave money.
  And they took her out of Scios
And off her course . . .
  And the boy came to, again, with the racket,
And looked out over the bows,
  and to eastward, and to the Naxos passage.
God-sleight then, god-sleight:

Ship stock fast in sea-swirl,
Ivy upon the oars, King Pentheus, 20
grapes with no seed but sea-foam,
Ivy in scupper-hole.
Aye, I, Acoetes, stood there,
and the god stood by me,
Water cutting under the keel,
Sea-break from stern forrards,
wake running off from the bow,
And where was gunwhale, there now was vine-trunk,
And tenthril where cordage had been,
grape-leaves on the rowlocks, 30
Heavy vine on the oarshafts,
And, out of nothing, a breathing,
hot breath on my ankles,
Beasts like shadows in glass,
a furred tail upon nothingness.
Lynx-purr, and heathery smell of beasts,
where tar smell had been,
Sniff and pad-foot of beasts,
eye-glitter out of black air.
The sky overshot, dry, with no tempest, 40
Sniff and pad-foot of beasts,
fur brushing my knee-skin,
Rustle of airy sheaths,
dry forms in the *aether*.
And the ship like a keel in ship-yard
slung like an ox in smith's sling,
Ribs stuck fast in the ways,
grape-cluster over pin-rack,
void air taking pelt.
Lifeless air become sinewed, 50
feline leisure of panthers,

Leopards sniffing the grape shoots by scupper-hole,
Crouched panthers by fore-hatch,
And the sea blue-deep about us,
  green-ruddy in shadows,
And Lyaeus: 'From now, Acoetes, my altars,
Fearing no bondage,
  fearing no cat of the wood,
Safe with my lynxes,
  feeding grapes to my leopards, 60
Olibanum is my incense,
  the vines grow in my homage.'

The back-swell now smooth in the rudder-chains,
Black snout of a porpoise
  where Lycabs had been,
Fish-scales on the oarsmen.
  And I worship.
I have seen what I have seen.
  When they brought the boy I said:
'He has a god in him, 70
  though I do not know which god.'
And they kicked me into the fore-stays.
I have seen what I have seen:
  Medon's face like the face of a dory,
Arms shrunk into fins. And you, Pentheus,
Had as well listen to Tiresias, and to Cadmus,
  or your luck will go out of you.
Fish-scales over groin muscles,
  lynx-purr amid sea . . .

EZRA POUND

107

I Had a Duck-billed Platypus

I had a duck-billed platypus when I was up at Trinity,
With whom I soon discovered a remarkable affinity.
He used to live in lodgings with myself and Arthur Purvis,
And we all went up together for the Diplomatic Service.
I had a certain confidence, I own, in his ability,
He mastered all the subjects with remarkable facility;
And Purvis, though more dubious, agreed that he was
    clever,
But no one else imagined he had any chance whatever.

I failed to pass the interview, The Board with wry grimaces
Took exception to my boots and then objected to my
    braces, 10
And Purvis too was failed by an intolerant examiner
Who said he had his doubts as to his sock-suspenders'
    stamina.
Our summary rejection, though we took it with urbanity,
Was naturally wounding in some measure to our vanity.
The bitterness of failure was considerably mollified,
However, by the ease with which our platypus had qualified.

The wisdom of the choice, it soon appeared, was
    undeniable;
There never was a diplomat more thoroughly reliable.
The creature never acted with undue precipitation O,
But gave to every question his mature consideration O. 20

He never made rash statements his enemies might hold
him to,
He never stated anything, for no one ever told him to,
And soon he was appointed, so correct was his behaviour,
Our Minister (without Portfolio) to Trans-Moravia.

My friend was loved and honoured from the Andes to
Esthonia,
He soon achieved a pact between Peru and Patagonia,
He never vexed the Russians nor offended the Rumanians,
He pacified the Letts and yet appeased the Lithuanians,
Won approval from his masters down in Downing Street so
wholly, O,
He was soon to be rewarded with the grant of a Portfolio, 30
When, on the Anniversary of Greek Emancipation,
Alas! He laid an egg in the Bulgarian Legation.

This untoward occurrence caused unheard-of repercussions,
Giving rise to epidemics of sword-clanking in the Prussians.
The Poles began to threaten, and the Finns began to flap at
him,
Directing all the blame for this unfortunate mishap at him;
While the Swedes withdrew entirely from the Anglo-Saxon
dailies
The right of photographing the Aurora Borealis,
And, all efforts at rapprochement in the meantime proving
barren,
The Japanese in self-defence annexed the Isle of Arran. 40

My platypus, once thought to be more cautious and more
tentative
Than any other living diplomatic representative,
Was now a sort of warning to all diplomatic students

Of the risks attached to negligence, the perils of
imprudence.
Beset and persecuted by the forces of reaction O,
He reaped the consequences of his ill-considered action O;
And, branded in the Honours List as 'Platypus, Dame Vera',
Retired, a lonely figure, to lay eggs at Bordighera.

PATRICK BARRINGTON

108

Hymn to Rover

When on that day the last bark rings
To call the dog-like throng,
Rover shall rise and don his wings,
And raise his voice in song;
  He'll raise his voice in song and sing,
  In ecstasy of dog-like things.

And weaving patterns with their tails,
The joyous dog-like hosts,
Will lead him through celestial vales,
And miles and miles of posts,
  To meadows full of gopher holes,
  Which he can sniff and dig for moles.

Then shall I shout and throw a stick,
And bounce his ball and hide his bone,
Or stop and help him find his tick,
And call him to his home;
  His home where he can take his ease,
  In sunny spots and scratch his fleas.

And I shall take him by the hand,
And feed him mush, and pull his ears,
And he will grin, and understand,
And lick away these tears.
  On that great day of the final bark,
  Rover (as usual) will beat the lark.

SARAH BINKS

109

Hawk Roosting

I sit in the top of the wood, my eyes closed.
Inaction, no falsifying dream
Between my hooked head and hooked feet:
Or in sleep rehearse perfect kills and eat.

The convenience of the high trees!
The air's buoyancy and the sun's ray
Are of advantage to me;
And the earth's face upward for my inspection.

My feet are locked upon the rough bark.
It took the whole of Creation
To produce my foot, my each feather:
Now I hold Creation in my foot

Or fly up, and revolve it all slowly –
I kill where I please because it is all mine.
There is no sophistry in my body:
My manners are tearing off heads –

The allotment of death.
For the one path of my flight is direct
Through the bones of the living.
No arguments assert my right:

The sun is behind me.
Nothing has changed since I began.
My eye has permitted no change.
I am going to keep things like this.

TED HUGHES

110

Kingfishers in British Columbia

A mad kingfisher
rocketing about in the
red fog at sunrise

now sits
on the alder
post that tethers the floats
angrily awaiting his mate.
Here she

comes, like a left wing
three-quarter cutting through toward
the goal in sun-lamped
fog at Rosslyn Park at half
past three in halcyon days.

MALCOLM LOWRY

111

To a Skylark

Hail to thee, blithe Spirit!
Bird thou never wert,
That from heaven, or near it,
Pourest thy full heart
In profuse strains of unpremeditated art.

Higher still and higher
From the earth thou springest,
Like a cloud of fire,
The blue deep thou wingest,
And singing still dost soar, and soaring ever singest. 10

In the golden light'ning
Of the sunken sun
O'er which clouds are bright'ning,
Thou dost float and run,
Like an unbodied joy whose race is just begun.

The pale purple even
Melts around thy flight;
Like a star of heaven
In the broad daylight
Thou art unseen, but yet I hear thy shrill delight: 20

Keen as are the arrows
Of that silver sphere,
Whose intense lamp narrows
In the white dawn clear
Until we hardly see, we feel that it is there.

All the earth and air
With thy voice is loud,
As, when night is bare,
From one lonely cloud
The moon rains out her beams, and heaven is overflow'd. 30

What thou art we know not;
What is most like thee?
From rainbow clouds there flow not
Drops so bright to see
As from thy presence showers a rain of melody;

Like a Poet hidden
In the light of thought,
Singing hymns unbidden,
Till the world is wrought
To sympathy with hopes and fears it heeded not: 40

Like a high-born maiden
In a palace tower,
Soothing her love-laden
Soul in secret hour
With music sweet as love, which overflows her bower:

Like a glow-worm golden
In a dell of dew,
Scattering unbeholden
Its aërial hue
Among the flowers and grass, which screen it from the
view: 50

Like a rose embowered
In its own green leaves,
By warm winds deflowered,

Till the scent it gives
Makes faint with too much sweet these heavy-wingèd
thieves.

Sound of vernal showers
On the twinkling grass,
Rain-awakened flowers,
All that ever was
Joyous, and clear, and fresh, thy music doth surpass. 60

Teach us, Sprite or Bird,
What sweet thoughts are thine:
I have never heard
Praise of love or wine
That panted forth a flood of rapture so divine.

Chorus Hymeneal,
Or triumphal chaunt,
Match'd with thine would be all
But an empty vaunt —
A thing wherein we feel there is some hidden want. 70

What objects are the fountains
Of thy happy strain?
What fields, or waves, or mountains?
What shapes of sky or plain?
What love of thine own kind? what ignorance of pain?

With thy clear keen joyance
Languor cannot be:
Shadow of annoyance
Never came near thee:
Thou lovest; but ne'er knew love's sad satiety. 80

Waking or asleep
  Thou of death must deem
Things more true and deep
  Than we mortals dream,
Or how could thy notes flow in such a crystal stream?

We look before and after,
  And pine for what is not:
Our sincerest laughter
  With some pain is fraught;
Our sweetest songs are those that tell of saddest thought. 90

Yet if we could scorn
  Hate, and pride, and fear;
If we were things born
  Not to shed a tear,
I know not how thy joy we ever should come near.

Better than all measures
  Of delightful sound,
Better than all treasures
  That in books are found,
Thy skill to poet were, thou scorner of the ground! 100

Teach me half the gladness
  That thy brain must know,
Such harmonious madness
  From my lips would flow,
The world should listen then, as I am listening now!

PERCY BYSSHE SHELLEY

112

Ode on a Grecian Urn

Thou still unravish'd bride of quietness,
  Thou foster-child of silence and slow time,
Sylvan historian, who canst thus express
  A flowery tale more sweetly than our rhyme:
What leaf-fring'd legend haunts about thy shape
  Of deities or mortals, or of both,
    In Tempe or the dales of Arcady?
What men or gods are these? What maidens loth?
  What mad pursuit? What struggle to escape?
    What pipes and timbrels? What wild ecstasy? 10

Heard melodies are sweet, but those unheard
  Are sweeter; therefore, ye soft pipes, play on;
Not to the sensual ear, but, more endear'd,
  Pipe to the spirit ditties of no tone:
Fair youth, beneath the trees, thou canst not leave
  Thy song, nor ever can those trees be bare;
    Bold Lover, never, never canst thou kiss,
Though winning near the goal – yet, do not grieve;
  She cannot fade, though thou hast not thy bliss,
    For ever wilt thou love, and she be fair! 20

Ah, happy, happy boughs! that cannot shed
  Your leaves, nor ever bid the Spring adieu;
And, happy melodist, unwearied,
  For ever piping songs for ever new;
More happy love! more happy, happy love!
  For ever warm and still to be enjoy'd,
    For ever panting, and for ever young;
All breathing human passion far above,
  That leaves a heart high-sorrowful and cloy'd,
    A burning forehead, and a parching tongue. 30

Who are these coming to the sacrifice?
  To what green altar, O mysterious priest,
Lead'st thou that heifer lowing at the skies,
  And all her silken flanks with garlands drest?
What little town by river or sea shore,
  Or mountain-built with peaceful citadel,
    Is emptied of this folk, this pious morn?
And, little town, thy streets for evermore
  Will silent be; and not a soul to tell
    Why thou art desolate, can e'er return. 40

O Attic shape! Fair attitude! with brede
  Of marble men and maidens overwrought,
With forest branches and the trodden weed;
  Thou, silent form, dost tease us out of thought
As doth eternity: Cold Pastoral!
  When old age shall this generation waste,
    Thou shalt remain, in midst of other woe
Than ours, a friend to man, to whom thou say'st,
  'Beauty is truth, truth beauty', – that is all
    Ye know on earth, and all ye need to know.

JOHN KEATS

113

Sonnet CXVI

Let me not to the marriage of true minds
Admit impediments. Love is not love
Which alters when it alteration finds,
Or bends with the remover to remove:
O no! it is an ever-fixèd mark
That looks on tempests, and is never shaken;
It is the star to every wandering bark,
Whose worth's unknown, although his height be taken.
Love's not Time's fool, though rosy lips and cheeks
Within his bending sickle's compass come;
Love alters not with his brief hours and weeks,
But bears it out ev'n to the edge of doom.
  If this be error, and upon me proved,
  I never writ, nor no man ever loved.

WILLIAM SHAKESPEARE

114

Sonnet

How do I love thee? Let me count the ways.
I love thee to the depth and breadth and height
My soul can reach, when feeling out of sight
For the ends of Being and ideal Grace.
I love thee to the level of every day's
Most quiet need, by sun and candlelight.
I love thee freely, as men strive for Right;
I love thee purely, as they turn from Praise.
I love thee with the passion put to use
In my old griefs, and with my childhood's faith;
I love thee with a love I seemed to lose
With my lost saints, – I love thee with the breath,
Smiles, tears, of all my life! – and, if God choose,
I shall but love thee better after death.

ELIZABETH BARRETT BROWNING

115

Porphyria's Lover

The rain set early in to-night,
  The sullen wind was soon awake,
It tore the elm-tops down for spite,
  And did its worst to vex the lake:
  I listened with heart fit to break,
When glided in Porphyria; straight
  She shut the cold out and the storm,
And kneeled and made the cheerless grate
  Blaze up, and all the cottage warm;
  Which done, she rose, and from her form   10
Withdrew the dripping cloak and shawl,
  And laid her soiled gloves by, untied
Her hat and let the damp hair fall,
  And, last, she sat down by my side
  And called me. When no voice replied,
She put my arm about her waist,
  And made her smooth white shoulder bare,
And all her yellow hair displaced,
  And, stooping, made my cheek lie there,
  And spread o'er all her yellow hair,   20
Murmuring how she loved me – she
  Too weak, for all her heart's endeavour,
To set its struggling passion free
  From pride, and vainer ties dissever,
  And give herself to me for ever.
But passion sometimes would prevail,
  Nor could to-night's gay feast restrain
A sudden thought of one so pale
  For love of her, and all in vain:

So, she was come through wind and rain. 30
Be sure I looked up at her eyes
Happy and proud; at last I knew
Porphyria worshipped me; surprise
Made my heart swell, and still it grew
While I debated what to do.
That moment she was mine, mine, fair,
Perfectly pure and good: I found
A thing to do, and all her hair
In one long yellow string I wound
Three times her little throat around, 40
And strangled her. No pain felt she;
I am quite sure she felt no pain.
As a shut bud that holds a bee,
I warily oped her lids: again
Laughed the blue eyes without a stain.
And I untightened next the tress
About her neck; her cheek once more
Blushed bright beneath my burning kiss:
I propped her head up as before,
Only, this time my shoulder bore 50
Her head, which droops upon it still:
The smiling rosy little head,
So glad it has its utmost will,
That all it scorned at once is fled,
And I, its love, am gained instead!
Porphyria's love: she guessed not how
Her darling one wish would be heard.
And thus we sit together now,
And all night long we have not stirred,
And yet God has not said a word!

ROBERT BROWNING

116

My Last Duchess

FERRARA

That's my last Duchess painted on the wall,
Looking as if she were alive. I call
That piece a wonder now: Frà Pandòlf's hands
Worked busily a day, and there she stands.
Will't please you sit and look at her? I said
'Frà Pandolf' by design, for never read
Strangers like you that pictured countenance,
The depth and passion of its earnest glance,
But to myself they turned (since none puts by
The curtain I have drawn for you, but I) 10
And seemed as they would ask me, if they durst,
How such a glance came there; so, not the first
Are you to turn and ask thus. Sir, 'twas not
Her husband's presence only, called that spot
Of joy into the Duchess' cheek: perhaps
Frà Pandolf chanced to say 'Her mantle laps
Over my lady's wrist too much,' or 'Paint
Must never hope to reproduce the faint
Half-flush that dies along her throat:' such stuff
Was courtesy, she thought, and cause enough 20
For calling up that spot of joy. She had
A heart – how shall I say? – too soon made glad,
Too easily impressed; she liked whate'er
She looked on, and her looks went everywhere.
Sir, 'twas all one! My favour at her breast,
The dropping of the daylight in the West,
The bough of cherries some officious fool

Broke in the orchard for her, the white mule
She rode with round the terrace — all and each
Would draw from her alike the approving speech, 30
Or blush, at least. She thanked men, — good! but thanked
Somehow — I know not how — as if she ranked
My gift of a nine-hundred-years-old name
With anybody's gift. Who'd stoop to blame
This sort of trifling? Even had you skill
In speech — (which I have not) — to make your will
Quite clear to such an one, and say, 'Just this
Or that in you disgusts me; here you miss,
Or there exceed the mark' — and if she let
Herself be lessoned so, nor plainly set 40
Her wits to yours, forsooth, and made excuse,
— E'en then would be some stooping; and I choose
Never to stoop. Oh sir, she smiled, no doubt,
Whene'er I passed her; but who passed without
Much the same smile? This grew; I gave commands;
Then all smiles stopped together. There she stands
As if alive. Will't please you rise? We'll meet
The company below, then. I repeat,
The Count your master's known munificence
Is ample warrant that no just pretence 50
Of mine for dowry will be disallowed;
Though his fair daughter's self, as I avowed
At starting, is my object. Nay, we'll go
Together down, sir. Notice Neptune, though,
Taming a sea-horse, thought a rarity,
Which Claus of Innsbruck cast in bronze for me!

ROBERT BROWNING

117

A Subaltern's Love-Song

Miss J. Hunter Dunn, Miss J. Hunter Dunn,
Furnish'd and burnish'd by Aldershot sun,
What strenuous singles we played after tea,
We in the tournament – you against me!

Love-thirty, love-forty, oh! weakness of joy,
The speed of a swallow, the grace of a boy,
With carefullest carelessness, gaily you won,
I am weak from your loveliness, Joan Hunter Dunn.

Miss Joan Hunter Dunn, Miss Joan Hunter Dunn,
How mad I am, sad I am, glad that you won. 10
The warm-handled racket is back in its press,
But my shock-headed victor, she loves me no less.

Her father's euonymus shines as we walk,
And swing past the summer-house, buried in talk,
And cool the verandah that welcomes us in
To the six-o'clock news and a lime-juice and gin.

The scent of the conifers, sound of the bath,
The view from my bedroom of moss-dappled path,
As I struggle with double-end evening tie,
For we dance at the Golf Club, my victor and I. 20

On the floor of her bedroom lie blazer and shorts
And the cream-coloured walls are be-trophied with sports,
And westering, questioning settles the sun
On your low-leaded window, Miss Joan Hunter Dunn.

The Hillman is waiting, the light's in the hall,
The pictures of Egypt are bright on the wall,
My sweet, I am standing beside the oak stair
And there on the landing's the light on your hair.

By roads 'not adopted', by woodlanded ways,
She drove to the club in the late summer haze, 30
Into nine-o'clock Camberley, heavy with bells
And mushroomy, pine-woody, evergreen smells.

Miss Joan Hunter Dunn, Miss Joan Hunter Dunn
I can hear from the car-park the dance has begun.
Oh! full Surrey twilight! importunate band!
Oh! strongly adorable tennis-girl's hand!

Around us are Rovers and Austins afar,
Above us, the intimate roof of the car,
And here on my right is the girl of my choice,
With the tilt of her nose and the chime of her voice, 40

And the scent of her wrap, and the words never said,
And the ominous, ominous dancing ahead.
We sat in the car park till twenty to one
And now I'm engaged to Miss Joan Hunter Dunn.

JOHN BETJEMAN

118

The Braw Wooer

Last May a braw° wooer cam doun the lang glen, — handsome
And sair° wi' his love he did deave° me; — greatly — deafened
I said there was naething I hated like men —
The deuce° gae wi'm, to believe me, believe me; — devil
The deuce gae wi'm to believe me.

He spake o' the darts in my bonie black een°, — eyes
And vow'd for my love he was diein',
I said he might die when he liket — for Jean —
The Lord forgie me for liein', for liein';
The Lord forgie me for liein'! — 10

A weel-stocket mailen°, himself for the laird, — farm
And marriage aff-hand, were his proffers;
I never loot° on that I keen'd it, or car'd, — let
But thought I might have waur° offers, waur offers; — worse
But thought I might hae waur offers.

But what wad ye think? — in a fortnight or less —
The deil tak his taste to gae near her!
He up the *Gate-slack* to my black cousin, Bess —
Guess ye how, the jad°! I could bear her, could bear her; — hussy
Guess ye how, the jad! I could bear her. — 20

But a' the neist week, as I petted wi' care,
I gaed to the tryst o' Dalgarnock;
And wha but my fine fickle wooer was there,
I glowr'd as I'd seen a warlock°, a warlock, — demon, sorcerer
I glowr'd as I'd seen a warlock.

But owre my left shouther I gae him a blink,
  Lest neibours might say I was saucy;
My wooer he caper'd as he'd been in drink,
  And vow'd I was his dear lassie, dear lassie,
  And vow'd I was his dear lassie. 30

I spier'd for° my cousin fu' couthy° and sweet, asked after / pleasant
  Gin° she had recover'd her hearin', If, whether
And how her new shoon fit her auld shachl't° feet, shambling
  But heavens! how he fell a swearin', a swearin',
  But heavens! how he fell a swearin'.

He begged, for gudesake, I wad be his wife,
  Or else I wad kill him wi' sorrow;
So e'en to preserve the poor body in life,
  I think I maun° wed him to-morrow, to-morrow; must
  I think I maun wed him to-morrow.

ROBERT BURNS

119

Plucking the Rushes

Green rushes with red shoots,
Long leaves bending to the wind –
You and I in the same boat
Plucking rushes at the Five Lakes.
We started at dawn from the orchid-island:
We rested under the elms till noon.
You and I plucking rushes
Had not plucked a handful when night came!

An anonymous Chinese poem
translated by ARTHUR WALEY

120

The River-Merchant's Wife: A Letter

While my hair was still cut straight across my forehead
I played about the front gate, pulling flowers.
You came by on bamboo stilts, playing horse,
You walked about my seat, playing with blue plums.
And we went on living in the village of Chokan:
Two small people, without dislike or suspicion.

At fourteen I married My Lord you.
I never laughed, being bashful.
Lowering my head, I looked at the wall.
Called to, a thousand times, I never looked back. 10

At fifteen I stopped scowling,
I desired my dust to be mingled with yours
Forever and forever and forever.
Why should I climb the look out?

At sixteen you departed,
And went into far Ku-to-yen, by the river of swirling eddies,
And you have been gone five months.
The monkeys make sorrowful noise overhead.
You dragged your feet when you went out.

By the gate now, the moss is grown, the different mosses, 20
Too deep to clear them away!
The leaves fall early this autumn, in wind.
The paired butterflies are already yellow with August
Over the grass in the West garden;

They hurt me. I grow older.
If you are coming down through the narrows of the river
    Kiang
Please let me know beforehand,
And I will come out to meet you
  As far as Cho-fu-sa.

LI PO

Translated by EZRA POUND
from the Japanese version by RIHAKU

121

A Birthday

My heart is like a singing bird
  Whose nest is in a watered shoot;
My heart is like an apple-tree
  Whose boughs are bent with thick-set fruit;
My heart is like a rainbow shell
  That paddles in a halcyon sea;
My heart is gladder than all these
  Because my love is come to me.

Raise me a dais of silk and down;
  Hang it with vair and purple dyes;
Carve it in doves, and pomegranates,
  And peacocks with a hundred eyes;
Work it in gold and silver grapes,
  In leaves, and silver fleur-de-lys;
Because the birthday of my life
  Is come, my love is come to me.

CHRISTINA ROSSETTI

122

The Constant Lover

Out upon it, I have lov'd
  Three whole days together;
And am like to love three more,
  If it prove fair weather.

Time shall molt away his wings
  Ere he shall discover
In the whole wide world again
  Such a constant lover.

But the spite on't is, no praise
  Is due at all to me:
Love with me had made no stays
  Had it any been but she.

Had it any been but she
  And that very face,
There had been at least ere this
  A dozen dozen in her place.

SIR JOHN SUCKLING

123

Love Turned to Hatred

I will not love one minute more, I swear,
No, not a minute; not a sigh or tear
Thou get'st from me, or one kind look again,
Though thou shouldst court me to 't and wouldst begin.
I will not think of thee but as men do
Of debts and sins, and then I'll curse thee too:
For thy sake woman shall be now to me
Less welcome, than at midnight ghosts shall be:
I'll hate so perfectly, that it shall be
Treason to love that man that loves a she;
Nay, I will hate the very good, I swear,
That's in thy sex, because it doth lie there;
Their very virtue, grace, discourse, and wit,
And all for thee; what, wilt thou love me yet?

SIR JOHN SUCKLING

124

An Irish Monk

ON LINDISFARNE, ABOUT 650 A.D.

A hesitation of the tide
betrays this island, daily.

On Iona, at dusk
(ago, how long ago?)
often (did it happen?)
I saw the Lord walking
in the surf amidst the gulls,
calling, 'Come. Have joy in Me.'

Yes, with these eyes.

Now, on strange rocks 10
(faintly through the wall)
echoing, the same sea roars.

Detail is my toil.
In chapel, verse by verse –
in the kitchen, loaf by loaf –
with my pen, word by word –

by imitation,
illumination –
spark upon spark,
striking spark. 20

The patience of the bricklayer
is assumed in the dream of the architect.

On the road coming, five days travel, a Pict
woman (big mouth and small bones) gave me
shelter, and laughed (part scorn, part
pity) at my journey, 'What do you hope for,
even if you get there, that you couldn't
have had twice over in Ireland?'

Then I told her of the darkness amongst the
barbarians, and of the great light in the 30
monasteries at home, and she replied, 'Will
they thank you for that, you so young and
naive, and why should you go, you out of
so many?'

And I said that I heard a voice calling, and
she said, 'So men dream, are unsatisfied,
wear their legs out with walking, and you
scarcely a boy out of school.'

So she laughed, and I leaned my head on my
hands, feeling the thickness of dust
in each palm.

Then she told me there was not another of

her race left in that valley, not one,
nothing left. 'And all in three generations.
Once even Rome feared us. Now my children
are mongrels. And my husband has left me.
No matter. Or great matter. I am still a
Pict.'

Then she fed me, put herbs on my feet, wished
me well, and I blessed her but she said, 50
'Save that for yourself, you will need it,
when your heart turns rancid, and your
joints begin to stiffen on the foreign
roads. Remember me, when you come,
returning.'

So she mocked; and sometimes, even now, ten
years later, I hear it as I waken (receding
in a dream), that laughter, broad, without
malice.

Returning, 60
in the mind, still there,
home:
– devout green hills
– intimate peat smoke
– a cow-bell beseeching
– warm fleece in my bed
– fresh water, fresh, a brook

Here:
– rain clouds like beggars' rags
– stench of burned weed 70

– fret of the chain-mail sea
– hard knees on cold stone
– dry saliva, salt fish

The gulls cry:
– believe
– achieve

The bells reply:
– some
– some

At the lowest ebb 80
you can leave dryshod
this fitful island.

GAEL TURNBULL

125

Dover Beach

The sea is calm to-night.
The tide is full, the moon lies fair
Upon the straits; – on the French coast the light
Gleams and is gone; the cliffs of England stand,
Glimmering and vast, out in the tranquil bay.
Come to the window, sweet is the night-air!
Only, from the long line of spray
Where the sea meets the moon-blanch'd land,

Listen! you hear the grating roar
Of pebbles which the waves draw back, and fling, 10
At their return, up the high strand,
Begin, and cease, and then again begin,
With tremulous cadence slow, and bring
The eternal note of sadness in.

Sophocles long ago
Heard it on the Aegaean, and it brought
Into his mind the turbid ebb and flow
Of human misery; we
Find also in the sound a thought,
Hearing it by this distant northern sea. 20

The Sea of Faith
Was once, too, at the full, and round earth's shore
Lay like the folds of a bright girdle furl'd.
But now I only hear
Its melancholy, long, withdrawing roar,
Retreating, to the breath
Of the night-wind, down the vast edges drear
And naked shingles of the world.

Ah, love, let us be true
To one another! for the world, which seems 30
To lie before us like a land of dreams,
So various, so beautiful, so new,
Hath really neither joy, nor love, nor light,
Nor certitude, nor peace, nor help for pain;
And we are here as on a darkling plain
Swept with confused alarms of struggle and flight,
Where ignorant armies clash by night.

MATTHEW ARNOLD

126

Green Flows the River of Lethe—O

Green flows the river of Lethe–O
Long Lethe river
Where the fire was in the veins – and grass is growing
Over the fever –
The green grass growing. . . .

I stood near the Cities of the Plains;
And the young girls were chasing their hearts like the gay
butterflies
Over the fields of summer –
O evanescent velvets fluttering your wings
Like winds and butterflies on the Road from Nothing to
Nowhere! 10

But in the summer drought
I fled, for I was a Pillar of Fire, I was Destruction
Unquenched, incarnate and incarnadine.

I was Annihilation
Yet white as the Dead Sea, white as the Cities of the Plains.
For I listened to the noontide and my veins
That threatened thunder and the heart of roses.

I went the way I would –
But long is the terrible Street of the Blood
That had once seemed only part of the summer redness: 20
It stretches forever, and there is no turning
But only fire, annihilation, burning.

I thought the way of the Blood would never tire.
But now only the red clover
Lies over the breath of the lion and the mouth of the
lover –

And green flows Lethe river–O
Long Lethe river
Over Gomorrah's city and the fire. . . .

EDITH SITWELL

127

Remember now thy Creator

Remember now thy Creator in the days of thy youth, while the evil days come not, nor the years draw nigh, when thou shalt say, I have no pleasure in them;

While the sun, or the light, or the moon, or the stars, be not darkened, nor the clouds return after the rain:

In the day when the keepers of the house shall tremble, and the strong men shall bow themselves, and the grinders cease because they are few, and those that look out of the windows be darkened,

And the doors shall be shut in the streets, when the sound of the grinding is low, and he shall rise up at the voice of the bird, and all the daughters of musick shall be brought low;

Also when they shall be afraid of that which is high, and fears shall be in the way, and the almond tree shall flourish, and the grasshopper shall be a burden, and desire shall fail: because man goeth to his long home, and the mourners go about the streets:

Or ever the silver cord be loosed, or the golden bowl be broken, or the pitcher be broken at the fountain, or the wheel broken at the cistern.

Then shall the dust return to the earth as it was: and the spirit shall return unto God who gave it.

ECCLESIASTES 12: 1-7

128

Lines

FROM THE
PROLOGUE
TO THE
Canterbury Tales

Whan that° Aprillè with his shourès soote° — When; sweet showers
The droghte of March hath percèd to the roote,
And bathèd every veyne in swich licour° — such liquid, sap
Of which vertu° engendred is the flour; — By power of which
Whan Zephirus° eek° with his swetè breeth — west wind; moreover
Inspirèd hath in every holt° and heeth° — grove; heath
The tendre croppès,° and the yongè sonne — shoots
Hath in the Ram his halfè cours y-ronne,
And smalè foweles maken melodye,
That slepen al the nyght with open eye, —
So priketh hem° Nature in hir corages,° — — stirs them; their hearts
Thanne longen° folk to goon° on pilgrimages, — long; go
And palmeres for to seken° straungè strondes,° — seek; foreign shores
To fernè halwes kowthe° in sondry londes; — distant shrines known
And specially, from every shirès ende
Of Engèlond, to Caunturbury they wende,
The hooly blisful martir for to seke,
That hem hath holpen° whan that they were seeke. — helped

GEOFFREY CHAUCER

129

Church Going

Once I am sure there's nothing going on
I step inside, letting the door thud shut.
Another church: matting, seats, and stone,
And little books; sprawlings of flowers, cut
For Sunday, brownish now; some brass and stuff
Up at the holy end; the small neat organ;
And a tense, musty, unignorable silence,
Brewed God knows how long. Hatless, I take off
My cycle-clips in awkward reverence,

Move forward, run my hand around the font. 10
From where I stand, the roof looks almost new –
Cleaned or restored? Someone would know: I don't.
Mounting the lectern, I peruse a few
Hectoring large-scale verses, and pronounce
'Here endeth' much more loudly than I'd meant.
The echoes snigger briefly. Back at the door
I sign the book, donate an Irish sixpence,
Reflect the place was not worth stopping for.

Yet stop I did: in fact I often do,
And always end much at a loss like this, 20
Wondering what to look for; wondering, too,
When churches fall completely out of use
What we shall turn them into, if we shall keep
A few cathedrals chronically on show,
Their parchment, plate and pyx in locked cases,
And let the rest rent-free to rain and sheep.
Shall we avoid them as unlucky places?

Or, after dark, will dubious women come
To make their children touch a particular stone;
Pick simples for a cancer; or in some 30
Advised night see walking a dead one?
Power of some sort or other will go on
In games, in riddles, seemingly at random;
But superstition, like belief, must die,
And what remains when disbelief has gone?
Grass, weedy pavement, brambles, buttress, sky,

A shape less recognisable each week,
A purpose more obscure. I wonder who
Will be the last, the very last, to seek
This place for what it was; one of the crew 40
That tap and jot and know what rood-lofts were?
Some ruin-bibber, randy for antique
Or Christmas-addict, counting on a whiff
Of gown-and-bands and organ-pipes and myrrh?
Or will he be my representative,

Bored, uninformed, knowing the ghostly silt
Dispersed, yet tending to the cross of ground
Through suburb scrub because it held unspilt
So long and equably what since is found
Only in separation – marriage, and birth, 50
And deaths, and thoughts of these – for whom was built
This special shell? For, though I've no idea
What this accoutred frowsty barn is worth,
It pleases me to stand in silence here;

A serious house on serious earth it is,
In whose blent air all our compulsions meet,
Are recognized, and robed as destinies.

And that much never can be obsolete,
Since someone will forever be surprising
A hunger in himself to be more serious, 60
And gravitating with it to this ground,
Which, he once heard, was proper to grow wise in,
If only that so many dead lie round.

PHILIP LARKIN

130

The Last Hour of Faustus

FROM

The Tragical History of Dr Faustus

Faustus speaks

Ah, Faustus,
Now hast thou but one bare hour to live,
And then thou must be damned perpetually!
Stand still, you ever-moving spheres of Heaven,
That time may cease, and midnight never come.
Fair Nature's eye, rise, rise again and make
Perpetual day; or let this hour be but
A year, a month, a week, a natural day,
That Faustus may repent and save his soul!

O lente, lente, currite noctis equi! 10
The stars move still, time runs, the clock will strike,
The Devil will come, and Faustus must be damned.
O, I'll leap up to my God! Who pulls me down?
See, see where Christ's blood streams in the firmament!
One drop would save my soul – half a drop: ah, my Christ!
Ah, rend not my heart for naming of my Christ!
Yet will I call on him: O spare me, Lucifer! –
Where is it now? 'tis gone; and see where God
Stretcheth out his arm, and bends his ireful brows!
Mountain and hills come, come and fall on me, 20
And hide me from the heavy wrath of God!
No! no!
Then will I headlong run into the earth;
Earth gape! O no, it will not harbour me!
You stars that reigned at my nativity,
Whose influence hath allotted death and hell,
Now draw up Faustus like a foggy mist
Into the entrails of yon labouring clouds,
That when they vomit forth into the air,
My limbs may issue from their smoky mouths, 30
So that my soul may but ascend to Heaven.

(The clock strikes the half hour)

Ah, half the hour is past! 'twill all be past anon!
O God!
If thou wilt not have mercy on my soul,
Yet for Christ's sake whose blood hath ransomed me,
Impose some end to my incessant pain;
Let Faustus live in hell a thousand years –
A hundred thousand, and – at last – be saved!
O, no end is limited to damned souls!
Why wert thou not a creature wanting soul? 40

Or why is this immortal that thou hast?
Ah, Pythagoras' metempsychosis! were that true,
This soul should fly from me, and I be changed
Unto some brutish beast! all beasts are happy,
For, when they die,
Their souls are soon dissolved in elements;
But mine must live, still to be plagued in hell.
Curst be the parents that engendered me!
No, Faustus: curse thyself: curse Lucifer
That hath deprived thee of the joys of Heaven. 50

(The clock strikes twelve)

O, it strikes, it strikes! Now, body, turn to air,
Or Lucifer will bear thee quick to hell.
O soul, be changed into little water-drops,
And fall into the ocean – ne'er be found.

(Devils enter)

My God! my God! look not so fierce on me!
Adders and serpents, let me breathe awhile!
Ugly hell, gape not! come not, Lucifer!
I'll burn my books – Ah Mephistophilis!

CHRISTOPHER MARLOWE

131

Reason has Moons

Reason has moons, but moons not hers
  Lie mirror'd on her sea,
Confounding her astronomers,
  But oh, delighting me.

RALPH HODGSON

132

Lucifer in Starlight

On a starr'd night Prince Lucifer uprose.
Tired of his dark dominion swung the fiend
Above the rolling ball in cloud part screen'd,
Where sinners hugg'd their spectre of repose.
Poor prey to his hot fit of pride were those.
And now upon his western wing he lean'd,
Now his huge bulk o'er Afric's sands careen'd,
Now the black planet shadow'd Arctic snows.
Soaring through wider zones that prick'd his scars
With memory of the old revolt from Awe,
He reach'd a middle height, and at the stars,
Which are the brain of heaven, he look'd, and sank.
Around the ancient track march'd, rank on rank,
The army of unalterable law.

GEORGE MEREDITH

133

In the Wide Awe and Wisdom of the Night

In the wide awe and wisdom of the night
I saw the round world rolling on its way,
Beyond significance of depth or height,
Beyond the interchange of dark and day.
I marked the march to which is set no pause,
And that stupendous orbit, round whose rim
The great sphere sweeps, obedient unto laws
That utter the eternal thought of Him.

I compassed time, outstripped the starry speed,
And in my still soul apprehended space,
Till, weighing laws which these but blindly heed,
At last I came before Him face to face –
And knew the Universe of no such span
As the august infinitude of Man.

SIR CHARLES G. D. ROBERTS

134

Welsh Night

FROM

Under Milk Wood

FIRST VOICE *(very softly)*

To begin at the beginning:

It is spring, moonless night in the small town, starless and bible-black, the cobblestreets silent and the hunched, courters'-and-rabbits' wood limping invisible down to the sloeblack, slow, black, crowblack, fishingboat-bobbing sea. The houses are blind as moles (though moles see fine to-night in the snouting, velvet dingles) or blind as Captain Cat there in the muffled middle by the pump and the town clock, the shops in mourning, the Welfare Hall in widows' weeds. And all the people of the lulled and dumbfound town are sleeping now.

Listen. It is night moving in the streets, the processional salt slow musical wind in Coronation Street and Cockle Row, it is the grass growing on Llaregyb Hill, dewfall, starfall, the sleep of birds in Milk Wood.

Listen. It is night in the chill, squat chapel, hymning in bonnet and brooch and bombazine black, butterfly choker and bootlace bow, coughing like nannygoats, sucking mintoes, fortywinking hallelujah; night in the four-ale, quiet as a domino; in Ocky Milkman's lofts like a mouse with gloves; in Dai Bread's bakery flying like black flour. It is to-night in Donkey Street, trotting silent, with seaweed on its hooves, along the cockled cobbles, past curtained fernpot, text and trinket, harmonium, holy dresser, watercolours done by hand, china dog and rosy tin teacaddy. It is night neddying among the snuggeries of babies.

Look. It is night, dumbly, royally winding through the Coronation cherry trees; going through the graveyard of Bethesda with winds gloved and folded, and dew doffed; tumbling by the Sailors Arms.

DYLAN THOMAS

135

Hymn to Diana

Queen and huntress, chaste and fair,
Now the sun is laid to sleep,
Seated in thy silver chair,
State in wonted manner keep:
Hesperus entreats thy light,
Goddess excellently bright.

Earth, let not thy envious shade
Dare itself to interpose;
Cynthia's shining orb was made
Heaven to clear when day did close:
Bless us then with wishèd sight,
Goddess excellently bright.

Lay thy bow of pearl apart,
And thy crystal-shining quiver;
Give unto the flying hart
Space to breathe, how short soever:
Thou that mak'st a day of night,
Goddess excellently bright.

BEN JONSON

136

Golden Slumbers

Golden slumbers kiss your eyes,
Smiles awake you when you rise.
Sleep, pretty wantons, do not cry,
And I will sing a lullaby.
Rock them, rock them, lullaby.

Care is heavy, therefore sleep you;
You are care, and care must keep you;
Sleep, pretty wantons, do not cry,
And I will sing a lullaby:
Rock them, rock them, lullaby.

THOMAS DEKKER

137

Night Bells

Two bells   six bells   two bells   six bells
On a blue pavilion
Out across a smooth blue pavilion
And between each bell
One clear cry of a woman
'Lord God you made the night too long too long.'

CARL SANDBURG

138

Snail

Little snail,
Dreaming you go.
Weather and rose
Is all you know.

Weather and rose
Is all you see,
Drinking
The dewdrop's
Mystery.

LANGSTON HUGHES

139

The Sick Rose

O Rose, thou art sick!
The invisible worm,
That flies in the night,
In the howling storm,

Has found out thy bed
Of crimson joy;
And his dark secret love
Does thy life destroy.

WILLIAM BLAKE

140

Farmers

Man to the plough,
Wife to the cow,
Girl to the yarn,
Boy to the barn,
And your rent will be netted;
But
Man tally-ho,
Miss Piano,
Wife silk and satin,
Boy Greek and Latin,
And you'll soon be gazetted.

ANONYMOUS

141

Girl's-Eye View of Relatives

FIRST LESSON

The thing to remember about fathers is, they're men.
A girl has to keep it in mind.
They are dragon-seekers, bent on improbable rescues.
Scratch any father, you find
Someone chock-full of qualms and romantic terrors,
Believing change is a threat –
Like your first shoes with heels on, like your first bicycle
It took such months to get.

Walk in strange woods, they warn you about the snakes
there.
Climb, and they fear you'll fall.
Books, angular boys, or swimming in deep water –
Fathers mistrust them all.
Men are the worriers. It is difficult for them
To learn what they must learn:
How you have a journey to take and very likely,
For a while, will not return.

TURN OF THE SCREW

Girl cousins condescend. They wear
Earrings, and dress like fashion's sample,
Have speaking eyes and curly hair.
And parents point to their example.
But the boy cousins one's allotted
Are years too young for one. Or spotted.

TRIOLET AGAINST SISTERS

Sisters are always drying their hair.
  Locked into rooms, alone,
They pose at the mirror, shoulders bare,
Trying this way and that their hair,
Or fly importunate down the stair
  To answer a telephone.
Sisters are always drying their hair,
  Locked into rooms, alone.

THE ADVERSARY

A mother's hardest to forgive.
Life is the fruit she longs to hand you,
Ripe on a plate. And while you live,
Relentlessly she understands you.

PHYLLIS MCGINLEY

142

Birds, Bags, Bears, and Buns

The common cormorant or shag
Lays eggs inside a paper bag.
The reason you will see, no doubt,
It is to keep the lightning out,
But what these unobservant birds
Have never noticed is that herds
Of wandering bears may come with buns
And steal the bags to hold the crumbs.

ANONYMOUS

143

The Prize Cat

Pure blood domestic, guaranteed,
Soft-mannered, musical in purr,
The ribbon had declared the breed,
Gentility was in the fur.

Such feline culture in the gads,
No anger ever arched her back –
What distance since those velvet pads
Departed from the leopard's track!

And when I mused how Time had thinned
The jungle strains within the cells,
How human hands had disciplined
Those prowling optic parallels;

I saw the generations pass
Along the reflex of a spring,
A bird had rustled in the grass,
The tab had caught it on the wing:

Behind the leap so furtive-wild
Was such ignition in the gleam,
I thought an Abyssinian child
Had cried out in the whitethroat's scream.

E. J. PRATT

144

Cats

Cats, no less liquid than their shadows,
Offer no angles to the wind,
They slip, diminished, neat, through loopholes
Less than themselves; will not be pinned

To rules or routes for journeys; counter-
Attack with non-resistance; twist
Enticing through the curving fingers
And leave an angered, empty fist.

They wait, obsequious as darkness,
Quick to retire, quick to return;
Admit no aims or ethics; flatter
With reservations; will not learn

To answer to their names; are seldom
Truly owned till shot and skinned.
Cats, no less liquid than their shadows,
Offer no angles to the wind.

A. S. J. TESSIMOND

145

Cheerio my Deario

(*By* ARCHY THE COCKROACH)

well boss i met
mehitabel the cat
trying to dig a
frozen lamb chop
out of a snow
drift the other day

a heluva comedown
that is for me archy
she says a few
brief centuries 10
ago one of old
king
tut
ankh
amens favourite
queens and today
the village scavenger
but wotthehell
archy wotthehell
its cheerio 20
my deario that
pulls a lady through

see here mehitabel
i said i thought

you told me that
it was cleopatra
you used to be
before you
transmigrated into
the carcase of a cat 30
where do you get
this tut
ankh
amen stuff
question mark

i was several
ladies my little
insect says she
being cleopatra was
only an incident 40
in my career
and i was always getting
the rough end of it
always being
misunderstood by some
strait laced
prune faced bunch
of prissy mouthed
sisters of uncharity
the things that 50
have been said
about me archy
exclamation point

and all simply
because i was a

live dame
the palaces i have
been kicked out of
in my time
exclamation point 60

but wotthehell
little archy wot
thehell
its cheerio
my deario
that pulls a
lady through
exclamation point

framed archy always
framed that is the 70
story of all my lives
no chance for a dame
with the anvil chorus
if she shows a little
motion it seems to
me only yesterday
that the luxor local
number one of
the ladies axe
association got me in 80
dutch with king tut and
he slipped me the
sarcophagus always my
luck yesterday an empress
and today too
emaciated to interest

a vivisectionist but
toujours gai archy
toujours gai and always
a lady in spite of hell
and transmigration 90
once a queen
always a queen
archy
period

one of her
feet was frozen
but on the other three
she began to caper and
dance singing its 100
cheerio my deario
that pulls a lady
through her morals may
have been mislaid somewhere
in the centuries boss but
i admire her spirit
archy

DON MARQUIS

146

The Bishop Orders his Tomb at Saint Praxed's Church

ROME, 15–

Vanity, saith the preacher, vanity!
Draw round my bed: is Anselm keeping back?
Nephews – sons mine . . . ah God, I know not! Well –
She, men would have to be your mother once,
Old Gandolf envied me, so fair she was!
What's done is done, and she is dead beside.
Dead long ago, and I am Bishop since,
And as she died so must we die ourselves,
And thence ye may perceive the world's a dream.
Life, how and what is it? As here I lie 10
In this state-chamber, dying by degrees,
Hours and long hours in the dead night, I ask
'Do I live, am I dead?' Peace, peace seems all.
Saint Praxed's ever was the church for peace;
And so, about this tomb of mine. I fought
With tooth and nail to save my niche, ye know:
– Old Gandolf cozened me, despite my care;
Shrewd was that snatch from out the corner South
He graced his carrion with, God curse the same!
Yet still my niche is not so cramped but thence 20
One sees the pulpit o' the epistle-side,
And somewhat of the choir, those silent seats,
And up into the aery dome where live
The angels, and a sunbeam's sure to lurk:
And I shall fill my slab of basalt there,
And 'neath my tabernacle take my rest,
With those nine columns round me, two and two,

The odd one at my feet where Anselm stands:
Peach-blossom marble all, the rare, the ripe
As fresh-poured red wine of a mighty pulse. 30
– Old Gandolf with his paltry onion-stone,
Put me where I may look at him! True peach
Rosy and flawless: how I earned the prize!
Draw close: that conflagration of my church
– What then? So much was saved if aught were missed!
My sons, ye would not be my death? Go dig
The white-grape vineyard where the oil-press stood,
Drop water gently till the surface sink,
And if ye find. . . . Ah God, I know not, I! . . .
Bedded in store of rotten fig-leaves soft, 40
And corded up in a tight olive-frail,
Some lump, ah God, of lapis lazuli,
Big as a Jew's head cut off at the nape,
Blue as a vein o'er the Madonna's breast . . .
Sons, all I have bequeathed you, villas, all,
That brave Frascati villa with its bath,
So, let the blue lump poise between my knees,
Like God the Father's globe on both his hands
Ye worship in the Jesu Church so gay,
For Gandolf shall not choose but see and burst! 50
Swift as a weaver's shuttle fleet our years:
Man goeth to the grave, and where is he?
Did I say basalt for my slab, sons? Black –
'Twas ever antique-black I meant! How else
Shall ye contrast my frieze to come beneath?
The bas-relief in bronze ye promised me,
Those Pans and Nymphs ye wot of, and perchance
Some tripod, thyrsus, with a vase or so,
The Saviour at his sermon on the mount,
Saint Praxed in a glory, and one Pan 60

Ready to twitch the Nymph's last garment off,
And Moses with the tables . . . but I know
Ye mark me not! What do they whisper thee,
Child of my bowels, Anselm? Ah, ye hope
To revel down my villas while I gasp
Bricked o'er with beggar's mouldy travertine
Which Gandolf from his tomb-top chuckles at!
Nay, boys, ye love me – all of jasper, then!
'Tis jasper ye stand pledged to, lest I grieve
My bath must needs be left behind, alas! 70
One block, pure green as a pistachio-nut,
There's plenty jasper somewhere in the world –
And have I not Saint Praxed's ear to pray
Horses for ye, and brown Greek manuscripts,
And mistresses with great smooth marbly limbs?
– That's if ye carve my epitaph aright,
Choice Latin, picked phrase, Tully's every word,
No gaudy ware like Gandolf's second line –
Tully, my masters? Ulpian serves his need!
And then how I shall lie through centuries, 80
And hear the blessed mutter of the mass,
And see God made and eaten all day long,
And feel the steady candle-flame, and taste
Good strong thick stupefying incense-smoke!
For as I lie here, hours of the dead night,
Dying in state and by such slow degrees,
I fold my arms as if they clasped a crook,
And stretch my feet forth straight as stone can point,
And let the bedclothes, for a mortcloth, drop
Into great laps and folds of sculptor's-work: 90
And as yon tapers dwindle, and strange thoughts
Grow, with a certain humming in my ears,
About the life before I lived this life,

And this life too, popes, cardinals and priests,
Saint Praxed at his sermon on the mount,
Your tall pale mother with her talking eyes,
And new-found agate urns as fresh as day,
And marble's language, Latin pure, discreet,
– Aha, *Elucescebat* quoth our friend?
No Tully, said I, Ulpian at the best! 100
Evil and brief hath been my pilgrimage.
All lapis, all, sons! Else I give the Pope
My villas! Will ye ever eat my heart?
Ever your eyes were as a lizard's quick,
They glitter like your mother's for my soul,
Or ye would heighten my impoverished frieze,
Piece out its starved design, and fill my vase
With grapes, and add a vizor and a Term,
And to the tripod ye would tie a lynx
That in his struggle throws the thyrsus down, 110
To comfort me on my entablature
Whereon I am to lie till I must ask
'Do I live, am I dead?' There, leave me, there!
For ye have stabbed me with ingratitude
To death – ye wish it – God, ye wish it! Stone –
Gritstone, a-crumble! Clammy squares which sweat
As if the corpse they keep were oozing through –
And no more lapis to delight the world!
Well go! I bless ye. Fewer tapers there,
But in a row: and, going, turn your backs 120
– Ay, like departing altar-ministrants,
And leave me in my church, the church for peace,
That I may watch at leisure if he leers –
Old Gandolf, at me, from his onion-stone,
As still he envied me, so fair she was!

ROBERT BROWNING

147

Passing By

There is a Lady sweet and kind,
Was never face so pleased my mind;
I did but see her passing by,
And yet I love her till I die.

Her gesture, motion, and her smiles,
Her wit, her voice, my heart beguiles,
Beguiles my heart, I know not why,
And yet I love her till I die.

Cupid is wingèd and doth range,
Her country so my love doth change:
But change she earth, or change she sky,
Yet will I love her till I die.

ANONYMOUS

148

Whenas in Silks

Whenas in silks my Julia goes
Then, then (methinks) how sweetly flows
That liquefaction of her clothes.

Next, when I cast mine eyes and see
That brave vibration each way free,
– O how that glittering taketh me!

ROBERT HERRICK

149

A Sweet Disorder

A sweet disorder in the dress
Kindles in clothes a wantonness: –
A lawn about the shoulders thrown
Into a fine distraction:
An erring lace, which here and there
Enthrals the crimson stomacher:
A cuff neglectful, and thereby
Ribbands to flow confusedly:
A winning wave, deserving note,
In the tempestuous petticoat:
A careless shoe-string, in whose tie
I see a wild civility:
Do more bewitch me, than when art
Is too precise in every part.

ROBERT HERRICK

150

To His Coy Mistress

Had we but world enough, and time,
This coyness, Lady, were no crime.
We would sit down, and think which way
To walk, and pass our long love's day.
Thou by the Indian Ganges' side
Shouldst rubies find; I by the tide
Of Humber would complain. I would
Love you ten years before the Flood;
And you should, if you please, refuse
Till the conversion of the Jews. 10
My vegetable love should grow
Vaster than empires, and more slow.
An hundred years should go to praise
Thine eyes, and on thy forehead gaze;
Two hundred to adore each breast;
But thirty thousand to the rest:
An age, at least, to every part,
And the last age should show your heart.
For, Lady, you deserve this state;
Nor would I love at lower rate. 20
But, at my back, I always hear
Time's winged chariot hurrying near:
And yonder, all before us lie
Deserts of vast eternity.
Thy beauty shall no more be found;
Nor, in the marble vault, shall sound
My echoing song. Then worms shall try
That long preserved virginity:
And your quaint honour turn to dust;
And into ashes all my lust. 30

The grave's a fine and private place,
But none, I think, do there embrace.
  Now, therefore, while the youthful hue
Sits on thy skin like morning dew,
And while thy willing soul transpires
At every pore with instant fires,
Now let us sport us while we may;
And now, like amorous birds of prey,
Rather at once our time devour,
Than languish in his slow-chapt power. 40
Let us roll all our strength, and all
Our sweetness, up into one ball;
And tear our pleasures, with rough strife,
Thorough the iron gates of life.
  Thus, though we cannot make our sun
Stand still, yet we will make him run.

ANDREW MARVELL

151

She Dwelt Among the Untrodden Ways

She dwelt among the untrodden ways
  Beside the springs of Dove;
A maid whom there were none to praise
  And very few to love:

A violet by a mossy stone
  Half hidden from the eye!
– Fair as a star, when only one
  Is shining in the sky.

She lived unknown, and few could know
  When Lucy ceased to be;
But she is in her grave, and oh,
  The difference to me!

WILLIAM WORDSWORTH

152

She Walks in Beauty

She walks in beauty, like the night
  Of cloudless climes and starry skies;
And all that's best of dark and bright
  Meet in her aspect and her eyes:
Thus mellow'd to that tender light
  Which heaven to gaudy day denies.

One shade the more, one ray the less,
  Had half impair'd the nameless grace
Which waves in every raven tress,
  Or softly lightens o'er her face;
Where thoughts serenely sweet express
  How pure, how dear their dwelling-place.

And on that cheek and o'er that brow
  So soft, so calm, yet eloquent,
The smiles that win, the tints that glow
  But tell of days in goodness spent,
A mind at peace with all below,
  A heart whose love is innocent.

LORD BYRON

153

Go by Brooks

Go by brooks, love,
Where fish stare,
Go by brooks,
I will pass there.

Go by rivers,
Where eels throng,
Rivers, love,
I won't be long.

Go by oceans,
Where whales sail,
Oceans, love,
I will not fail.

LEONARD COHEN

154

Hynd Horn

Hynd Horn's bound, love, and Hynd Horn's free,
  With a hey lillelu, and a how lo lan;
Where was ye born, or in what countrie?
  And the birk and the broom blows bonnie.

'In good greenwood, there I was born,
And all my forbears me beforn.

'O seven long years I served the King,
And as for wages I never gat nane;

'But ae sight o' his ae daughter.
And that was through an auger-bore.' 10

Seven long years he served the King.
And it's a' for the sake of his daughter Jean.

The King an angry man was he;
He sent young Hynd Horn to the sea.

He's gi'en his love a silver wand
Wi' seven silver laverocks sittin' thereon.

She's gi'en to him a gay gold ring
Wi' seven bright diamonds set therein.

'As lang's these diamonds keep their hue,
Ye'll know I am a lover true: 20

'But when the ring turns pale and wan,
Ye may ken that I love anither man.'

He hoist up sails and awa' sailed he
Till that he came to a foreign countrie.

One day as he looked his ring upon,
He saw the diamonds pale and wan.

He's left the seas and he's come to the land,
And the first that he met was an auld beggar man.

'What news, what news? thou auld beggar man,
For it's seven years sin I've seen land.' 30

'No news,' said the beggar, 'no news at a',
But there is a wedding in the King's ha'.

'But there is a wedding in the King's ha',
That has halden these forty days and twa.'

'Cast off, cast off thy auld beggar weed,
And I'll gi'e thee my gude grey steed:

'And lend to me your wig o' hair
To cover mine, because it is fair.'

'My begging weed is na for thee,
Your riding steed is na for me.' 40

But part by right and part by wrang
Hynd Horn has changed wi' the beggar man.

The auld beggar man was bound for to ride,
But young Hynd Horn was bound for the bride.

When he came to the King's gate,
He sought a drink for Hynd Horn's sake.

The bride came trippin' down the stair,
Wi' the scales o' red gowd in her hair;

Wi' a cup o' the red wine in her hand,
And that she gae to the auld beggar man. 50

Out o' the cup he drank the wine,
And into the cup he dropt the ring.

'O got ye this by sea or land?
Or got ye it of a dead man's hand?'

'I got it na by sea nor land,
But I got it, madam, of your own hand.'

'O I'll cast off my gowns o' brown,
And beg with you frae town to town.

'O I'll cast off my gowns o' red,
And I'll beg wi' you to win my bread. 60

'O I'll take the scales o' gowd frae my hair,
And I'll follow you for evermair.'

She cast awa' the brown and the red,
And she's followed him to beg her bread.

She has ta'en the scales o' gowd frae her hair
And she's followed him for evermair.

But atween the kitchen and the ha'
He has let his cloutie cloak down fa'.

And the red gowd shinèd over him a'.
With a hey lillelu, and a how lo lan; 70
And the bride frae the bridegroom was stown awa'
And the birk and the broom blows bonnie.

ANONYMOUS

155

True Love

As I walked out one evening,
Walking down Bristol Street,
The crowds upon the pavement
Were fields of harvest wheat.

And down by the brimming river
I heard a lover sing
Under an arch of the railway:
'Love has no ending.

I'll love you, dear, I'll love you
  Till China and Africa meet, 10
And the river jumps over the mountain
  And the salmon sing in the street.

I'll love you till the ocean
  Is folded and hung up to dry,
And the seven stars go squawking
  Like geese about the sky.

The years shall run like rabbits,
  For in my arms I hold
The Flower of the Ages,
  And the first love of the world.' 20

But all the clocks in the city
  Began to whirr and chime:
'O let not Time deceive you,
  You cannot conquer Time.

In the burrows of the Nightmare
  Where Justice naked is,
Time watches from the shadow
  And coughs when you would kiss.

In headaches and in worry
  Vaguely life leaks away, 30
And Time will have his fancy
  Tomorrow or today.

Into many a green valley
  Drifts the appalling snow;

Time breaks the threaded dances
  And the diver's brilliant bow.

O plunge your hands in water,
  Plunge them in up to the wrist;
Stare, stare in the basin
  And wonder what you've missed. 40

The glacier knocks in the cupboard,
  The desert sighs in the bed,
And the crack in the tea-cup opens
  A lane to the land of the dead.

Where the beggars raffle the banknotes
  And the Giant is enchanting to Jack,
And the Lily-white Boy is a Roarer,
  And Jill goes down on her back.

O look, look in the mirror,
  O look in your distress; 50
Life remains a blessing
  Although you cannot bless.

O stand, stand at the window
  As the tears scald and start;
You shall love your crooked neighbor
  With your crooked heart.'

It was late, late in the evening,
  The lovers they were gone;
The clocks had ceased their chiming,
  And the deep river ran on.

W. H. AUDEN

156

A Valediction Forbidding Mourning

As virtuous men pass mildly away
  And whisper to their souls to go,
Whilst some of their sad friends do say,
  'The breath goes now,' and some say, 'No:'

So let us melt, and make no noise,
  No tear-floods, nor sigh-tempests move;
'Twere profanation of our joys
  To tell the laity our love.

Moving of th'earth brings harms and fears;
  Men reckon what it did, and meant.
But trepidation of the spheres,
  Though greater far, is innocent.

Dull sublunary lovers' love –
  Whose soul is sense – cannot admit
Absence, because it doth remove
  Those things which elemented it.

But we by a love so much refined
  That ourselves know not what it is,
Inter-assured of the mind,
  Care less eyes, lips, and hands to miss.

Our two souls, therefore, which are one,
  Though I must go, endure not yet
A breach, but an expansion,
  Like gold to airy thinness beat.

If they be two, they are two so
   As stiff twin compasses are two;
Thy soul, the fixed foot, makes no show
   To move, but doth, if th'other do.

And though it in the center sit,
   Yet, when the other far doth roam,
It leans and harkens after it,
   And grows erect, as that comes home.

Such wilt thou be to me, who must,
   Like th'other foot, obliquely run;
Thy firmness makes my circle just,
   And makes me end where I begun.

JOHN DONNE

157

A Hymn to God the Father

Wilt thou forgive that sin where I begun,
  Which is my sin, though it were done before?
Wilt thou forgive those sins, through which I run,
And do run still: though still I do deplore?
  When thou hast done, thou hast not done,
    For I have more.

Wilt thou forgive that sin by which I've won
  Others to sin? and, made my sin their door?
Wilt thou forgive that sin which I did shun
A year, or two: but wallowed in, a score?
    When thou hast done, thou hast not done,
      For I have more.

I have a sin of fear, that when I have spun
  My last thread, I shall perish on the shore;
Swear by thy self, that at my death thy sun
  Shall shine as he shines now, and heretofore;
    And, having done that, Thou hast done,
      I fear no more.

JOHN DONNE

158

Death

Death, be not proud, though some have called thee
Mighty and dreadful, for thou art not so:
For those whom thou think'st thou dost overthrow
Die not, poor Death; nor yet canst thou kill me.
From Rest and Sleep, which but thy picture be,
Much pleasure, then from thee much more must flow;
And soonest our best men with thee do go —
Rest of their bones and souls' delivery!
Thou'rt slave to fate, chance, kings, and desperate men,
And dost with poison, war, and sickness dwell;
And poppy or charms can make us sleep as well
And better than thy stroke. Why swell'st thou then?
One short sleep past, we wake eternally,
And death shall be no more: Death, thou shalt die!

JOHN DONNE

159
Charity

Though I speak with the tongues of men and of angels, and have not charity, I am become as sounding brass, or a tinkling cymbal.

And though I have the gift of prophecy, and understand all mysteries, and all knowledge; and though I have all faith, so that I could remove mountains, and have not charity, I am nothing.

And though I bestow all my goods to feed the poor, and though I give my body to be burned, and have not charity, it profiteth me nothing. 10

Charity suffereth long, and is kind; charity envieth not; charity vaunteth not itself, is not puffed up,

Doth not behave itself unseemly, seeketh not her own, is not easily provoked, thinketh no evil;

Rejoiceth not in iniquity, but rejoiceth in the truth;

Beareth all things, believeth all things, hopeth all things, endureth all things.

Charity never faileth: but whether there be prophecies, they shall fail; whether there be tongues, they shall cease; whether there be knowledge, it shall vanish away. 20

For we know in part, and we prophesy in part.

But when that which is perfect is come, then that which is in part shall be done away.

When I was a child, I spake as a child, I understood as a child, I thought as a child: but when I became a man I put away childish things.

For now we see through a glass, darkly; but then face to face: now I know in part; but then shall I know even as also I am known.

And now abideth faith, hope, charity, these three;
but the greatest of these is charity. I CORINTHIANS 13: 1-13

160

Love

Love bade me welcome; yet my soul drew back,
  Guilty of dust and sin.
But quick-eyed Love, observing me grow slack
  From my first entrance in,
Drew nearer to me, sweetly questioning
  If I lack'd anything.

'A guest,' I answer'd, 'worthy to be here.'
  Love said, 'You shall be he.'
'I, the unkind, ungrateful? Ah, my dear!
  I cannot look on Thee.'
Love took my hand, and smiling did reply,
  'Who made the eyes but I?'

'Truth, Lord; but I have marr'd them; let my shame
  Go where it doth deserve.'
'And know you not,' says Love, 'who bore the blame?'
  'My dear, then I will serve.'
'You must sit down,' says Love, 'and taste my meat.'
  So I did sit and eat.

GEORGE HERBERT

161

Virtue

Sweet day! so cool, so calm, so bright!
  The bridal of the earth and sky –
The dew shall weep thy fall to-night;
  For thou must die.

Sweet rose, whose hue angry and brave
  Bids the rash gazer wipe his eye,
Thy root is ever in the grave,
  And thou must die.

Sweet Spring, full of sweet days and roses,
  A box where sweets compacted lie,
My music shows ye have your closes,
  And all must die.

Only a sweet and virtuous soul,
  Like seasoned timber, never gives,
But, though the whole world turn to coal,
  Then chiefly lives.

GEORGE HERBERT

162

Hail, Holy Light

FROM

Paradise Lost, Book III

Hail, holy Light, offspring of Heaven first-born!
Or of th' Eternal coeternal beam
May I express thee unblamed? since God is light,
And never but in unapproached light
Dwelt from eternity, dwelt then in thee,
Bright effluence of bright essence increate!
Or hear'st thou rather pure ethereal stream,
Whose fountain who shall tell? before the Sun,
Before the Heavens, thou wert, and at the voice
Of God, as with a mantle, didst invest 10
The rising world of waters dark and deep,
Won from the void and formless Infinite!
Thee I revisit now with bolder wing,
Escaped the Stygian Pool, though long detained
In that obscure sojourn, while in my flight,
Through utter and through middle darkness borne,
With other notes than to th' Orphean lyre
I sung of Chaos and eternal Night,
Taught by the Heavenly Muse to venture down
The dark descent, and up to reascend, 20
Though hard and rare: thee I revisit safe,
And feel thy sovran vital lamp; but thou
Revisit'st not these eyes, that roll in vain
To find thy piercing ray, and find no dawn;
So thick a drop serene hath quenched their orbs,
Or dim diffusion veiled. Yet not the more
Cease I to wander where the Muses haunt

Clear spring, or shady grove, or sunny hill,
Smit with the love of sacred song: but chief
Thee, Sion, and the flowery brooks beneath, 30
That wash thy hallowed feet, and warbling flow,
Nightly I visit: nor sometimes forget
Those other two equalled with me in fate,
So were I equalled with them in renown,
Blind Thamyris and blind Maeonides,
And Tiresias and Phineus, prophets old:
Then feed on thoughts that voluntary move
Harmonious numbers; as the wakeful bird
Sings darkling, and, in shadiest covert hid,
Tunes her nocturnal note. Thus with the year 40
Seasons return; but not to me returns
Day, or the sweet approach of even or morn,
Or sight of vernal bloom, or summer's rose,
Or flocks, or herds, or human face divine;
But cloud instead and ever-during dark
Surrounds me, from the cheerful ways of men
Cut off, and for the book of knowledge fair,
Presented with a universal blank
Of Nature's works, to me expunged and rased,
And wisdom at one entrance quite shut out. 50
So much the rather thou, Celestial Light,
Shine inward, and the mind through all her powers
Irradiate; there plant eyes; all mist from thence
Purge and disperse, that I may see and tell
Of things invisible to mortal sight.

JOHN MILTON

163

Last Chorus

FROM

Samson Agonistes

All is best, though we oft doubt,
What the unsearchable dispose
Of Highest Wisdom brings about,
And ever best found in the close.
Oft he seems to hide his face,
But unexpectedly returns,
And to his faithful champion hath in place
Bore witness gloriously; whence Gaza mourns,
And all that band them to resist
His uncontrollable intent;
His servants he, with new acquist
Of true experience from this great event,
With peace and consolation hath dismissed
And calm of mind, all passion spent.

JOHN MILTON

164

On His Blindness

When I consider how my light is spent
Ere half my days, in this dark world and wide,
And that one talent which is death to hide
Lodged with me useless, though my soul more bent
To serve therewith my Maker, and present
My true account, lest He returning chide, –
'Doth God exact day-labour, light denied?'
I fondly ask: – But Patience, to prevent
That murmur, soon replies, 'God doth not need
Either man's work, or His own gifts; who best
Bear His mild yoke, they serve Him best. His state
Is kingly; thousands at His bidding speed
And post o'er land and ocean without rest;
They also serve who only stand and wait.'

JOHN MILTON

165

The Unsleeping

I soothe to unimagined sleep
The sunless bases of the deep.
And then I stir the aching tide
That gropes in its reluctant side.

I heave aloft the smoking hill;
To silent peace its throes I still.
But ever at its heart of fire
I lurk, an unassuaged desire.

I wrap me in the sightless germ
An instant or an endless term;
And still its atoms are my care,
Dispersed in ashes or in air.

I hush the comets one by one
To sleep for ages in the sun;
The sun resumes before my face
His circuit of the shores of space.

The mount, the star, the germ, the deep,
They all shall wake, they all shall sleep.
Time, like a flurry of wild rain,
Shall drift across the darkened pane.

Space, in the dim predestined hour,
Shall crumble like a ruined tower.
I only, with unfaltering eye,
Shall watch the dreams of God go by.

SIR CHARLES G. D. ROBERTS

166

December 29, 1170

CHORUS FROM

Murder in the Cathedral

Does the bird sing in the South?
Only the sea-bird cries, driven inland by the storm.
What sign of the spring of the year?
Only the death of the old: not a stir, not a shoot, not a
breath.
Do the days begin to lengthen?
Longer and darker the day, shorter and colder the night.
Still and stifling the air: but a wind is stored up in the East.
The starved crow sits in the field, attentive; and in the wood
The owl rehearses the hollow note of death.
What signs of a bitter spring? 10
The wind stored up in the East.
What, at the time of the birth of Our Lord, at
Christmastide,
Is there not peace upon earth, goodwill among men?
The peace of this world is always uncertain, unless men
keep the peace of God.
And war among men defiles this world, but death in the
Lord renews it,
And the world must be cleaned in the winter, or we shall
have only
A sour spring, a parched summer, an empty harvest.
Between Christmas and Easter what work shall be done?
The ploughman shall go out in March and turn the same
earth
He has turned before, the bird shall sing the same song. 20
When the leaf is out on the tree, when the elder and may

Burst over the stream, and the air is clear and high,
And voices trill at windows, and children tumble in front
    of the door,
What work shall have been done, what wrong
Shall the bird's song cover, the green tree cover, what wrong
Shall the fresh earth cover? We wait, and the time is short
But waiting is long.

T. S. ELIOT

167

The Swimmer's Moment

For everyone
The swimmer's moment at the whirlpool comes,
But many at that moment will not say
'This is the whirlpool, then.'
By their refusal they are saved
From the black pit, and also from contesting
The deadly rapids, and emerging in
The mysterious, and more ample, further waters.
And so their bland-blank faces turn and turn
Pale and forever on the rim of suction
They will not recognize.
Of those who dare the knowledge
Many are whirled into the ominous centre
That, gaping vertical, seals up
For them an eternal boon of privacy,
So that we turn away from their defeat
With a despair, not for their deaths, but for
Ourselves, who cannot penetrate their secret
Nor even guess at the anonymous breadth
Where one or two have won:
(The silver reaches of the estuary).

MARGARET AVISON

168

The Cold Green Element

At the end of the garden walk
the wind and its satellite wait for me;
their meaning I will not know
        until I go there,
but the black-hatted undertaker

who, passing, saw my heart beating in the grass,
is also going there. Hi, I tell him,
a great squall in the Pacific blew a dead poet
        out of the water,
who now hangs from the city's gates.

Crowds depart daily to see it, and return
with grimaces and incomprehension;
if its limbs twitched in the air
        they would sit at its feet
peeling their oranges.

And turning over I embrace like a lover
the trunk of a tree, one of those
for whom the lightning was too much
        and grew a brilliant
hunchback with a crown of leaves.

The ailments escaped from the labels
of medicine bottles are all fled to the wind;

I've seen myself lately in the eyes
        of old women,
spent streams mourning my manhood,

in whose old pupils the sun became
a bloodsmear on broad catalpa leaves
and hanging from ancient twigs,
        my murdered selves
sparked the air like the muted collisions

of fruit. A black dog howls down my blood,
a black dog with yellow eyes;
he too by someone's inadvertence
        saw the bloodsmear
on the broad catalpa leaves.

But the furies clear a path for me to the worm
who sang for an hour in the throat of a robin,
and misled by the cries of young boys
        I am again
a breathless swimmer in that cold green element.

IRVING LAYTON

169

Anyone Lived in a Pretty How Town

anyone lived in a pretty how town
(with up so floating many bells down)
spring summer autumn winter
he sang his didn't he danced his did.

Women and men (both little and small)
cared for anyone not at all
they sowed their isn't they reaped their same
sun moon stars rain

children guessed (but only a few
and down they forgot as up they grew
autumn winter spring summer)
that noone loved him more by more

when by now and tree by leaf
she laughed his joy she cried his grief
bird by snow and stir by still
anyone's any was all to her

someones married their everyones
laughed their cryings and did their dance
(sleep wake hope and then) they
said their nevers they slept their dream

stars rain sun moon
(and only the snow can begin to explain

how children are apt to forget to remember
with up so floating many bells down)

one day anyone died i guess
(and noone stooped to kiss his face)
busy folk buried them side by side
little by little and was by was

all by all and deep by deep
and more by more they dream their sleep
noone and anyone earth by april
wish by spirit and if by yes.

Women and men (both dong and ding)
summer autumn winter spring
reaped their sowing and went their came
sun moon stars rain

E. E. CUMMINGS

170

The Apprentice Priestling

A boy not ten years old
   they are giving to the temple!
      Oh, it's cold!

MASAOKA SHIKI

Translated by H. G. HENDERSON

171

Song of the Horseman

Córdoba.
Remote and lonely.

Jet-black mare and full round moon,
With olives in my saddle bags,
Although I know the road so well
I shall not get to Córdoba.

Across the plain, across the wind,
Jet-black mare and full red moon,
Death is gazing down upon me,
Down from the towers of Córdoba.

Ay! The road so dark and long.
Ay! My mare so tired yet brave.
Death is waiting for me there
Before I get to Córdoba.

Córdoba.
Remote and lonely.

F. GARCÍA LORCA

Translated by ROY CAMPBELL

172

Home After Three Months Away

Gone now the baby's nurse,
a lioness who ruled the roost
and made the Mother cry.
She used to tie
gobbets of porkrind in bowknots of gauze –
three months they hung like soggy toast
on our eight foot magnolia tree,
and helped the English sparrows
weather a Boston winter.

Three months, three months! 10
Is Richard now himself again?
Dimpled with exaltation,
my daughter holds her levee in the tub.
Our noses rub,
each of us pats a stringy lock of hair –
they tell me nothing's gone.
Though I am forty-one,
not forty now, the time I put away
was child's-play. After thirteen weeks
my child still dabs her cheeks 20
to start me shaving. When
we dress her in her sky-blue corduroy,
she changes to a boy,
and floats my shaving brush
and washcloth in the flush. . . .

Dearest, I cannot loiter here
in lather like a polar bear.

Recuperating, I neither spin nor toil.
Three stories down below,
a choreman tends our coffin's length of soil, 30
and seven horizontal tulips blow.
Just twelve months ago,
these flowers were pedigreed
imported Dutchmen; now no one need
distinguish them from weed.
Bushed by the late spring snow,
they cannot meet
another year's snowballing enervation.

I keep no rank nor station.
Cured, I am frizzled, stale and small.

ROBERT LOWELL

173

In Time of 'The Breaking of Nations'

JEREMIAH 51: 20

I

Only a man harrowing clods
  In a slow silent walk
With an old horse that stumbles and nods
  Half asleep as they stalk.

II

Only thin smoke without flame
  From the heaps of couch-grass;
Yet this will go onward the same
  Though Dynasties pass.

III

Yonder a maid and her wight
  Come whispering by:
War's annals will cloud into night
  Ere their story die.

THOMAS HARDY

174

God's Grandeur

The world is charged with the grandeur of God.
It will flame out, like shining from shook foil;
It gathers to a greatness, like the ooze of oil
Crushed. Why do men then now not reck his rod?
Generations have trod, have trod, have trod;
And all is seared with trade; bleared, smeared with toil;
And wears man's smudge and shares man's smell: the soil
Is bare now, nor can foot feel, being shod.
And for all this, nature is never spent;
There lives the dearest freshness deep down things;
And though the last lights off the black West went
Oh, morning, at the brown brink eastward, springs –
Because the Holy Ghost over the bent
World broods with warm breast and with ah! bright wings.

GERARD MANLEY HOPKINS

175

This Lime-Tree Bower My Prison

Well, they are gone, and here I must remain,
This lime-tree bower my prison! I have lost
Beauties and feelings, such as would have been
Most sweet to my remembrance even when age
Had dimmed my eyes to blindness! They, meanwhile,
Friends, whom I never more may meet again,
On springy heath, along the hill-top edge,
Wander in gladness, and wind down, perchance,
To that still roaring dell, of which I told;
The roaring dell, o'erwooded, narrow, deep, 10
And only speckled by the mid-day sun;
Where its slim trunk the ash from rock to rock
Flings arching like a bridge; – that branchless ash,
Unsunned and damp, whose few poor yellow leaves
Ne'er tremble in the gale, yet tremble still,
Fanned by the water-fall! and there my friends
Behold the dark green file of long lank weeds,
That all at once (a most fantastic sight!)
Still nod and drip beneath the dripping edge
Of the blue clay-stone.

Now, my friends emerge 20
Beneath the wide wide Heaven – and view again
The many-steepled tract magnificent
Of hilly fields and meadows, and the sea,
With some fair bark, perhaps, whose sails light up
The slip of smooth clear blue betwixt two Isles
Of purple shadow! Yes! they wander on

In gladness all; but thou, methinks, most glad,
My gentle-hearted Charles! for thou hast pined
And hungered after Nature, many a year,
In the great City pent, winning thy way 30
With sad yet patient soul, through evil and pain
And strange calamity! Ah! slowly sink
Behind the western ridge, thou glorious Sun!
Shine in the slant beams of the sinking orb,
Ye purple heath-flowers! richlier burn, ye clouds!
Live in the yellow light, ye distant groves!
And kindle, thou blue Ocean! So my friend
Struck with deep joy may stand, as I have stood,
Silent with swimming sense; yea, gazing round
On the wide landscape, gaze till all doth seem 40
Less gross than bodily; and of such hues
As veil the Almighty Spirit, when yet he makes
Spirits perceive his presence.

A delight
Comes sudden on my heart, and I am glad
As I myself were there! Nor in this bower,
This little lime-tree bower, have I not marked
Much that has soothed me. Pale beneath the blaze
Hung the transparent foliage; and I watched
Some broad and sunny leaf, and loved to see
The shadow of the leaf and stem above 50
Dappling its sunshine! And that walnut-tree
Was richly tinged, and a deep radiance lay
Full on the ancient ivy, which usurps
Those fronting elms, and now, with blackest mass
Makes their dark branches gleam a lighter hue
Through the late twilight: and though now the bat
Wheels silent by, and not a swallow twitters,

Yet still the solitary humble-bee
Sings in the bean-flower! Henceforth I shall know
That Nature ne'er deserts the wise and pure; 60
No plot so narrow, be but Nature there,
No waste so vacant, but may well employ
Each faculty of sense, and keep the heart
Awake to Love and Beauty! and sometimes
'Tis well to be bereft of promised good,
That we may lift the soul, and contemplate
With lively joy the joys we cannot share.
My gentle-hearted Charles! when the last rook
Beat its straight path along the dusky air
Homewards, I blest it! deeming its black wing 70
(Now a dim speck, now vanishing in light)
Had crossed the mighty Orb's dilated glory,
While thou stood'st gazing; or, when all was still,
Flew creeking o'er my head, and had a charm
For thee, my gentle-hearted Charles, to whom
No sound is dissonant which tells of life.

SAMUEL TAYLOR COLERIDGE

176

No Doctors Today, Thank You

They tell me that euphoria is the feeling of feeling
    wonderful; well, today I feel euphorian,
Today I have the agility of a Greek god and the appetite of
    a Victorian.
Yes, today I may even go forth without my galoshes;
Today I am a swashbuckler, would anybody like me to
    buckle any swashes?
This is my euphorian day,
I will ring welkins and before anybody answers I will run
    away.
I will tame me a caribou
And bedeck it with marabou.
I will pen me my memoirs.
Ah youth, youth! What Euphorian days them was!
I wasn't much of a hand for the boudoirs,
I was generally to be found where the food was.
Does anybody want any flotsam?
I've gotsam.
Does anybody want any jetsam?
I can getsam.
I can play 'Chopsticks' on the Wurlitzer,
I can speak Portuguese like a Berlitzer.
I can don or doff my shoes without tying or untying the
    laces because I am wearing moccasins,
And I practically know the difference between serums and
    antitoccasins.
Kind people, don't think me purse-proud, don't set me
    down as vainglorious,
I'm just a little euphorious.

OGDEN NASH

177

Birthday

Mother, let me congratulate you on
the birthday of your son.
You worry so much about him. Here he lies,
he earns little, his marriage was unwise,
he's long, he's getting thin, he hasn't shaved.
Oh, what a miserable loving gaze!
I should congratulate you if I may
mother on your worry's birthday.
It was from you that he inherited
devotion without pity to this age
and arrogant and awkward in his faith
from you he took his faith, the Revolution.
You didn't make him prosperous or famous,
and fearlessness is his only talent.
Open up his windows,
let in the twittering in the leafy branches,
kiss his eyes open.
Give him his notebook and his ink bottle,
give him a drink of milk and watch him go.

YEVGENY YEVTUSHENKO

Translated by
PETER LEVI *and* ROBIN MILNER-GULLAND

178

The Cocky Walkers

Grouped nightly at the cold, accepted wall,
Carved with a gaslight chisel the lean heads
Cry out unwittingly for Rembrandt's needle.
These are the flashy saplings whose domain
I cannot enter.
They burn at lip and finger the stuffed paper;
The trouser-pocket boys, the cocky walkers,
Sons of old mothers, with their hats askew
Hummock the shoulder to the little flower
That lights the palm into a nightmare land, 10
A bloody basin of the sterile moon,
That lights the face that sprouts the cigarette
Into a sudden passion of fierce colour.
Down the cold corridor of winter nights
I see a thousand groups that keep
The fag alight, at walls, and in the sharp
Stern corners of the street:
These are the sprigs; flash boys, uncaught,
Treading the reedy springboard of green days.
Theirs is a headiness for they 20
Have burned their lives up to the quarter-mark.
The days move by them and the chill nights hold them
In an old, unthought conspiracy for they
Tinkle upon tin feet that send no root.
I see them at the cold, accepted wall,
The trouser-pocket boys, the cocky walkers.

MERVYN PEAKE

179

On the Move

'MAN, YOU GOTTA GO'

The blue jay scuffling in the bushes follows
Some hidden purpose, and the gust of birds
That spurts across the field, the wheeling swallows,
Have nested in the trees and undergrowth.
Seeking their instinct, or their poise, or both,
One moves with an uncertain violence
Under the dust thrown by a baffled sense
Or the dull thunder of approximate words.

On motorcycles, up the road, they come:
Small, black, as flies hanging in heat, the Boys, 10
Until the distance throws them forth, their hum
Bulges to thunder held by calf and thigh.
In goggles, donned impersonality,
In gleaming jackets trophied with the dust,
They strap in doubt – hiding it, robust –
And almost hear a meaning in their noise.

Exact conclusion of their hardiness
Has no shape yet, but from known whereabouts
They ride, direction where the tires press.
They scare a flight of birds across the field: 20
Much that is natural, to the will must yield.
Men manufacture both machine and soul,
And use what they imperfectly control
To dare a future from the taken routes.

It is a part solution, after all.
One is not necessarily discord
On earth; or damned because, half animal,
One lacks direct instinct, because one wakes
Afloat on movement that divides and breaks.
One joins the movement in a valueless world, 30
Choosing it, till, both hurler and hurled,
One moves as well, always toward, toward.

A minute holds them, who have come to go:
The self-defined, astride the created will
They burst away; the towns they travel through
Are home for neither bird nor holiness,
For birds and saints complete their purposes.
At worst, one is in motion; and at best,
Reaching no absolute, in which to rest,
One is always nearer by not keeping still.

THOM GUNN

180

The Fights

What an elusive target
the brain is! Set up
like a coconut on a flexible stem
it has 101 evasions.
A twisted nod slues a punch
a thin gillette's width
past a brain, or
a rude brush-cut to the chin
tucks one brain safe under another.
Two of these targets are 10
set up to be knocked down
for 25 dollars or a million.

In that TV picture in the parlor
the men, who linked move to move
in a chancy dance,
are abstractions only.
Come to ringside, with two
experts in there! See
each step or blow pivoted,
balanced and sudden as gunfire. 20
See muscles wriggle, shine
in sweat like windshield rain.

In stinking dancehalls, in
the forums of small towns,
punches are cheaper but
still pieces of death.
For the brain's the target

with its hungers
and code of honor. See
in those stinking little towns, 30
with long counts, swindling judges,
how fury ends with the last gong.
No matter who's the cheated one
they hug like a girl and man.

It's craft and
the body rhythmic and terrible,
the game of struggle.
We need something of its nature
but not this;
for the brain's the target 40
and round by round it's whittled
til nothing's left of a man
but a jerky bum, humming
with a gentleness less than human.

MILTON ACORN

181

The Top Hat

Whether it's just a gag or the old geezer's
A bit queer in the head, it's still refreshing
To see someone walking up Bay Street
With toes out of shoes, patched trousers, frayed suit-coat,
And on his head the biggest shiniest top hat
Since Abe Lincoln
                                        and walking as if the whole
Damn street belonged to him
                                                        which at this moment for my money
It does.

RAYMOND SOUSTER

182

Wishes of an Elderly Man at a Garden Party

I wish I loved the Human Race;
I wish I loved its silly face;
I wish I liked the way it walks;
I wish I liked the way it talks;
And when I'm introduced to one
I wish I thought *What Jolly Fun!*

SIR WALTER RALEIGH

183

Selections

FROM THE

Rubáiyát of Omar Khayyám of Naishápúr

Awake! for Morning in the Bowl of Night
Has flung the Stone that puts the Stars to Flight:
  And Lo! the Hunter of the East has caught
The Sultán's Turret in a Noose of Light.

Dreaming when Dawn's Left Hand was in the Sky
I heard a Voice within the Tavern cry,
  'Awake, my Little ones, and fill the Cup
Before Life's Liquor in its Cup be dry.'

And, as the Cock crew, those who stood before
The Tavern shouted – 'Open then the Door! 10
  You know how little while we have to stay,
And, once departed, may return no more.'

Come, fill the Cup, and in the Fire of Spring
The Winter Garment of Repentance fling:
  The Bird of Time has but a little way
To fly – and Lo! the Bird is on the Wing.

With me along some Strip of Herbage strown,
That just divides the desert from the sown,
  Where name of Slave and Sultán scarce is known,
And pity Sultán Máhmúd on his Throne. 20

Here with a Loaf of Bread beneath the Bough,
A Flask of Wine, a Book of Verse – and Thou

Beside me singing in the Wilderness –
And Wilderness is Paradise enow.

'How sweet is mortal Sovranty!' – think some:
Others – 'How blest the Paradise to come!'
Ah, take the Cash in hand and waive the Rest;
Oh, the brave Music of a *distant* Drum!

The Worldly Hope men set their Hearts upon
Turns Ashes – or it prospers; and anon, 30
Like Snow upon the Desert's dusty Face
Lighting a little Hour or two – is gone.

Myself when young did eagerly frequent
Doctor and Saint, and heard great Argument
About it and about: but evermore
Came out by the same Door as in I went.

With them the seed of Wisdom did I sow,
And with mine own hand wrought to make it grow;
And this was all the Harvest that I reap'd –
'I came like Water, and like Wind I go.' 40

There was the Door to which I found no Key;
There was the Veil through which I might not see:
Some little talk awhile of ME and THEE
There was – and then no more of THEE and ME.

The Moving Finger writes; and, having writ,
Moves on: nor all thy Piety nor Wit
Shall lure it back to cancel half a Line,
Nor all thy Tears wash out a Word of it.

EDWARD FITZGERALD

184

The Darkling Thrush

I leant upon a coppice gate
When frost was spectre-gray,
And winter's dregs made desolate
The weakening eye of day.
The tangled bine-stems scored the sky
Like strings of broken lyres,
And all mankind that haunted nigh
Had sought their household fires.

The land's sharp features seemed to be
The century's corpse outleant, 10
His crypt the cloudy canopy,
The wind his death-lament.
The ancient pulse of germ and birth
Was shrunken, hard, and dry.
And every spirit upon earth
Seemed fervourless as I.

At once a voice arose among
The bleak twigs overhead,
In a full-hearted evensong
Of joy illimited; 20
An aged thrush, frail, gaunt, and small,
In blast-beruffled plume,
Had chosen thus to fling his soul
Upon the growing gloom.

So little cause for carollings
Of such ecstatic sound
Was written on terrestrial things
Afar or nigh around,
That I could think there trembled through
His happy good-night air   30
Some blessed hope, whereof he knew,
And I was unaware.

THOMAS HARDY

185

Ah! Sun-flower

Ah, Sun-flower! weary of time,
Who countest the steps of the sun;
Seeking after that sweet golden clime,
Where the traveller's journey is done;

Where the Youth pined away with desire,
And the pale Virgin shrouded in snow,
Arise from their graves, and aspire
Where my sun-flower wishes to go.

WILLIAM BLAKE

186

He Who Binds to Himself

He who binds to himself a Joy
Doth the winged life destroy;
But he who kisses the Joy as it flies
Lives in Eternity's sunrise.

WILLIAM BLAKE

187

On Wenlock Edge

On Wenlock Edge the wood's in trouble;
  His forest fleece the Wrekin heaves;
The gale, it plies the saplings double,
  And thick on Severn snow the leaves.

'Twould blow like this through holt and hanger
  When Uricon the city stood:
'Tis the old wind in the old anger,
  But then it threshed another wood.

Then, 'twas before my time, the Roman
  At yonder heaving hill would stare:
The blood that warms an English yeoman,
  The thoughts that hurt him, they were there.

There, like the wind through woods in riot,
  Through him the gale of life blew high;
The tree of man was never quiet:
  Then 'twas the Roman, now 'tis I.

The gale, it plies the saplings double,
  It blows so hard, 'twill soon be gone:
To-day the Roman and his trouble
  Are ashes under Uricon.

A. E. HOUSMAN

188

Her Strong Enchantments Failing

Her strong enchantments failing,
  Her towers of fear in wreck,
Her limbecks dried of poisons
  And the knife at her neck,

The Queen of air and darkness
  Begins to shrill and cry,
'O young man, O my slayer,
  To-morrow you shall die.'

O Queen of air and darkness,
  I think 'tis truth you say,
And I shall die to-morrow;
  But you will die to-day.

A. E. HOUSMAN

189

Fishes' Heaven

Fish (fly-replete, in depth of June,
Dawdling away their wat'ry noon)
Ponder deep wisdom, dark or clear,
Each secret fishy hope or fear.
Fish say, they have their Stream and Pond;
But is there anything Beyond?
This life cannot be All, they swear,
For how unpleasant, if it were!
One may not doubt that, somehow, Good
Shall come of Water and of Mud; 10
And, sure, the reverent eye must see
A Purpose in Liquidity.
We darkly know, by Faith we cry,
The future is not Wholly Dry.
Mud unto mud! – Death eddies near –
Not here the appointed End, not here!
But somewhere, beyond Space and Time,
Is wetter water, slimier slime!
And there (they trust) there swimmeth One
Who swam ere rivers were begun, 20
Immense, of fishy form and mind,
Squamous, omnipotent, and kind;
And under that Almighty Fin,
The littlest fish may enter in.
Oh! never fly conceals a hook,
Fish say, in the Eternal Brook,
But more than mundane weeds are there,
And mud, celestially fair;
Fat caterpillars drift around,

And Paradisal grubs are found; 30
Unfading moths, immortal flies,
And the worm that never dies.
And in that Heaven of all their wish,
There shall be no more land, say fish.

RUPERT BROOKE

190

The Fisherman

Although I can see him still,
The freckled man who goes
To a grey place on a hill
In grey Connemara clothes
At dawn to cast his flies,
It's long since I began
To call up to the eyes
This wise and simple man.
All day I'd looked in the face

What I had hoped 'twoud be 10
To write for my own race
And the reality;
The living men that I hate,
The dead man that I loved,
The craven man in his seat,
The insolent unreproved,
And no knave brought to book
Who has won a drunken cheer,
The witty man and his joke
Aimed at the commonest ear, 20
The clever man who cries
The catch-cries of the clown,
The beating down of the wise
And great Art beaten down.

Maybe a twelvemonth since
Suddenly I began,
In scorn of this audience,
Imagining a man,
And his sun-freckled face,
And grey Connemara cloth, 30
Climbing up to a place
Where stone is dark under froth,
And the down-turn of his wrist
When the flies drop in the stream;
A man who does not exist,
A man who is but a dream;
And cried, 'Before I am old
I shall have written him one
Poem maybe as cold
And passionate as the dawn.'

WILLIAM BUTLER YEATS

191

The Choice

FROM

'A Dialogue of Self and Soul'

My Self. A living man is blind and drinks his drop.
What matter if the ditches are impure?
What matter if I live it all once more?
Endure that toil of growing up;
The ignominy of boyhood; the distress
Of boyhood changing into man;
The unfinished man and his pain
Brought face to face with his own clumsiness;

The finished man among his enemies? –
How in the name of Heaven can he escape 10
That defiling and disfigured shape
The mirror of malicious eyes
Casts upon his eyes until at last
He thinks that shape must be his shape?
And what's the good of an escape
If honour find him in the wintry blast?

I am content to live it all again
And yet again, if it be life to pitch
Into the frog-spawn of a blind man's ditch,
A blind man battering blind men; 20
Or into that most fecund ditch of all,
The folly that man does
Or must suffer, if he woos
A proud woman not kindred of his soul.

I am content to follow to its source
Every event in action or in thought;
Measure the lot; forgive myself the lot!
When such as I cast out remorse
So great a sweetness flows into the breast
We must laugh and we must sing, 30
We are blest by everything,
Everything we look upon is blest.

WILLIAM BUTLER YEATS

192

Death

Nor dread nor hope attend
A dying animal;
A man awaits his end
Dreading and hoping all;
Many times he died,
Many times rose again,
A great man in his pride
Confronting murderous men
Casts derision upon
Supersession of breath;
He knows death to the bone –
Man has created death.

WILLIAM BUTLER YEATS

193

Dirge Without Music

I am not resigned to the shutting away of loving hearts in
the hard ground.
So it is, and so it will be, for so it has been, time out of
mind:
Into the darkness they go, the wise and the lovely. Crowned
With lilies and with laurel they go; but I am not resigned.

Lovers and thinkers, into the earth with you.
Be one with the dull, the indiscriminate dust.
A fragment of what you felt, of what you knew,
A formula, a phrase remains, – but the best is lost.

The answers quick & keen, the honest look, the laughter,
the love,
They are gone. They have gone to feed the roses. Elegant
and curled
Is the blossom. Fragrant is the blossom. I know. But I do
not approve.
More precious was the light in your eyes than all the roses
in the world.

Down, down, down into the darkness of the grave
Gently they go, the beautiful, the tender, the kind;
Quietly they go, the intelligent, the witty, the brave.
I know. But I do not approve. And I am not resigned.

EDNA ST VINCENT MILLAY

194

And Death Shall Have No Dominion

And death shall have no dominion.
Dead men naked they shall be one
With the man in the wind and the west moon;
When their bones are picked clean and the clean bones
    gone,
They shall have stars at elbow and foot;
Though they go mad they shall be sane,
Though they sink through the sea they shall rise again;
Though lovers be lost love shall not;
And death shall have no dominion.

And death shall have no dominion. 10
Under the windings of the sea
They lying long shall not die windily;
Twisting on racks when sinews give way,
Strapped to a wheel, yet they shall not break;
Faith in their hands shall snap in two,
And the unicorn evils run them through;
Split all ends up they shan't crack;
And death shall have no dominion.

And death shall have no dominion.
No more may gulls cry at their ears 20
Or waves break loud on the seashores;
Where blew a flower may a flower no more
Lift its head to the blows of the rain;
Though they be mad and dead as nails,

Heads of the characters hammer through daisies;
Break in the sun till the sun breaks down,
And death shall have no dominion.

DYLAN THOMAS

195

The Isles of Greece

FROM

Don Juan

The isles of Greece, the isles of Greece!
  Where burning Sappho loved and sung,
Where grew the arts of war and peace,
  Where Delos rose, and Phoebus sprung!
Eternal summer gilds them yet,
But all, except their sun, is set.

The mountains look on Marathon –
  And Marathon looks on the sea;
And musing there an hour alone,
  I dream'd that Greece might still be free; 10
For standing on the Persians' grave,
I could not deem myself a slave.

A king sate on the rocky brow
  Which looks o'er sea-born Salamis;
And ships, by thousands, lay below,
  And men in nations; – all were his!
He counted them at break of day –
And when the sun set where were they?

Must *we* but weep o'er days more blest?
  Must *we* but blush? – Our fathers bled. 20
Earth! render back from out thy breast
  A remnant of our Spartan dead!
Of the three hundred grant but three,
To make a new Thermopylae!

What, silent still? and silent all?
  Ah! no; – the voices of the dead
Sound like a distant torrent's fall,
  And answer, 'Let one living head,
But one arise, – we come, we come!'
'Tis but the living who are dumb.

LORD BYRON

196

All That's Past

Very old are the woods;
  And the buds that break
Out of the briar's boughs,
  When March winds wake,
So old with their beauty are –
  Oh, no man knows
Through what wild centuries
  Roves back the rose.

Very old are the brooks;
  And the rills that rise
Where snow sleeps cold beneath
  The azure skies
Sing such a history
  Of come and gone,
Their every drop is as wise
  As Solomon.

Very old are we men;
  Our dreams are tales
Told in dim Eden
  By Eve's nightingales;
We wake and whisper awhile,
  But, the day gone by,
Silence and sleep like fields
  Of amaranth lie.

WALTER DE LA MARE

197

Echo

'Who called?' I said, and the words
   Through the whispering glades,
Hither, thither, baffled the birds –
   'Who called? Who called?'

The leafy boughs on high
   Hissed in the sun;
The dark air carried my cry
   Faintingly on:

Eyes in the green, in the shade,
   In the motionless brake,
Voices that said what I said
   For mockery's sake:

'Who cares?' I bawled through my tears;
   The wind fell low:
In the silence, 'Who cares? Who cares?'
   Wailed to and fro.

WALTER DE LA MARE

198

To S. R. Crockett

Blows the wind to-day, and the sun and the rain are flying,
  Blows the wind on the moors to-day and now,
Where about the graves of the martyrs the whaups are
    crying,
  My heart remembers how!

Grey recumbent tombs of the dead in desert places,
  Standing stones on the vacant wine-red moor,
Hills of sheep, and the homes of the silent vanished races,
  And winds, austere and pure:

Be it granted me to behold you again in dying,
  Hills of home! and to hear again the call;
Hear about the graves of the martyrs the peewees crying,
  And hear no more at all.

ROBERT LOUIS STEVENSON

199

Cities and Thrones and Powers

Cities and Thrones and Powers
  Stand in Time's eye,
Almost as long as flowers,
  Which daily die:
But, as new buds put forth
  To glad new men,
Out of the spent and unconsidered Earth
  The Cities rise again.

This season's Daffodil,
  She never hears
What change, what chance, what chill,
  Cut down last year's;
But with bold countenance,
  And knowledge small,
Esteems her seven days' continuance
  To be perpetual.

So Time that is o'er-kind
  To all that be,
Ordains us e'en as blind,
  As bold as she:
That in our very death,
  And burial sure,
Shadow to shadow, well persuaded, saith,
  'See how our works endure!'

RUDYARD KIPLING

200

Death the Leveller

The glories of our blood and state
  Are shadows, not substantial things;
There is no armour against Fate;
  Death lays his icy hand on kings:
    Sceptre and Crown
    Must tumble down,
And in the dust be equal made
With the poor crookèd scythe and spade.

Some men with swords may reap the field,
  And plant fresh laurels where they kill:
But their strong nerves at last must yield;
  They tame but one another still:
    Early or late
    They stoop to fate,
And must give up their murmuring breath
When they, pale captives, creep to death.

The garlands wither on your brow;
  Then boast no more your mighty deeds!
Upon Death's purple altar now
  See where the victor-victim bleeds.
    Your heads must come
    To the cold tomb:
Only the actions of the just
Smell sweet and blossom in their dust.

JAMES SHIRLEY

201

Song

FROM

Cymbeline

Fear no more the heat o' the sun,
  Nor the furious winter's rages;
Thou thy worldly task hast done,
  Home art gone, and ta'en thy wages;
Golden lads and girls all must,
As chimney-sweepers, come to dust.

Fear no more the frown o' the great,
  Thou art past the tyrant's stroke:
Care no more to clothe and eat;
  To thee the reed is as the oak;
The Sceptre, Learning, Physic, must
All follow this, and come to dust.

Fear no more the lightning-flash,
  Nor the all-dreaded thunder-stone;
Fear not slander, censure rash;
  Thou hast finish'd joy and moan:
All lovers young, all lovers must
Consign to thee, and come to dust.

No exorciser harm thee!
  Nor no witchcraft charm thee!
Ghost unlaid forbear thee!
  Nothing ill come near thee!
Quiet consummation have;
And renowned be thy grave!

WILLIAM SHAKESPEARE

202

Song

Adieu, farewell earths blisse,
This world uncertaine is,
Fond are lifes lustfull joyes,
Death proves them all but toyes,
None from his darts can flye,
I am sick, I must dye:
  Lord have mercy on us.

Rich men, trust not in wealth,
Gold cannot buy you health,
Phisick himself must fade. 10
All things, to end are made,
The plague full swift goes bye,
I am sick, I must dye:
  Lord have mercy on us.

Beauty is but a flowre,
Which wrinckles will devoure,
Brightness falls from the ayre,
Queenes have died yong, and faire,
Dust hath closde *Helens* eye.
I am sick, I must dye: 20
  Lord have mercy on us.

Strength stoopes unto the grave,
Wormes feed on *Hector* brave,
Swords may not fight with fate,
Earth still holds ope her gate.
Come, come, the bells do crye.
I am sick, I must dye:
  Lord have mercy on us.

Wit with his wantonesse,
Tasteth deaths bitterness: 30
Hels executioner,
Hath no eares for to heare
What vaine art can reply.
I am sick, I must dye:
  Lord have mercy on us.

Haste therefore eche degree,
To welcome destiny:
Heaven is our heritage,
Earth but a players stage,
Mount wee unto the sky. 40
I am sick, I must dye:
  Lord have mercy on us.

THOMAS NASHE

203

I Love All Beauteous Things

I love all beauteous things,
  I seek and adore them;
God hath no better praise,
And man in his hasty days
  Is honoured for them.

I too will something make
  And joy in the making;
Altho' to-morrow it seem
Like the empty words of a dream
  Remembered on waking.

ROBERT BRIDGES

204

I Give You the End of a Golden String

I give you the end of a golden string;
  Only wind it into a ball,
It will lead you in at Heaven's gate,
  Built in Jerusalem's wall.

WILLIAM BLAKE

How Does a Poem Mean?

AN ESSAY BY JOHN CIARDI

'Bitzer,' said Thomas Gradgrind, your definition of a horse.'

'Quadruped. Gramnivorous. Forty teeth, namely twenty-four grinders, four eye-teeth, and twelve incisive. Sheds coat in the spring; in marshy countries sheds hoofs too. Hoofs hard, but requiring to be shod with iron. Age known by marks in mouth.' Thus (and much more) Bitzer.

'Now girl number twenty,' said Mr Gradgrind, 'you know what a horse is.'

CHARLES DICKENS, *Hard Times*

The School of Hard Facts over which Mr Gradgrind presided was a school of fixed answers. Mr Gradgrind would have agreed with a recent anthologist who wrote that the inspection of a poem should be as certain as a chemical analysis. Mr Gradgrind would have assured himself that he was a first-class critic, of poetry as of horses. 'Now girl number twenty,' he would have said looking up from his analysis, 'you know what a poem is.'

This essay originally appeared in *Introduction to Literature* published by Houghton Mifflin Co., Boston, 1960. It is reprinted by permission of the author and the publisher.

Today, a century later than Mr Gradgrind's School of Hard Facts, the idea is still current that the methods of measurement evolved by the physical sciences can be applied to all human processes. And there still lingers the belief that a dictionary definition is a satisfactory description of an idea or of an experience.

There are many grounds on which dictionary definitions can be disputed, but only one need concern us here. Bitzer's definition of a horse was a dictionary definition. Note that it is put almost exclusively in terms of classification. In those terms, it may do as a table of physical characteristics of *Equus caballus*. But what can it possibly say of the experience one has had of the living animal? No horseman ever rode a 'gramnivorous quadruped.' No gambler ever bet on one. No sculptor ever dreamed one out of a block of stone. For horseman, gambler, and sculptor are involved in a living relation to a living animal, *and the kind of relation is expressed in the language each has evolved for his experience.* ('A good-winded bay', says the horseman, 'but he has a mouth like iron and won't answer to the bit. He's had bad schooling.' Or the gambler: 'A good four-year-old. Better than his performance to date. And a good mudder. He's due to win, especially on a wet track. And at nice odds.' Or the sculptor: 'The set of the stone suggested a rearing posture: the line of force curving down the haunches repeated in the straining line of the neck with the mouth held hard-down by the bit.') Whatever the 'gramnivorous quadruped' may be to the biologist, these three ways of speaking are three experiences of the living horse. As Tip O'Neill once wrote in a fine sarcastic line: 'There's not a wedding in the world that's worth a running horse.' Now try the line revised: 'There is not a marriage ceremony in existence worthy of comparison with a gramnivorous quadruped of the genus *Equus caballus* in rapid motion.'

The point is that *the language of experience is not the language of classification.* A boy burning with ambition to become a jockey does not study a text on zoology. He watches horses, he listens to what is said by those who have spent their lives around horses, he rides them, trains them, feeds them, curries them, pets them. He lives with intense feelings toward them. He may never learn how many incisors a horse has, nor how many yards of intestines. What does it matter? He is concerned with a *feel,* a response-to, a sense of the character and reaction of the living animal. And zoology cannot give him that. Not all the anatomizing of all the world's horses could teach a man horse-sense.

So for poetry. The concern is not to arrive at a definition and to close the book, but to arrive at an experience. There will never be a complete system for 'understanding' or for 'judging' poetry. Understanding and critical judgement are admirable goals, but neither can take place until the poem has been experienced, and even then there is always some part of every good work of art that can never be fully explained or categorized. It still remains true that the reader who has experienced most fully will finally be the best judge.

Poetry has only a remote place in the gross of our culture. As has, for example, the opera. Therefore, Americans generally need to be taught in school how to experience both poetry and the opera. In Milan, on the other hand, no one need go to school in order to learn how to experience an opera: the Milanese do not study opera, they *inhale* it. They would have to go to school to learn, for example, how to watch a baseball game in an experienceable way. Certainly no one in The Bronx need go to that school: in The Bronx it is baseball that is inhaled as a living thing, and opera and poetry that have to be learned.

If the reader cared enough for poetry, he would have no need to study it. He would *live into it.* As the Milanese citizen becomes an encyclopedia of opera information, and as even retarded boys in The Bronx are capable of reciting endlessly detailed baseball statistics, so the passionate reader of poetry becomes alive to it by natural process.

Any teaching of the poem by any other method owes the poem an apology. What greater violence can be done to the poet's experience than to drag it into an early morning classroom and to go after it as an item on its way to a Final Examination? The apology must at least be made. It is the experience, not the Final Examination, that counts. Though one must note with care – as in the case of the baseball fan – that passionate learning is full of very technical stuff. Why else would baseball statistics give rise to such heated arguments as one can hear throughout the season?

And in poetry there is the step beyond: once one has learned to experience the poem as a poem, there inevitably arrives a sense that one is also experiencing himself as a human being. It must certainly have been this second experience (to put it in another way, the point at which Art for Art's sake becomes Art for Life's sake) that Matthew Arnold had in mind when he wrote: 'The grand power of poetry is its interpretative power . . . the power of so dealing with things as to awaken in us a wonderfully full, new, and intimate sense of them, and of our relations with them.' But the grand power of a good sermon is also its interpretative power, and a sermon, it must be remembered, is not a poem.

Paradise Lost, is in one sense, a rhymed sermon written to justify God's ways to man. So is Michael Wigglesworth's *The*

Day of Doom. Wigglesworth was a Puritan clergyman of the Massachusetts Bay Colony and for over two centuries Puritan children memorized large sections of his poem as part of their church training. Wigglesworth's theology is every bit as sound and as comprehensive as Milton's. Yet today *The Day of Doom* is all but unknown except as a scholar's curio. The difference is not in content but in the fact that Milton wrote a poem whereas Wigglesworth wrote only doggerel. Poetry, it follows, is more than simply 'something to say.' Nor is it simply an elaborate way of saying something or nothing.

W. H. Auden was once asked what advice he would give a young man who wished to become a poet. Auden replied that he would ask the young man why he wanted to write poetry. If the answer was 'because I have something important to say,' Auden would conclude that there was no hope for that young man as a poet. If on the other hand the answer was something like 'because I like to hang around words and overhear them talking to one another,' then that young man was at least interested in a fundamental part of the poetic process and there was hope for him.

When one 'message-hunts' a poem (i.e., goes through the poem with no interest except in its paraphraseable content) he is approaching the writing as did the young man with 'something important to say.' He is giving it the Wigglesworth treatment. The common question from which such an approach begins is 'WHAT Does the Poem Mean?' His mind closed on that point of view, the reader tends to 'interpret' the poem rather than to experience it, seeking only what he can make over from it into a prose statement (or Examination answer) and forgetting in the process that it was originally a poem. Thus, students are too often headed by their teachers in the direction of reciting, almost like Bitzer: 'Keats.

"When I have fears that I may cease to be." Sonnet. Irregular. Consisting of three quatrains and a couplet, the third quatrain consisting of very close rhymes, thus: "hour, more, power, shore." Written on the theme of the vanity of earthly wishes, but given a strong romantic coloration of individualistic aspiration for the good pleasures of the world.'

Poor Keats!

For WHAT DOES THE POEM MEAN? is too often a self-destroying approach to poetry. A more useful way of asking the question is HOW DOES A POEM MEAN? Why does it build itself into a form out of images, ideas, rhythms? How do these elements become the meaning? How are they inseparable from the meaning? As Yeats wrote:

> *O body swayed to music, o quickening glance,*
> *How shall I tell the dancer from the dance?*

What the poem is, is inseparable from its own performance of itself. The dance is in the dancer and the dancer is in the dance. Or put in another way: where is the 'dance' when no one is dancing it? and what man is a 'dancer' except when he is dancing?

Above all else, poetry is a performance. Keats' overt subject in his sonnet was his own approaching death. But note this about poetry: Keats took the same *self-delighting pains* in writing about his death as he took in poems on overtly happy subjects, such as 'On First Looking into Chapman's Homer' or the 'Ode to a Nightingale.' Here is the complete sonnet:

> *When I have fears that I may cease to be*
> *Before my pen has glean'd my teeming brain,*
> *Before high piled books, in charactery,*
> *Hold like rich garners the full ripened grain;*

When I behold upon the night's starred face,
Huge cloudy symbols of a high romance,
And think that I may never live to trace
Their shadows with the magic hand of chance;
And when I feel, fair creature of an hour,
That I shall never look upon thee more,
Never have relish in the faery power
Of unreflecting love; — then on the shore
Of the wide world I stand alone, and think
Till love and fame to nothingness do sink.

If this sonnet means 'the vanity of human wishes given a strong romantic coloration, *etc.*,' why did Keats take the trouble to bring his rhythms to a stop at the end of the fourth and eighth lines and in the middle of the twelfth? Sonnets normally divide into 'octet' (the first eight lines) and 'sestet' (the final six lines). Note that Keats' divisions occur in a very nearly symmetrical pattern. Why did Keats spend so much care on symmetry? What has symmetry to do with 'the vanity of earthly wishes'? Why, too, did Keats bother to compare his mind to a field of grain, and the books he felt himself able to write, to storage bins? An elaborate figure. Why did Keats bother to construct it? Why did he search out such striking phrases as 'the magic hand of chance'? If Keats were really convinced that all human wishes are vain, why did he wish to phrase his idea with such earthly care? If *nothingness* is all, why bother to make *the something* a poem is?

Robert Frost provided a valuable clue when he spoke of 'the pleasure of taking pains.' The paradox here is simply verbal. Frost meant precisely what the German critic Baumgarten meant when he spoke of the central impulse toward poetry (and toward all art) as the *Spieltrieb,* the play-impulse.

An excellent native example of the play-impulse in poetry is the child clapping its hands in response to a Mother Goose rhyme. What does a child care for 'meaning'? What on earth is the 'meaning' of the following poem?

> *High Diddle diddle*
> *The cat and the fiddle*
> *The cow jumped over the moon;*
> *The little dog laughed*
> *To see such craft*
> *And the dish ran away with the spoon.*

'Preposterous,' says Mr Gradgrind. But the child is wiser: he is busy having a good time with the poem. The poem pleases and involves him. He responds to it in an immediate muscular way. He recognizes its performance at once and wants *to act with it.*

This is the first level of play. As rhythm is the first element of music. The child claps hands, has fun, and the play involves practically no thoughtful activity. Beyond this level of response, there begins the kind of play whose pleasure lies for the poet in overcoming meaningful and thoughtful (and 'feelingful') difficulties, and for the reader in identifying with the poet in that activity.

Nor is the word 'difficulty' one to be afraid of. Chess is a play-activity, yet it is play only because the players deliberately make the game difficult in order to overcome the difficulties. The equation is simple: no difficulty, no fun. No chess player finds any real pleasure in playing an obviously inferior opponent. *Every game ever invented by mankind is a way of making things hard for the fun of it. The great fun, of course, is in making the hard look easy.* Too much difficulty is painful. The Freshman football coach does not send his squad to play last year's Rose Bowl winner. Neither does he send it to play grammar school teams. He tries to find opponents who will give his players a real chance to extend themselves, win or lose, and he hopes bit by bit to develop them for harder play.

Learning to experience poetry is not a radically different process from that of learning any other kind of play. The way to develop a poetic sense is by using it. And one of the real joys of the play-impulse is in the sudden discovery that one is getting better at it than he had thought he would be.

It is this self-delighting play-impulse that the literalist and message-hunter overlooks, just as Mr Gradgrind overlooked the living fun it is to ride a horse, even an undefined horse.

To summarize these same points in more formal terms: *no matter how serious the overt message of a poem, the unparaphraseable and undiminishable life of the poem lies in the way it performs itself through the difficulties it imposes upon itself*. The way *in which* it means is *what* it means.

What for example does a dance 'mean'? Or what does music 'mean'? Or what does a juggler 'mean' when we watch him with such admiration of his skill? All of these forms – and poetry with them – have meaning only as they succeed in being good performances.

One sees a wizard of a poet tossing his words in the air and catching them and tossing them again – what a grand stunt! Then suddenly one may be astonished to find that the poet is not simply juggling cups, saucers, roses, rhymes and other random objects, but the very stuff of life. And discovering that, one discovers that seeing the poet's ideas flash so in the air, seeing them performed under such control, is not only a reward in itself, but a living experience that deepens every man's sense of life. One finds himself more alert to life, surer of his own emotions, wiser than he would have been without that experience. — And he thought he was just watching a show!

But only a poem can illustrate how a poem works. One of the purposes of this volume is to provide beginning students with a reasonable bulk of poems from the great tradition of English and American poetry. But great as are the virtues of wide reading, they amount to nothing unless the reading goes deep as well as wide. It is good to read much. It is even more important to read a little in greater depth, for every poem one reads closely will teach him something about how to read another poem.

What should such a close reading take into consideration?

Here is a poem, one of the master lyrics of American poetry, perhaps the best known poem by an American poet:

STOPPING BY WOODS
ON A SNOWY EVENING

Robert Frost

Whose woods these are I think I know.
His house is in the village though;
He will not see me stopping here
To watch his woods fill up with snow.

My little horse must think it queer
To stop without a farmhouse near
Between the woods and frozen lake
The darkest evening of the year.

He gives his harness bells a shake
To ask if there is some mistake.

The only other sound's the sweep
Of easy wind and downy flake.

The woods are lovely, dark and deep.
But I have promises to keep,
And miles to go before I sleep,
*And miles to go before I sleep.**

Note that the poem begins as a simple description of events, but that it ends in a way that suggests meanings far beyond the specific description. This movement *from the specific to the general* is one of the basic formulas of poetry. Many poems follow exactly this progression from the specific to the general, but the generalization is, in a sense, divided from the specific description or narration, and even seems additional to the specific action rather than intrinsically part of it. It is this sense of division that is signified when one speaks of 'a tacked-on moral.' Frost, however, is painstakingly careful to avoid the tacked-on moral. Everything in the poem pretends, on one level, to be part of the incident narrated. Yet one cannot miss the feeling that by the end of the poem, Frost has referred to something much more far-reaching than stopping by woods or than driving home to go to bed. There can be little doubt, in fact, that part of Frost's own pleasure in this poem was in making the larger intent *grow out* of the poem rather than in tacking it on. It is in the poem's own performance of itself that the larger meaning is made to emerge from the specific incident. A careful look at that performance will teach a great deal about the nature of poetry.

The poem begins with a situation. A man – knowing Robert Frost, we know it is a Vermont or New Hampshire man – is on his way somewhere at night-fall. It is snowing and as he passes a patch of woods he stops to watch the easy down-drift of the snow into the dark woods. We are told two other things: first that the man is familiar with these parts (he knows who owns these woods and where he lives) and second that no one sees him stop. More could be read into this opening (for example: why doesn't he say what errand he is on? why does he say he knows whose woods these are? what is the significance of watching another man's woods in this way?). Such questions can be multiplied almost endlessly without losing real point, but for present purposes let us assume that we have identified scene one of the poem's performance without raising these questions.

Note that the scene is set in the simplest possible terms. We have no trouble sensing that the man stopped because the scene moved him, but he neither tells us that it is beautiful nor that it moved him. A student writer, always ready to overdo, might have said that he was moved to stop and 'to fill his soul with the slow steady stately sinking of that crystalline loveliness into the glimmerless profundities of the hushed primeval wood.' Frost prefers to avoid such a spate of words, and to speak the incident in the simplest terms.

His choice illustrates two basic principles of writing of which every sensitive reader should be aware. Frost stated the first principle himself in 'The Mowing' when he wrote 'Anything *more* than the truth would have seemed too *weak*.' (Italics mine.) Understatement is one of the principal sources of power in English poetry.

The second principle here illustrated is to let the action speak for itself. A good novelist who wishes us to know a character does not tell us that character is good or bad and leave it at that. Rather, he introduces the character, shows him in action, and lets his actions speak for him. This process is spoken of as *characterization in action*. One of the skills of a good poet is to enact his experiences rather than to talk about having had them. '*Show* it, don't *tell* it,' he says, 'make it happen, don't talk about its happening.'

One part of this poem's performance, in fact, is *to act out* (and thereby to make us act out – i.e., *feel out* – i.e., *identify with*) just why the speaker did stop. The man is the principal actor of this little 'drama of why' and in scene one he is the only character. In scene two (starting with the beginning of stanza two), however, a 'foil' is introduced. In drama, a 'foil' is a character who 'plays against' a more important character; by presenting a different point of view or an opposed set of motives, the foil moves the more important character to react in ways that might not have found expression without such opposition. The more important character is thus more fully revealed, to the reader and to himself. The foil here is the horse.

The horse forces the first question in the drama of why. Why did the man stop? Until he comes to realize that his 'little horse must think it queer' to stop this way, he has not asked himself why he stopped; he simply did. But he senses that the horse is confused by the stop. He imagines how the horse must feel about it – what *is* there to stop for out here in the cold, away from bin and stall and all that any self-respecting horse would value on such a night?

In imagining the horse's question, the man is of course led to examine his own reasons. In stanza two this question arises only as a feeling within the man. In stanza three, however, the horse acts definitely. He gives his harness bells a shake.

'What's wrong,' he seems to say, 'what are we doing here?'

By now, obviously, the horse, without losing its identity as a horse has also become a symbol. A symbol is something that stands for something else. That something else may, perhaps, be taken as the order of life that does not understand why a man stops in the wintry middle of nowhere to watch snow come down. (Could the dark and the snowfall symbolize a death wish? that hunger for the last rest that man may feel, but not a beast?) So there is the man, there is that other order of life, and there is the third presence – the movement of the inanimate wind and snow (the all-engulfing?) across both their lives – with the difference that the man knows the second darkness of the dark while the horse does not.

The man has no ready answer to this combination of forces. They exist and he feels them – all three of them, himself included. We sense that he would like to remain here longer to ponder these forces, perhaps to yield to their total. But a fourth force prompts him. That fourth force can be given many names. It is almost certainly better, in fact, to give it many names than attempt to limit it to one. Social obligation, responsibility, personal commitment, duty, or just the realization that a man cannot indulge a mood forever – all of these things and more. He has a long way to go and it is time to be getting there (so there's something to be said for the horse, too). We find the man's inner conflict dramatized to this point by the end of scene two (which coincides with the end of stanza three).

Then and only then – his feelings dramatized in the cross tug of motives he has given form to – does the poet, a little sadly, venture on the comment of his final scene. 'The woods are lovely, dark and deep.' The very sound of the syllables lingers over the thought. But there is something to do yet before he can yield to the lovely dark-and-deep. 'Not yet,' he seems to say, 'not yet.' He has a long way to go – miles to go before he can sleep. Yes, miles to go. He repeats the line and the performance ends.

But why the repetition? The first time Frost writes 'And miles to go before I sleep' there can be little doubt that he means, 'I have a long way to go yet before I can get to bed tonight.' The second time he says it, however, 'miles to go' and 'sleep' are suddenly transformed into symbols. What is the 'something else' these symbols stand for? Hundreds of people have asked Mr Frost that question in one form or another, and Mr Frost has always turned the question away with a joke. He has turned it away primarily *because he cannot answer it*. He could answer some part of it. But some part is not enough.

For a symbol is like a rock dropped into a pool: it sends out ripples in all directions, and the ripples are in motion. Who can say where the last ripple disappears? One may have a sense that he at least knows approximately the center point of all those ripples, the point at which the stone struck the water. Yet even then he has trouble marking it precisely. How does one make a mark on water? Oh, very well – the center point of 'miles to go' is probably approximately in the neighborhood of being close to meaning, perhaps, 'the road of life,' and 'before I sleep' is maybe that close to meaning 'before I take my final rest.' (That rest-in-darkness that seemed so temptingly 'lovely dark-and-deep' for the moment of the mood.) But the ripples continue to move and the light to change on the water and the longer one watches the more changes he sees. And such shifting-and-being-at-the-same-instant is of the very sparkle and life of poetry. Of poetry and of life itself. For the poem is a dynamic and living thing. One experiences it as one experiences life – as everybody but Mr Gradgrind experiences life. One is never done with it: every time he looks he sees something new, and it changes even as he watches. And that very sense of continuity in fluidity is one of the kinds of knowledge, one of the ways of knowing, that only the arts can teach, poetry foremost among them.

Frost himself certainly did not ask what the lines 'meant.' They came to him and he received them; he 'felt right' about them. And what he 'felt right about' may perhaps be called their 'meaning,' but it is far more to the point to describe it as 'their long possibility of meaning.' For the poem is not a statement but a performance of forces, not an essay on life but a re-enactment, and just as men must search their lives over and over again for the meaning of their deepest experiences, so the performance of a true poem is endless in being not a meaning but an act of existence.

Now look at the poem in another way. Did Frost know what he was going to do when he began? Considering the poem simply as a piece of juggling one cannot fail to respond to the magnificent turn at the end where, with one flip, seven of the simplest words in the language suddenly dazzle full of never-ending waves of thought and feeling; or – more precisely – of felt-thought. Certainly an equivalent stunt by a juggler – could there be such an equivalent – would bring the house down. Was it to cap his performance with that grand stunt that Frost wrote the poem?

Far from it; the fact that must not be overlooked is that *Frost did not know he was going to write those lines until he wrote them*. Then a second fact must be registered: *he wrote them because, for the fun of it, he had got himself into trouble*.

Let us start by saying that Frost began by playing a game

with himself. The most usual way of writing a four line stanza with four feet to the line, is to rhyme the third line with the first, and the fourth line with the second. Even that much rhyme is so difficult that many poets and almost all the anonymous ballad makers do not bother to rhyme the first and third lines at all, settling for two rhymes in four lines. For the fact is that English is a rhyme-poor language. In Italian and in French, for example, so many words end with the same sounds that rhyming is relatively easy. English, being a more agglomerate language, has far more final sounds, hence fewer of them rhyme. When an Italian poet writes a line ending with 'vita' (life) he has literally hundreds of possible rhyme words available. When an English poet writes 'life' at the end of a line, he can summon 'strife, wife, knife, fife, rife' and then he is in trouble. Now 'life-strife,' and 'life-rife' and 'life-wife' seem to offer a combination of ideas that are possibly related by more than rhyme. Inevitably, therefore, the poets have had to work, re-work, and over-work these combinations until the sparkle has gone out of them. Readers are normally tired of these combinations. When one encounters 'life-strife' he is certainly entitled to suspect that the poet did not really want to say 'strife' — that if there had been in English such a word as, say, 'hife' meaning 'infinite peace and harmony,' he would gladly have used that word instead of 'strife.' So one feels that the writing is haphazard: that the rhyme is making the poet say things he doesn't really feel, and which, therefore, the reader does not feel. One likes to see the rhymes fall into place, but he must end up with the belief that it is the poet who is deciding what is said and not the rhyme scheme.

So rhyme is a kind of game, and an especially difficult one in English. As in every game, the fun of rhyme is to set one's difficulties high and then to meet them skillfully. As Frost himself once defined freedom, it consists of 'moving easy in harness.'

In 'Stopping by Woods on a Snowy Evening' Frost took a long chance. He decided to rhyme not two lines, but three in each stanza. Not even Frost could have sustained that much rhyme in a long poem (as Dante, for example, with the advantage of writing in Italian sustained triple rhyme for thousands of lines in *The Divine Comedy*). He would have known instantly, therefore, when he took that first chance, that he was going to write a short poem. He would have had that much foretaste of it. So the first stanza emerged rhymed a a b a. And with the certain sense that this was to be a short poem, Frost decided to take a chance and redouble: in English three rhymes in four lines is enough – there is no need to rhyme the fourth line. For the fun of it, however, Frost set himself to pick up that loose rhyme and weave it into the pattern – thereby accepting the all but impossible burden of quadruple rhyme.

The miracle is that it worked. Despite that enormous freight of rhyme, the poem not only came out as a neat pattern, but managed to do so with no sense of strain. It is this unstrained fulfilment of one's difficulties Frost means by 'moving easy in harness.' Despite all his self-imposed restrictions the poem *seems* to go effortlessly. Every word falls into place as naturally as if there were no rhyme restricting the choice.

That ease is part of the success of the performance. One watches the skill-man juggle two balls, then three, then four – and every addition makes the trick more wonderful, but unless he makes the hard trick *seem* as easy as the easy one, then all is lost.

The real point, however, is not only that Frost took on a hard rhyme-trick and made it look easy. It is rather as if a juggler, carried away, had tossed up one more ball than he could really handle – and then amazed himself by actually handling it. So with the real triumph of this poem. Frost could not have known what a stunning effect his repetition of the last line was going to produce. He could not even have known he was going to repeat the line. He simply found himself up against a difficulty he probably had not foreseen: in picking up the rhyme from the third line of stanza one and carrying it over into stanza two, he had created an endless chain-link form. Each stanza left a hook sticking out for the next stanza to catch. So by stanza four, feeling the poem rounding to its end, Frost had to do something about his third-line rhyme.

He might have tucked it back in a third line rhyming with 'know/though/snow' of stanza one. That would have worked out to the mathematical symmetry of using each rhyme four times. But though such a device might be defensible in theory, a rhyme repeated after eleven lines is so far from its original rhyme sound that its feeling as rhyme must certainly be lost, and what good is theory if the reader is not moved by the writing?

It must have been in some such quandary that the final repetition suggested itself – a suggestion born of the very difficulty of what the poet had set out to do. So the point beyond mere ease in handling a hard thing: that the very difficulty of the restrictions the poet imposed upon himself offered the opportunity to do better than he had imagined. What – aside from having that happen to oneself – could be more self-delighting than to participate in its happening by one's reader-identification with the poem?

You will observe one further point: that the human-insight

of the poem, and the technicalities of the poetic devices are inseparable. Each feeds the other. This interplay is the poem's meaning, a matter not of WHAT IT MEANS (nobody can say entirely what a good poem means) but HOW IT MEANS — a process one can come much closer to discussing.

Is it too frivolous to have compared this process to the act of juggling? Consider the following parable based on a short story by Anatole France, 'The Juggler of Notre Dame.'

The juggler wandered France from fair to fair and whenever he saw a chance to earn a few pennies he unrolled his rug, lay on his back, and juggled his paraphernalia with his hands and feet. It was all he knew how to do, he did it well, and he was happy in the doing.

As he grew older, however, misfortunes crowded him. One winter's day, ill and tired, he took refuge in a monastery and by the time he had recovered he decided to remain there. It was a pleasant monastery dedicated to the Virgin and each of the monks and brothers set himself a special task in her honor. One illuminated manuscripts to offer her, another decorated her altar, another raised flowers. Only the juggler had no productive art, only he produced nothing that could be set in place before her and stay tangibly in place. (This rendering takes a few liberties with the original for the sake of making a point.)

Finally, in despair, the juggler took to stealing into the chapel when no one else was about. There he would unroll his rug and juggle before the Virgin's statue. It was all he had to offer, the one thing he could do well.

One day a passing brother discovered the juggler at work before the statue and summoned the other monks in horror to witness the profanation of the chapel. Soon all the windowsills were lined with the heads of outraged monks come to verify the horrible report. They were just about to rush in and put an end to the sacrilege, when before their eyes the Virgin descended smiling from her pedestal and wiped the sweat from the juggler's brow. The offering was acceptable.

A note to residual Gradgrinds: This parable is not a religious excursion. It is an allegory. An allegory is a story in which each character and element is more important as a symbol (as something else) than as its presumably-literal self. Then all these symbols-put-together acquire further meanings by their interaction upon one another. — What does the Virgin stand for in poetic terms? What do the monks stand for? The juggler? How does juggling relate to Frost's definition of freedom (in poetry)? Why should juggling produce the miracle? How does the parable mean what it means?

Modernist Poetry and the Plain Reader's Rights

AN ESSAY BY ROBERT GRAVES WITH LAURA RIDING

Let us assume for the moment that poetry not characteristically 'modernist' presents no difficulty to the plain reader: for the complaint against modernist poetry turns on its differences from traditional poetry. These differences would seem to justify themselves if their effect were to bring poetry any nearer the plain reader; even traditional poetry, it is sometimes charged, has a tendency to withdraw itself from him. But the sophistications of advanced modern poetry seem only to widen the breach. In the poetry of Mr E. E. Cummings, for example, who may be considered to illustrate the divorce of advanced contemporary poetry from the standards of ordinary common sense, is to be found apparently not only a disregard of common sense, but an insult to it. Such poetry seems to say: 'Keep out! This is a private performance.'

But does the poet really mean to keep the public out? If, after a careful examination of poems that seem only to be part of the high-brow's game of baiting the low-brow, they still resist all reasonable efforts to understand him, then we must conclude that such work is, after all, merely a joke at

This essay originally appeared in *The Common Asphodel*. It is reprinted by permission of International Authors N.V.

the plain reader's expense and return him to his newspapers and his Shakespeare – let us assume for the moment that he has no difficulty in understanding Shakespeare. But if, on the other hand, we are able to extract from these poems the experiences which are expected of poetry, or at least see that the poet originally wrote them in all sincerity, then the plain reader must modify his critical attitude. In the first place, he must admit that what is called common intelligence is the mind in its least active state: that poetry demands a more vigorous imaginative effort than he has hitherto been willing to apply to it; and that, if anthologies compiled to refresh tired minds have indulged his lazy reading habits, poets can be pardoned for using exceptional means to make him do justice to their poems. Next, he must ask himself whether such innovations have not a place in the normal course of poetry-writing, and if he decides that they have, he must question the depth of his understanding of poetry which, like Shakespeare's, is taken for granted and ask whether a poet like Mr Cummings must not be taken seriously, at least for his effect on the future reading of poetry of any age or style.

To begin with, we shall choose one of Mr Cummings' earlier and simpler poems, which will nevertheless excite much the same hostility as his later work. It is unusually suitable for analysis, because the subject is of just the kind that the plain reader looks for in poetry. It appears, moreover, in Mr Louis Untermeyer's popular *Anthology of Modern American Poetry* side by side with the work of poets more willing than Mr Cummings to defer to the intelligence-level of the plain reader. It is all the more important to study because Mr Untermeyer seems personally hostile to Mr Cummings' work and yet to have been forced by the pressure of more advanced critical opinion to include it in a book where modernism in poetry means, in his own definition, simplicity ('the use of the language of everyday speech' and the discarding of that poetical padding which the plain reader and the plain critic enjoy more than Mr Untermeyer would admit). But Mr Untermeyer is speaking of a modernism no longer modern, that of such dead movements as Georgianism and Imagism which were supposedly undertaken in the interests of the plain reader. We are dealing here with a modernist who seems to feel no obligation to the plain reader, and to work solely in the interests of poetry.

SUNSET

stinging
gold swarms
upon the spires
silver

        chants the litanies the
great bells are ringing with rose
the lewd fat bells
                                        and a tall

wind
is dragging
the
sea

with

dream

-S

With so promising a title – though supplied, it appears, by Mr Untermeyer, since none of the poems in Mr Cummings' own volumes have titles – what barriers does the poem raise between itself and the plain reader? In what respect does it seem to sin against common intelligence?

The lines do not begin with capital letters. The spacing does not suggest any regular verse-form, though it seems to be systematic. There are no punctuation marks. But even if one can overlook these technical oddities, it still seems impossible to read the poem as a logical sequence. Many words essential to the coherence of the ideas suggested have been deliberately omitted; and the entire effect is so sketchy that the poem might be made to mean almost anything. If the author once had a precise meaning he seems to have lost it while writing the poem. Let us, however, assume for the sake of this argument that it is possible to discover the original poem at the back of the poet's mind; or at least to gather enough material from the poem as it stands from which to construct a poem that will satisfy all formal requirements, the poem that he perhaps meant to hint at with these fragments. As the naturalist Cuvier could reconstruct an extinct animal in full anatomical detail from a single tooth, let us restore this extinct poem from what Mr Cummings has permitted to survive.

First, we must decide whether there are any positive features in *Sunset* which will allow it to be judged as a formal poem and which must occur with much the same emphasis in the proposed rewriting. The title might be amplified because of a veiled literary reference in lines five and six to Rémy de Gourmont's *Litanies de la Rose*. It might reasonably include some acknowledgment of the poet's debt to French influences, and read: 'Sunset Piece: After Reading

Rémy de Gourmont.' The heavy *s* alliteration in the first seven lines, confirmed in the last by the solitary capitalized *S*, cannot be discarded: the context demands it. The first word, *stinging*, taken alone, suggests merely a sharp feeling; its purpose is to supply an emotional source from which the other *s* ideas may derive. In the second line *swarms* develops the alliteration; at the same time it colours *stinging* with the association of golden bees and softens it with the suppressed idea of buzzing. We are now ready for the more tender *s* word, *spires*, in the third line. *Silver*, the single word of the fourth line, brings us back to the contrast between cold and warm in the first and second lines (*stinging* suggests cold in contrast with the various suggestions of warmth in the *gold swarms*) because *silver* reminds one of cold water as gold does of warm light. Two suppressed *s* words play behind the scenes in this first part of the poem, both disguised in *silver* and *gold*, namely *sea* and *sun*. *Sea* does not actually occur until the twelfth line, when the *s* alliteration has flagged: separated from alliterative associations, it becomes the definite image *sea* around which the poem is to be built up. But once it has appeared there is little more to be said: the poem trails off, closing with the large *S* echo of the last line. The hyphen before this *S* detaches it from *dream* and sets it apart as the alliterative summary of the poem; in a realistic sense *-S* might stand for the alternation of quiet and hiss in wave movement. As a formal closing it leaves us with much the same feeling as at the start, but less acute, because the *z* sound has prevailed over the *s* sound with which the poem began. The sunset is over, the final impression is darkness and sleep, though the *-S* vaguely returns us to the two sharp *s*'s of the opening.

Another feature which would recur in the rewriting of

the poem is the deceleration of the rhythm in the last half indicated by the shortening of the lines and by the double spacing. In regular verse this would naturally mean line-lengthening, the closing of a ten-syllable stanza series with a twelve-syllable couplet, for example. No end-rhymes occur in the poem as it stands but the rhyme element is strong. Though the only obvious rhyme-sympathy is between *stinging* and *ringing*, many suppressed rhymes are present: not only *swinging* accompanying the idea of bells but *bees* and *seas, bells* and *swells, spires* and *fires*. In the rewritten poem a formal metrical scheme would have to be employed, but the choice would be governed by the character of the original poem. The rhythm would be gentle and simple, with few marked emphases. Monosyllables would prevail, with a noticeable recurrence of *ing* words; and *bells* would be repeated. Here, then, is a poem embodying the important elements of Mr Cummings' poem, but with normal spacing and punctuation and a regular verse-form. It contains no images not directly suggested by the original, but links up grammatically what appears to be an arrangement based on caprice.

SUNSET PIECE

After reading Rémy de Gourmont

White foam and vesper wind embrace.
The salt air stings my dazzled face
And sunset flecks the silvery seas
With glints of gold like swarms of bees
And lifts tall dreaming spires of light
To the imaginary sight,
So that I hear loud mellow bells
Swinging as each great wave swells,

Wafting God's perfumes on the breeze,
And chanting of sweet litanies
Where jovial monks are on their knees,
Bell-paunched and lifting glutton eyes
To windows rosy as the skies.

And this slow wind – how can my dreams forget? –
Dragging the waters like a fishing-net.

Mr Cummings, it may be assumed, felt bound to write the poem as he did in order to prevent it from becoming what we have made of it. To treat an old subject like sunset and avoid all the obvious poetical formulas, the poet must write in a new way if he is to evoke any fresh response in his readers at all. Not only does the rewritten version demand much less attention than the original, but it is difficult to feel respect for a poem that is full of reminiscences not only of Rémy de Gourmont, but of Wordsworth ('To the imaginary sight'), Milton (in the metrical variations taken from *L'Allegro*), Messrs Belloc and Chesterton ('Where jovial monks . . .' etc.) and Tagore in English translation ('Dragging the waters like a fishing-net'). Stale phrases such as 'vesper wind' and 'silver seas' have come to mean so little that they scarcely do their work in the poem. And yet we shall see that such phrases cannot be avoided if we are to revise the poem for the plain man. 'White foam' is understood from the sea setting, the movement of the poem, and the cold hissing implied in the sequence of *s*'s. 'Vesper wind' is suggested by *sunset, spires, monks, bells, tall wind.* 'Salt air,' besides resulting from the embrace of 'white foam' and 'vesper wind,' is built up from *stinging, sea* and *wind.* The transformations in the next three lines are fairly obvious.

'Imaginary sight' is necessary to remind the plain reader that the poem is not to be taken literally, a hint which Mr Cummings disdained to give. It should be noticed that 'imaginary' is the longest and slowest word in the poem yet adds nothing to the picture; in fact, makes it less real. The seventh and eighth lines express the connection between bells and waves which Mr Cummings leaves the reader to deduce, if he pleases. The ninth line is the expansion of the rose idea demanded by the context: *monks, spires, litanies* are all bound up with the Catholic symbolism of the rose; and in rewriting the poem it is impossible not to develop the literary associations of the rose as well (*wafting, perfumes*). The rose-windows of cathedrals are also obviously suggested. Unfortunately *lewd,* too strong a word for a formal sunset piece, has to be broken up into *jovial* and *glutton,* recalling the Christmas-annual type of monk. The analogy between *great bells* and *fat monks* has to be emphasized, thus introducing gratuitous words like *mellow, bell-paunched, on their knees,* etc. Instead of taking advantage of the natural associations latent in certain highly pictorial words, we have had to go over much unnecessary ground and have ended by merely being banal. In lengthening the metre of the last two lines to match the slowing down in the original piece, many superfluous words and images have had to be introduced here too. First of all, *slow* itself, as weakening to the concentration of the poem as the line 'To the imaginary sight.' Then, ' – how can my dreams forget? – ', to account grammatically for the vivid present tense in which the whole poem is written, and to put *dream* in its more logical position, since in the original poem it is doing double duty for a specific image (*fishing-net,* following from *dragging*) and the vagueness with which the image is felt.

The conclusion to be drawn from this exercise might be that poems must in future be written in skeleton style if poetry is not to die out. But the poetry of Mr Cummings is clearly more important as a sign of local irritation in the poetic body than as a model for a new tradition. The important thing to recognize, in a time of popular though superficial education, is the need of bringing home to the reading public the differences between good and bad poems, the very differences that we have been pointing out here. Poets in such a time, indeed, may forget that they have any function other than to teach the proper approach to poetry: there is an exaggerated though excusable tendency to suspend the writing of all poetry that is not critical in intention. (Rare exceptions, of course, occur: poets whose writing is so self-contained that they are not affected by staleness in traditional poems or obliged to attack them or escape from them.) Mr Cummings in this poem was really rewriting the other poem, the one we gave, into a good poem. But for the rarer poet there is no 'other poem'; there is only the poem which he writes. Mr Cummings' experimental technique, indeed, if further and more systematically developed, would become so complicated and so elaborate that the principal interest in his poems would be mathematical. Real poets, however, do not pursue innovation for its own sake: they are conservative in their methods so long as these ensure the proper security and delivery of the poem.

A poem's virtue does not lie in the way in which it is set down on paper, as a picture's does in the way it is set down on canvas. Method in poetry is not anything that can be discussed in terms of physical form. The poem is neither the paper, nor the type, nor the spoken syllables. It is as invisible and as inaudible as thought; and the only method that the real poet cares to use is one that will present the poem without making it either visible or audible: without turning it into a substitute for a painting or for music. Yet when conservatism of method, through its abuse by slack-minded poets, comes to mean the supplanting of poems by exercises in poetcraft, then there is a reasonable place for any innovation which brings up the important question: 'How should poetry be written?' and acts as a deterrent against writing in a worn-out style. Our suggestion is not that poets should imitate Mr Cummings, but that the appearance of poems like his and the attention they demand should make it harder for poetical exercises to be passed off as poetry. We may not accept his experimental version of the sunset piece, but once we have understood it we cannot return with satisfaction to the formal one.

Turning back for a closer comparison of the two versions, we see how much of the force of the original has been lost in the rewriting. We have begun each line with a capital letter, but the large final *S* which was one of the most important properties of the original has thus been eliminated, and a look of unnecessary importance has been given to words like *And, To* and *So.* In our use of normal spacing and verse-form we have had to disregard the significance of the double spacing and indentation, and of the variation in the length of the lines. Formal indentation can either be a guide to rhyming pairs or a sign that the first part of a line is missing, but it cannot denote musical rests of varying value as in the original of the poem. We have also expanded the suggested ideas by grammatic means and supplemented them with the words which seem to have been omitted. But in so doing we have sacrificed the compactness of the original and dispelled its carefully devised dreaminess. In fact, by formalizing the poem we have not added anything to it but on the contrary detracted from its value.

The expansion of the original by the addition of the suppressed words has necessarily multiplied the number of *s*'s, because the suppressed words show a high proportion of these. This alliteration, sustained over several couplets, does not match the alliteration of the original, especially since we have been obliged to use many *s*'s that have no sort of alliterative significance ('To windows rosy as the skies'). Neither has the gradual slowing down of the rhythm in the last half of the poem been effectively reproduced. In the original the slowing down extends over the sestet of this fragmentary sonnet (the fragmentary line, *-S,* being an alliterative hang-over). But because in the formal version the original simple octave develops a prolixity which destroys the proper balance between it and its sestet, we have had to abandon the sonnet-form and pack into two lines words which should have had the time-value of six. The best we have been able to do is to keep fourteen lines (or rather seven rhyming couplets, one of which has an extra line). The rhymes, too, in the formal version have mutilated the sense: they express the remoteness of the scene by a series of echoes rather than by silences – for the original lines can be regarded as sonnet-lines filled out with musical rests. By transposing the poem into a form in which a definite metrical scheme can be recognized we have entirely altered the character of the poem. We have not even been able to save the scraps of regular iambic rhythm with which we started.

Certain admissions must therefore be made. We must not only reject the formal version in favour of the original: we must admit that the original itself is an intensely formal poem. Indeed, its very virtuosity has caused it to be mistaken for a mere assemblage of words, a literary trick. But since it is proved capable of yielding the kind of experiences customarily expected from poetry, in fact the most ordinary of such experiences, our conclusion must be that the plain reader's approach to poetry is adequate only for poems as weak as the critical effort which he is ready to apply to them; and that Mr Cummings (to disregard the satiric hilarity in which many of his poems are written) really means to write serious poetry and to have it read with the critical sympathy it deserves. The importance of any new technical methods which he employs to bring this about lies not in their ultimate permanence or impermanence, but in their establishment of what the poet's rights are in his poem: how free he is to disregard the inferior critical efforts to which the poem will be submitted by the greater part of the poetry-reading public. What, then, of the plain reader's rights? They are, like the poet's, whatever his intelligence is able to make them.

It must be admitted that excessive interest in the technique of the poem can become morbid both in the poet and the reader, like the composing and solving of crossword puzzles. Once the sense of a poem with a technical soul, so to speak, is unriddled and its patterns plainly displayed, it is not fit for re-reading: as with the Sphinx in the fable, to allow the riddle to be guessed is equivalent to suicide. A poem of this kind is nevertheless able to stave off death by revealing, under closer examination, an unexpected reserve of new riddles; and so long as it is able to supply these it may continue to live as a poem. But clearly its surprises cannot last for ever; nor can we, as when reading the indestructible poem whose soul is not technical, go back to the beginning when we have done and start all over again as with a new poem.

How much more life is left in *Sunset* at this point? Have we come to an end? Or are there further reasons why it should continue to be called a poem, since it is a poem only so long as there is a possibility of its yielding still more meaning? Did we not, without assuming any formal verse-pattern, give a satisfactory explanation of the poem? Did we not also find it possible to give an entirely new view of it on the basis of its being a skeletonized sonnet? Did we not accept it as a non-grammatic construction, yet still make sense of it? But could we not show it to be potentially or even actually grammatic and make sense of it because it was so? Why not read *swarms* and *chants,* which we have been regarding as nominative plural nouns, as third person singular verbs, and read *silver* and *gold* as nouns, not as adjectives? The poem will then stand grammatically as follows:

> *Stinging gold swarms upon the spires.*
> *Silver [i.e. a voice or tone of silver] chants the litanies*
> *The great bells are ringing with rose –*
> *The lewd fat bells –*
> *And a tall wind is dragging the sea with dreams.*

And even if we had explored the technical possibilities in this poem of thirty-one words – the grammar, the metre and other technical aspects, the context and the association of images – we should still be left with the fact that it has thirty-one words, and perhaps find in it another formalism. Can it be a coincidence that this is also the standard length of the *tanka,* the dominant verse-form in Japanese poetry – thirty-one syllables, each of word value? The Japanese influence is further intimated by Mr Cummings' tendency to suggest and symbolize rather than to express in full. In Japanese, according to the conventional arrangement of the thirty-one word-units in lines of five, seven, five, seven, seven, this poem would be set down like this:

stinging gold swarms upon the
spires silver chants the litanies the great
bells are ringing with rose
the lewd fat bells and a tall
wind is dragging the sea with dreams.

But stronger than the Japanese influence in modern English and American poetry is the French, which in turn has borrowed much from the Japanese. Mallarmé, the father of symbolism, turned the act of suggestion in poetry into a science. He found the tradition of French poetry so exhausted by sterile laws of prosody that he had to practise poetry as a science to avoid malpractising it as an art. Rimbaud, with all Mallarmé's science behind him and endowed with a natural poetic mind, was able to practise poetry as an art again. Similarly Mr Cummings and other experimentalists – he is to be regarded rather as an inspired amateur than a scientist – may be preparing the way for an English or American Rimbaud. As M. Paul Valéry, the French critic and poet, says of Mallarmé and Rimbaud, discussing their employment of the vehicles of sense in poetry: 'What is only a system in Mallarmé becomes a domain in Rimbaud.' So modernist poets are developing resources to which a future poet will have easy access when he turns the newly opened-up territory into a personal poetic domain.

Although an elaborate system of poetic technique may come to flower in the work of a natural poet like Rimbaud, it may on the other hand fossilize in a convention as tyrannic as the one it was invented to supplant. There is more danger of this, however, in French poetry than in English.

M. Paul Valéry has even been made a member of the French Academy, in recognition of his formal influence on contemporary poetry. Although as traditional in form as Mr Cummings is modernist, he relies, like him, almost entirely on the effectiveness of images – on their power to evoke sensations, and on their strangeness. To describe how night hid from Narcissus his own beloved image in the fountain, he says that night slid between him and his image like 'a knife shearing a fruit in two.' What he means is that Narcissus and the image formed a whole as symmetrical as the halves of an apple before they are divided. Mr Cummings' images are as strange and as vivid as this ('gold swarms' or 'ringing with rose,' for example) ; but there is no question of making an academician of him or calling his most recent and more methodical phase 'Pope-ian,' as M. Valéry's last phase is known by his admirers as 'Racinian' after the master-craftsman of the most formal period in French poetry.

English modernist poets also imitate the French in the use of combinations of sounds to create a musical picture. This is, of course, nothing new in English poetry. Gray, one of the most traditional of English poets, wishing to give the picture of slow and painful descent down a steep mountain, writes:

As down the steep of Snowdon's shaggy side
He wound with toilsome march his long array.

But this usage has never been applied except as an occasional trope, and even as such has been discouraged rather than encouraged by criticism. It is considered tolerable only where the combinations of sounds add musicalness without taking away from the meaning; never where they over-represent or distort the meaning.

Musicalness in modern French verse means something

else: the treating of word-sounds as musical notes in which the meaning itself is to be found. This takes poetry even farther from its natural course than the Victorians took it with their coloratura effects. The bond between the Victorian poet and his reader was at least that of a common, though not an original, sentiment. The meaning of a poem was understood beforehand from the very title, and the persuasiveness of the word-music was intended to keep the poem vibrating in the memory long after it had been read. The bond, however, between the French modernist poet and his reader is one of technical ingenuity: the poet setting the meaning down in combinations of sounds, the reader interpreting words as combinations of sounds rather than as words. Actually, there is little poetic thought in Victorian poetry because of the compromise it makes between ideas and their pleasurable expression. But the compromise in modern French poetry, though less apparent, is still more destructive of poetic thought. It is between ideas and typography and as such implies the domination of ideas by mechanics. By giving the letters of words a separate personality we have a new psychology of letters entirely distinct from the psychology of images. A striking illustration of the attempt to reconcile these two psychologies is a poem of Rimbaud's on the colours of the vowels. It is plain that the colours associated with vowels will vary widely with the individual and may be determined by so irrelevant a cause as the colours of the alphabet-blocks which one used as a child. A better case might perhaps be made for the meaning-associations of consonants, particularly of combinations of consonants such as *st*, as in *stinging, strike, stench,* to denote sharp assault, and the final *nch,* as in *clinch, munch, wrench,* to denote strain. But it is only occasionally that the letters of a word imitate its meaning in this way; no general rule can be drawn from these examples. There are many more instances of letters out of harmony with word-meanings than of letters in harmony with them. Take the word *kiss,* for instance. Is this *iss* any gentler than the *iss* of *hiss*? Or is the *k* in *kiss* gentler than the *k* of *kick*? Logically, such a theory should mean that a French poem written in this way would produce the same effect on a person who did not understand French as one who did.

When it is remembered how such theories crowd the literary air, it will be realized what great restraint Mr Cummings has imposed on himself in the matter of alliteration and other tricks with letters. He would not, we feel, let such theories run away with him to the extent of forcing his choice of words to depend more on the sense of their sounds than on the sense of their images. His choice of *swarms,* for instance, is primarily determined by the three meanings combined in the word (the crowding sense, the bee-buzzing sense, and another hitherto not noted – the climbing sense associated with *spires* and the eye looking up to the light) ; not by the occurrence of *s* and *z* or by the presence of *warm* in *swarms,* though these are accidents of which he takes every advantage. And this is the way such things should happen in poetry: by coincidence. The poet appreciates and confirms rather than stage-manages. A certain amount of superstitious faith in language is necessary if the poet is to perform the sort of miracle expected of, and natural to, poetry.

Notes and Questions on the Poems

1. FERN HILL

See the notes on pastoral poetry (p. 501), symbol (p. 487), and transferred epithet (p. 516).

Thomas recalls the days he spent as a boy on a farm in Wales. The poet's techniques include: playful twisting of stock phrases, such as three variations on 'happy as the day is long' in lines 2, 11, and 38; repetition of simple images with cumulative effect; unobtrusive use of the creation story from Genesis to suggest the innocence of the young child, the fresh creation of the world with each new day in the child's life, and the eventual loss of this idyllic world. **l. 3 dingle** A small secluded ravine. **l. 9 windfall light** It is typical of Thomas to achieve such a multiplicity of meanings in a single phrase. The words can suggest any one of the following images, any combination of them, and may go far beyond: the subdued atmosphere at twilight as both the light and the wind fade together; the reflected patches of rosy sky and green foliage; the colours of the apples blown prematurely from the trees in autumn; the distinctive grey-green colour of the river surface at twilight, as the barely disturbed water reflects the darkened sky and the bordering foliage; shafts of light, like rivers, between the rows of trees in the orchard; the unexpected wealth added by this experience. **ll. 10-18 green, golden** The green is not only the grass, but also the poet's youth and the joy of fresh experience. The gold is the sun, the source of life and the blessing of God. **ll. 11, 13, 14, and 15** The opening words of these lines repeat those of the first stanza, thereby suggesting the child's sense of permanence and continuity. **l. 25 nightjars** Name given to the goatsucker and other birds of the genus. **l. 26 ricks** Haystacks. **l. 39** Each day presents a freshly created world; also, the child is reborn with each new day. Cf. ll. 32-33. **l. 40** Although Thomas revised this poem at least seventeen times, he was always dissatisfied with one word in this line. Can you identify the word and explain his dissatisfaction? **ll. 53-54** An effective realization in imagery of the paradoxical relationship of growth and decline. The sea's chains are the tides, controlled by the circling moon.

2. LOOK, STRANGER

See the notes on assonance, consonance, internal rhyme, and onomatopoeia (p. 514).

The speaker asks for the reader's attention, creates a vividly detailed scene for the eye and ear, and moves gently from the immediate landscape to a later appreciation of it. The scene is possibly set above the chalk cliffs of Dover, overlooking the English Channel. **l. 12 shingle** Stones and pebbles covering a beach. **l. 15** The arresting juxtaposition of adjectives is a feature of Auden's style.

3. THERE WAS A BOY

See the note on pastoral poetry (p. 501).

Wordsworth drew together his childhood memories in *The Prelude,* a remarkable long poem which illustrates the gradual shaping of the individual by the experiences and environment of early life. The excerpt from Book V (ll. 364-388), given here, was also published separately. It is difficult to be certain whether Wordsworth, at this stage of his life, believed in pantheism or in divine immanence. The pantheist describes God in terms of the spirit of Nature; a believer in divine immanence describes Nature in terms of God who pervades it. **l. 2 Winander** The scene is Lake Windermere ('Wynander's lake') in the English Lake District. **ll. 19-25**

Wordsworth felt that, in such moments of deep communion, Nature impressed its patterns on the depths of his mind and imagination.

Questions: Poems 1, 2, and 3

(a) Compare the responses of the three poets to their natural environments.

(b) Compare the effects achieved by the language, rhythm, and imagery of these poems.

4. SONNET: THE WORLD IS TOO MUCH WITH US

l. 13 Proteus A prophetic sea-god who tended the seals of Poseidon (Neptune); he could change his shape at will. **l. 14 Triton** A sea deity, son of Poseidon; he could raise or calm the sea by blowing a command on a conch shell.

6. AUTOBIOGRAPHICAL

This poem appears in Klein's novel *The Second Scroll* which symbolizes, in the life of a Jewish scholar, the religious history of the Jewish people. The book is divided into five chapters, each with a different form of gloss or commentary named for a letter of the Hebrew alphabet. 'Autobiographical' is Gloss Aleph, from the first letter. Klein grew up in the Jewish community in Montreal, and this poem conveys the contented absorption of the boy in all aspects of the life of his community. **ll. 1, 86 Jewboy** Klein uses a derisive term with pride. **l. 4 goy** Anyone who is not a Jew. A 'Sabbath-goy' is one who performs duties not permitted to a Jew on the Jewish Sabbath. **l. 5 Torah** Literally 'the Law', the five books of Moses. In the Jewish liturgy the Torah is read from a handwritten scroll of leather or parchment, which on certain occasions is carried in procession. **l. 24 Saturday night** The Sabbath ends at sunset, when it is customary to have a social gathering. **l. 29 maariv** The daily evening prayer. **l. 31 Volhynia** A province in southeastern Poland, and a part of the Russian Empire, where many Jews were slaughtered in the fighting which followed the Russian Revolution of 1917. **ll. 34-35** Every week the Jewish youngsters learned Hebrew and portions of the Bible; when their work was satisfactory pennies were dropped on their books to reward them. **l. 37** Friday night was the occasion of the family ceremony ushering in the Sabbath. The mother would light ritual candles for which she said a blessing. **l. 38 Warsovian** From Warsaw in Poland. **perruque** A wig. Upon marriage an orthodox Jewish woman customarily cut off her hair, to symbolize the fact that she no longer wished to be attractive to men other than her husband. **l. 40** In the middle of the eighteenth century there developed in Polish Judaism a great religious renaissance known as Hasidism. The founding leader was a teacher called Baal Shem Tov, 'Master of the Good Name.' Many stories are told of his miracles. **l. 65 the Haman rattle** In the annual festival of Purim, Jews celebrate their salvation from destruction at the hands of Haman, the chief minister of King Ahasuerus. As part of the celebration the story, as told in the Book of Esther, is read in the synagogue and the young people mark the reading of the name Haman by waving rattles. **l. 66** The Torah is divided into sections for reading on the Sabbath so that it is finished once a year. Simchas Torah – 'the Joy of the Law' – is the day on which the reading is both completed and begins again with the first chapter of Genesis; it is an occasion for celebrations.

7. HOME THOUGHTS FROM ABROAD

Probably written in 1838, while the poet was living in Italy. **l. 5 brushwood sheaf** Here, the growth of young shoots round the bole of the elm.

8. SNAKE

See the note on imitative harmony (p. 515).

Lawrence uses his reactions to the snake to expose what he sees as a conflict between the values and standards of natural man and those imposed by civilized life. The suggestiveness of the symbols, the extremely evocative imagery, and the internal dialogue blend to recreate both the physical experience and the spiritual crisis. **l. 4 carob** An evergreen with dark reddish berries, native to the Mediterranean region. **l. 18** Note that Lawrence mentions the forked tongue but not the fangs. **l. 21 Etna** A famous active volcano near Taormina, on the east coast of Sicily, where Lawrence lived for a time. **ll. 22-24** Is this the normal significance of black and gold? **l. 66 the albatross** In Coleridge's 'Rime of the Ancient Mariner', a sailor was punished for having wantonly killed an albatross. He was sentenced to wander, telling the story of his sin and of his redemption by love. It is interesting to compare Coleridge's and Lawrence's treatments of wanton brutality and its symbolic overtones.

9. A FIELD OF LIGHT

See the notes on cadence (p. 507) and juxtaposition (p. 492).

Roethke traces states of feeling by depicting the very delicate nuances of a natural setting. The landscape of the first part suggests isolation and stagnancy, and an incapacity for sensuous response to the beauty around him. The poet is driven to ask himself whether he has ever denied the forces of life by 'cursing the sun'. Immediately he is carried back in memory to earlier scenes, in which he had felt drawn to dark and enclosed vegetation, dank and rotting in the absence of sunlight. Even there, he recalls, he had celebrated his delight in the natural world. Fortified by this memory, he moves in the third part to a joyful affirmation of personal and natural well-being. **l. 24 viscid** Covered with a sticky secretion. **l. 43 The lovely diminutives** Roethke is enthusiastic about the myriad forms in nature — particularly small plants and animals, and small inanimate objects.

10. THE LONELY LAND

The visual drama of Canada's northland challenges the poet's command of language and metre. Apart from explicit statement, how has Smith suggested the strength and desolation of the northland?

Questions: Poems 4, 5, 6, 7, 8, 9, and 10

(a) From these poems select images that express each poet's appreciation of natural beauty.

(b) Does the poet gain any insight that goes beyond the appreciation of nature? If so, to what extent is nature the source of that insight?

(c) What is the relation between the poet's mood and the landscape?

(d) Compare the ways in which Klein in poem 6 (p. 8) and Thomas in poem 1 (p. 1) recollect their childhoods. Do you detect any similarities in style?

12. THE SHEPHERD TO HIS LOVE

See the note on pastoral poetry (p. 501).

l. 2 prove Experience; try. **l. 8 madrigal** An intricate part-song popular with the Elizabethans; here, any pastoral music. **l. 11 kirtle** Skirt **l. 21 meat** Food in general. **l. 25 swains** Rustic lovers.

13. THE NYMPH'S REPLY

See the note on pastoral poetry (p. 501).

l. 7 Philomel A poetic name for the nightingale. In the Greek myth, Philomela was assaulted by her brother-in-law, Tereus, who cut out her tongue so that she could not reveal his crime. The gods, pitying her, transformed her into a nightingale.

Questions: Poems 11, 12, 13, and 14

(a) How does each poet characterize pastoral life? Which poets distinguish between the ideal and reality; what is the basis for the choice they make between the two?

(b) Where does William Carlos Williams echo the sixteenth-century poets, and where does he show his poetry to be contemporary?

15. THE VILLAGE MASTER

The Deserted Village, from which these lines are taken, is a long poem published in 1770, recalling regretfully the charms of a village fallen into decay as a result of the Enclosure Movement. **l. 14 fault** In Goldsmith's day the 'l' in the word was not pronounced. **l. 16 cypher** Do arithmetic. **l. 17 terms** Legal agreements; or, divisions of the year in lawcourts and universities. **tides** Church festivals or sea tides. **l. 18 gauge** Measure exactly, particularly the capacity of a barrel.

16. ODE TO THE WEST WIND

See the notes on the ode (p. 500), apostrophe (p. 473), and terza rima (p. 516).

l. 18 Angels Here, in the original Greek sense of 'messengers'. **l. 21 Maenad** A female worshipper in the wild rituals of Dionysus, the Greek god of wine and sensual ecstasy. **l. 31 coil** A gently curling motion; a softly plashing sound. **l. 32 pumice** Hardened lava. **Baiae** A Roman port in Central Italy. **ll. 33-34** The Mediterranean Sea dreams of the Roman towers which it once mirrored at Baiae, whose ruins it now partially covers. **l. 57 lyre** The instrument which accompanied song or recitation in Greece; also, the wind-harp, a stringed instrument which made music when set in the wind. It became a favourite Romantic symbol for poetic inspiration. **l. 63** Shelley's passionate arguments for social and religious liberty had been denounced or ignored in England.

Questions: Poems 15, 16, and 17

(a) What is the occasion of the melancholy tone in each poem? Is that tone the only one? If not, what other tones are present?

(b) What specific event makes Emily Brontë and Shelley realize that autumn has come? What does autumn mean to each?

18. I HEAR AN ARMY CHARGING UPON THE LAND

Although Joyce's novels were among the most revolutionary of the century (see poem 19), his poetry was relatively conventional. This poem develops its note of despair entirely by means of powerfully evocative imagery. It is interesting to compare the poem with Shelley's vision of the charioteers in *Prometheus Unbound,* Act II, Scene iv, ll. 129-139.

19. THE HITHERANDTHITHERING WATERS OF

See the notes on archetype (p. 474), and portmanteau word (p. 503).

Finnegan's Wake, the long novel on which Joyce spent seventeen years, is ostensibly the recreation of a single night's dream. The dreamer is H. C. Earwicker (Eire-wicker, or dweller in Ireland), keeper of a public-house or tavern in Dublin; his dreams revolve around his family – his wife Anna, his two sons Shaun and Shem, and his daughter Iseult – and around minor incidents in his waking life. By developing an intricately punning dream-language of his own, drawn from many languages, and by expanding the major figures in the novel into universal symbols of masculinity and femininity, Joyce contrived to make all time and all space his subject-matter.

This excerpt is taken from a dialogue between two Irish washerwomen who, in the dream, are rinsing out Earwicker's 'dirty linen' in the River Liffey, which runs through Dublin. They stand on opposite banks discussing Earwicker's family; as day flows into night they move gradually down the widening stream, so that it becomes increasingly difficult to communicate from one bank to the other. In an astonishing feat of verbal orchestration, Joyce recreates the drowsiness of the washerwomen as their senses are invaded and overcome by the night-sounds about them, until finally they are metamorphosed into a stone and a tree-trunk. **ll. 1-2 chittering . . . bawk talk** A reference to the thin sounds and sudden reverses of direction of the bats and mice which are particularly active at twilight. 'Bawkie' is an old word for a bat. **ll. 4-5 my foos won't moos** An early draft of this line read, 'My feet won't move.' Joyce changed 'move' to 'moos' in order to draw on the German word 'Moos', meaning 'moss'; the suggestion is that the woman's feet have become mossy, as though she were a stone or a tree. The change from 'feet' to 'foos' deepens the effect of dream-like chant, in which all things flow into one another and seem to sleep. **ll. 5-6 elm . . . Shaun or Shem** Shaun (Sean; in English, 'John') is the blond, heroic son of Anna and Earwicker, and the builder of social order. Shem (a Hebrew name, given, for example, to Noah's eldest son) is dark, introverted, and brooding. In his dream, Earwicker frequently thinks of Shaun as a tree (an elm) and Shem as a stone. As the washerwomen discuss the two sons, they find their own feet taking root and their bodies growing heavy. **l. 6 Livia** The dreamer identifies his wife Anna with the Liffey, casting the name of the river in a form suitable to a Roman matron. Earwicker's full name for his wife is Anna Livia Plurabelle. **daughtersons** In this dream-world masculine and feminine characteristics are frequently transferred from one sex to the other.

Question: Poems 18 and 19

'I Hear an Army Charging Upon the Land' was written in Joyce's youth, while *Finnegan's Wake* was his last published work. Discuss some of the changes which the contrasting selections suggest in his approach to artistic communication.

20. LITTLE GREEN TREE

The mood and form are derived from those of the blues. In the six-line stanza of the traditional blues, lines 1 and 2 are repeated as lines 3 and 4.

I woke up this mornin'
With the blues all round my bed.

Yes, I woke up this mornin'
With the blues all round my bed.
Went to eat my breakfast,
Had the blues all in my bread.
Good Mornin' Blues

21. LINES FROM THE GARDEN OF PROSERPINE

Proserpine The beautiful daughter of Jupiter and Ceres (in Greek mythology Persephone, daughter of Zeus and Demeter). While walking in her garden, Proserpine was carried off by Pluto (Hades in Greek mythology) to be made queen of the Underworld. Her mother persuaded Jupiter to ordain that she return to earth twice a year. With each sojourn on earth she brought prosperous harvests to men.

The myth symbolizes the cycle of planting and harvest. The burial of Proserpine is the planting of the seed in the ground in spring or autumn; her absence from earth corresponds to the period of barrenness during the heat of summer or the cold of winter; her return to her mother Ceres is the reappearance of the crops and flowers.

Swinburne uses the myth as a vehicle for his conviction that growth and vitality are irrevocably consumed in death. His fatalism finds comfort in the fact that life's burdens also end in peaceful oblivion.

Notice how the balance and cadence of phrases suggest that Swinburne's statements are beyond doubt. The patterning of vowels and consonants, the rhyme scheme, and the placing of masculine and feminine line-endings make this stanza form a remarkably appropriate medium. See the note on rhyme (p. 513).

22. GIORNO DEI MORTI

Italian, 'The day of the dead'.

l. 1 cypresses Evergreen trees, usually symmetrical in form and frequently associated with death and mourning. l. 2 **surplices** Short outer garments of white linen worn by clergy and choristers in certain forms of divine service.

How do the repetitions and the pattern of line endings contribute to the description of the funeral procession?

Questions: Poems 20, 21, and 22

(a) How does the rhythm affect the mood of 'Little Green Tree' and 'Lines from *The Garden of Proserpine*'?

(b) How do the references to trees relate to the idea of death in 'Little Green Tree', 'Lines from *The Garden of Proserpine*', and 'Giorno Dei Morti'?

(c) Which do you find more effective, a direct statement of despair, or the suggestion of despair by imagery? Give reasons for your choice.

23. SELF PORTRAIT

Mr Lear's nonsense amuses both children and adults, but also discloses more of his nature than its light tone suggests. l. 20 **runcible** A nonsense word, possibly derived from *runcinate* – saw-toothed, and *rundle* – round. Lear also used the word in 'The Owl and the Pussy Cat' in the line 'They ate with a runcible spoon.' A three-pronged pickle fork has been named after it.

24. RICHARD CORY

As in the preceding poem, the character of the man cannot be deduced from external impressions alone; it is implied in the accumulation of detail.

25. A PEASANT

l. 1 **Prytherch** Pronounce *y* as *u* in but; *th* as in then; *ch* as in the Scottish word loch. l. 3 **gap of cloud** The tops of the Welsh hills are frequently enveloped in mist. l. 7 **clods that glint** The turned edge of the furrow is polished by the ploughshare.

Why does Thomas change the level of diction part way through the poem?

Questions: Poems 23, 24, and 25

(a) Why does the poet want his readers to think about the individual he presents?

(b) What tone is conveyed by each author's presentation of his subject?

26. THE AVERAGE

See the note on the sonnet (p. 511).

A poem from a series called *The Quest,* in which men seek to come to terms with various enigmas of life. Each poem deals with a different trail leading to failure; here, the average man is shown undertaking too ambitious a career.

Many of Auden's subtly ironic poems contrast illusion and truth. What forces the boy in this poem to recognize the truth?

27. THE UNKNOWN CITIZEN

This is a poet's ironic presentation of the lifeless conformity of the average citizen in a mass industrial society. Is Auden suggesting that we can or should return to the 'good old days'? **l. 9 scab** A worker who refuses to accept the policy of a union, usually when a strike has been called.

28. DEPARTMENTAL

See the note on the fable (p. 482).

l. 22 Formic Literally, pertaining to ants; from the Latin *formica,* meaning ant. **l. 25 Janizary** Historically, a member of the Turkish Sultan's military bodyguard. **l. 31 ichor** In classical mythology, the ethereal fluid that flowed in the veins of gods.

29. THE NEWSPAPER

See the notes on the mock epic (p. 481), satire (p. 511), and the heroic couplet (p. 478).

These excerpts are from Crabbe's long poem of the same name. They describe the London newspapers of the eighteenth century. **l. 1 I sing of News** An epic device. Vergil's *Aeneid* begins 'I sing of arms and the man who, exiled by fate from the shores of Troy, first came to Italy . . . ' **ll. 5-12** References to the names of a multitude of morning and evening newspapers. **l. 6** Crabbe employs the pun as one of his satirical devices. **l. 22** Praised on the day when they appear, and with a life-span of a single day. **l. 38 promiscuous** Used here to mean without a fixed place at table; or, undiscriminating in choice of food. **l. 53 runners** Men who gathered information for a newspaper. **l. 61 fair Tweed-side** The River Tweed marks, along part of its course, the border between England and Scotland. Scots law, up to 1856, allowed a declaration before witnesses to constitute a legal marriage without requiring any previous residence in Scotland; in order to avoid the restrictions imposed by English law it was necessary only to cross the border. **l. 80 Tyburn** A place of public execution in London up to 1783.

Questions: Poems 26, 27, 28, and 29

(a) What is being said about society in these poems? Is the poet amused or angry in each case?
(b) Which poets have a solution for the problems they raise?
(c) Do you think there is any place for the poet who points out faults without being able to correct them?

30. AN OLD WOMAN'S LAMENTATIONS

Translated very freely from *Le Grand Testament* by François Villon, the name adopted by the French poet Montcorbier (1431-c.1484). His sardonic, ribald, but very moving lyrics were championed by many writers in the first decades of the present century.

31. THE LOVE SONG OF J. ALFRED PRUFROCK

See the note on dramatic monologue (p. 479), juxtaposition (p. 492), allusion (p. 471), and irony (p. 490).

The title is calculated to convey the dissonance and wry flavour which permeate the poem. 'J. Alfred Prufrock' is a grotesquely unsuitable name for a singer of love songs; and it is not until we have read almost a hundred lines that we find reason to call the poem a love song at all.

The speaker, Prufrock, invites a companion to accompany him on a journey through run-down city streets. They are at once impelled to consider an 'overwhelming question'; but Prufrock refuses to take the question up, suggesting instead that his companion and he continue on their way to visit a lady friend. They soon arrive, and the remainder of the poem is occupied with images of the banal and futile existence in the home of Prufrock's friend; and with the doubts, hesitations, and self-recriminations of Prufrock himself, who is paralyzed before the momentous question which he cannot even articulate. The total impression of desperation and spiritual fatigue can be sensed directly in Prufrock, and indirectly in his society, which has produced only slums for the lonely men in shirtsleeves and sterile sophistication for the well-to-do. The poem is filled with references to inconsequential activities, such as taking tea or marmalade, or engaging in banal conversation: measuring out one's life with coffee spoons.

The key to reading this poem lies in recognizing its tone. Prufrock has the awareness and sensitivity to see through pretences, whether other people's or his own; but he has not the resolution necessary to shake off his apathy. Hence he speaks in a tone of self-deprecating irony. It is that element which provokes the deliberately childish rhythms and the mocking rhymes:

Oh, do not ask, 'What is it?'
Let us go and make our visit.

Every effort of Prufrock to compare himself with great figures of the past is defeated by the same self-irony. Is he like John the Baptist, martyred by a cruel woman? At once he has the humiliating thought: how would *his* head, with its little bald spot, look on a platter? No, he has nothing of the prophet in him.

The epigraph in Italian is from Dante's *Inferno,* XXVII, 61-66. These are the words of a damned soul who addressed Dante during his descent into Hell. 'If I believed my answer were being made to one who could ever return to the world, this flame would shake [i.e., this soul would speak] no more; but since, if what I hear is true, never from this abyss did living man return, I answer thee without fear of infamy.' The epigraph suggests that the poet considers himself and his readers to be living in a hell on earth. **ll. 2-3** This audacious conceit, perhaps the most famous in modern poetry, not only provides a setting, but establishes the clinical, unromantic atmosphere of a poem which dissects a diseased society. **l. 10 an overwhelming question** Prufrock's obsession with this question, which he cannot bring himself to ask, returns in lines 30, 45, 80, and 93. It becomes increasingly ominous throughout the poem, but we never learn what the question is. **ll. 13-14 Michelangelo** The Florentine artist Michelangelo Buonarroti (1475-1564), noted for the massive virility of his work. This juxtaposed couplet, with its inane ryhme, suggests vividly the debasing of great art to the status of a conversation piece for dilettantes. Life in the home of Prufrock's friend is characterized by such conversations. **ll. 15-22** What is the sustained metaphor in these lines? **ll. 23-34 there will be time, works and days** Phrases taken from *Works and Days,* a didactic poem by Hesiod, a Greek poet thought to have lived about the end of the eighth century B.C. It describes a depressed peasantry and a decadent aristocracy and gives advice on such matters as worthy and unworthy effort, choosing a wife, and lucky or unlucky days. What are the functions of this allusion? **l. 51** What fact about his life is Prufrock summing up so effectively? **l. 52 a dying fall** An allusion to the opening lines of *Twelfth Night.* **ll. 70-74** At the beginning of his only attempt to speak out directly, Prufrock trails off into silence (l. 72). He recognizes his ignoble lack of purpose, seeing himself as a crab scuttling away at every fright. **l. 92** A reworded allusion to the love poem 'To His Coy Mistress', ll. 41-42 (p. 243). All time and space would be condensed into one small sphere if the question were asked. **ll. 94-95 Lazarus** Apparently a blending of two Biblical allusions. One is to John 11: 1-44, where the brother of Martha and Mary, raised by Christ from the dead, returns to the grim world which he had left for a time. In the other, Luke 16: 19-31, a beggar is not allowed to return from the land of the dead to warn the rich about damnation. **ll. 96-98** What is the final fear that paralyzes Prufrock? **ll. 111-119** Prufrock wonders idly if he might be compared to Hamlet, who was also tortured by indecision and spiritual malaise, but he rejects the idea, and speaks of himself in terms that suggest Polonius. **l. 117 Full of high sentence** In Chaucer's description of the Clerk of Oxenford in the *Canterbury Tales*, this phrase is used in commendation. Here Eliot uses it to suggest pompous bombast. **l. 121** The fashion of having cuffs on trousers was new. Prufrock would like to be stylish.

Who might Prufrock's companion be? It is impossible to know precisely what 'overwhelming' question Prufrock has tried to ask and failed. Can you suggest some of the elements it might include?

32. A KISS

See the note on the triolet (p. 516).

33. SONNET XVIII: SHALL I COMPARE THEE TO A SUMMER'S DAY?

While Shakespeare's sonnets were probably written between 1592 and 1601, it is impossible to establish the precise date of each as they were published only in a pirated and slipshod edition in 1609. Scholars have not identified with certainty the young man whose friendship the poet treasures, or the woman with whom he is infatuated. In any case the sonnets are valued, not primarily for their biographical information, but for the cumulative power of their emotional statement and imagery. **l. 8 untrimm'd** Divested of ornament. **l. 10 ow'st** Ownest. **l. 12 to time thou grow'st** You acquire the same duration of life as time itself.

34. SONNET: BRIGHT STAR!

l. 4 Eremite Hermit. **ll. 13-14** In an earlier draft these lines read:

To hear, to feel her tender-taken breath,
Half passionless, and so swoon on to death.

36. THE ILL-TEMPERED LOVER

The thirteenth poem in the sequence of the same name. **l. 4 Sebastian** A Christian martyr, killed by Roman archers. The death of St. Sebastian is the subject of many well-known paintings.

37. THOMAS THE RHYMER

See the note on the ballad (p. 474).

Thomas the Rhymer was Thomas of Erceldoune, famous in the thirteenth century for his prophecies, which are reputed to have included predictions of the Battle of Bannockburn and the accession of James VI of Scotland to the English throne. This ballad recounts how he acquired the gift of prophecy. **l. 1 True Thomas** See lines 67-68. **l. 17 Harp and carp** Play and recite (as a minstrel). **l. 24 the Eildon Tree** The Eildon Hills in Roxburghshire, Scotland, associated with the legends of Thomas of Erceldoune. **l. 72 tryst** A private meeting at an appointed time and place.

Question: Poems 30, 31, 32, 33, 34, 35, 36, and 37
What relation between love and the passage of time is represented in each poem?

Question: Poems 33, 34, and 35
These are love sonnets from three different centuries. Show how from period to period the form has been treated more freely.

38. THE SONG OF THE MAD PRINCE

The questions heard and repeated by the mad prince bear on his tormenting obsession with the dead lady. Poems representing madness (such as Nos. 38 and 39) reveal the soul without its protection of reason. Why has the prince become mad? Is his madness of any use to him?

39. TOM O' BEDLAM'S SONG

These two stanzas are taken from a much longer poem which occurs in a number of versions of varying lengths.

Tom O' Bedlams were wandering beggars, who were either mad or pretended to be so. The name Bedlam comes from the Hospital of Saint Mary of Bethlehem, an asylum for the insane in London, which was miserably overcrowded in the sixteenth and seventeenth centuries, and discharged many more or less harmless patients to beg in the streets. Snatches of their street cries are woven into the refrain of this song. **l. 4 Moons** The moon was often associated with madness; hence the word lunatic from the Latin *luna,* meaning 'moon'. **ll. 13-15** The irrational arithmetic reflects his tortured mind. **l. 14 enragéd** Mad. **ll. 16-20** Disturbed or ironic references to the wards and cages of Bedlam, and to the barbarous treatment of the insane which was usual at the time.

Questions: Poems 38 and 39

(a) How is the idea of madness conveyed in 'The Song of the Mad Prince' and 'Tom O' Bedlam's Song'?

(b) The subject of each poem is involved with a world of fantasy, madness, or the supernatural. What relation does his mad vision in this realm bear to his earlier life?

40. SONG FOR SAINT CECILIA'S DAY, 1687

See the notes on imitative rhythm and imitative harmony (p. 515).

Saint Cecilia was a Christian martyr who has traditionally been associated with music. When the Academy of Music was founded at Rome in 1584, she was made the patron saint of church music. The poem was written as the libretto for a musical performance. **ll. 1-15** Dryden has united the account of creation in Genesis with the Platonic conception of an eternal Order underlying finite existence, and revealing its nature most fully in the harmonies of music and mathematics. **l. 8 Then cold . . . dry** A reference from medieval natural philosophy to the four elements: earth, fire, water, and air. **l. 15 diapason . . . Man** A swelling burst of harmony, here achieving its climax in the creation of man. **l. 17 Jubal** 'The father of all such as handle the harp and organ' (Genesis 4: 21). **l. 48 Orpheus** A legendary Greek bard who, by the power of his music, could charm animals and trees into following him. **l. 56 spheres** According to a doctrine accepted by Plato, the earth stood at the centre of nine transparent spheres, one inside another, which carried the planets and stars. As the spheres revolved they produced harmonies in which the eternal Order was more fully revealed than on earth. Only those qualified by understanding and proper living could hear the music of the revolving spheres. **ll. 61-63** Cf. I Corinthians 15: 52.

41. SONNET: IT IS NOT TO BE THOUGHT OF THAT THE FLOOD

Wordsworth had been greatly stirred by the spirit of liberty which inspired the French Revolution, although he regretted its excesses. In this sonnet he emulates Milton, making himself the voice for his country's conscience. **l. 4** The quotation is from Book II, Stanza 7, of Daniel's *Civil Wars* (1604). **ll. 5-6** Wordsworth may have in mind the Civil Wars of 1642-49, the struggle for political liberty which ended with the execution of Charles I.

Question: Poems 40 and 41

Aldous Huxley once said: 'Beauty is imprisoned, as it were, within the white spaces between the lines of a poem. . . .' Explain in what ways this may be true of 'Song for Saint Cecilia's Day, 1687' and Wordsworth's sonnet on freedom.

42. ANTHEM FOR DOOMED YOUTH

This sonnet is modelled on the choral anthem of the liturgy.

The first line of both octave and sestet would be sung by one part of the choir, the responses by the other part. The imagery of the poem is also liturgical. The octave presents the horrors of war through concrete details, envisaged in terms of the funeral service which the combatants are denied. **l. 1 passing-bells** The knell or death bell. **l. 4 orisons** Prayers. **l. 9** The candles are lit for prayers for the dead.

43. STRANGE MEETING

See the note on consonance and near-rhyme (p. 514).

This visionary meeting takes place, not in the hell which sinners enter after death, as in Dante's *Inferno*, but in a hell created by war and imposed on innocent living men. The poet's warning is here urgent and explicit. **l. 3 Titanic wars** Wars waged by the Titans, mythical giants imprisoned underground by Jupiter. **groined** A groined roof consists of a number of intersecting vaulted arches which can give the impression of being scooped out of the stone. With what other meanings does Owen invest the word here? **l. 5 fast** Bound, fixed. **l. 38 cess** This word achieves its force in the poem by evoking a number of connotations. Among them are: cess-pool, swamp or bog, and luck as in the phrase, 'Bad cess to you!'

44. THE TRUTH

The reference is to the fire raids during the blitz on London in 1940. How does this poem differ from a dramatic monologue?

45. WAR ON THE PERIPHERY

This deceptively simple poem reflects with irony on the tensions of civilian life in the years following the Second World War.

Question: Poems 42, 43, 44, and 45

Compare the treatment of the theme of war in Owen, Jarrell, and Johnston.

46. DUSK ON ENGLISH BAY

The poem gains its impact not only from the individual sensuous images, but from the fact that each image in the second half of the poem refers back and adds significance to its parallel in the first half, and it becomes apparent that the whole is a carefully designed unit. **English Bay** A residential area in Vancouver, British Columbia, with a popular bathing beach. **l. 11 long tamed whale of Point Grey** In the dusk, from the poet's vantage point the slightly elevated promontory, Point Grey, which lies some miles west along the shore, resembles a stationary whale. **ll. 13-14 a row of moons along the promenade** A boardwalk runs west along the beach. **l. 16 copper sulphate** Copper sulphate takes the form of blue crystals which lose water upon being heated, leaving a whitish residue. **l. 18 Gulf of Georgia** The Strait of Georgia lies between Vancouver and Vancouver Island. **ll. 20-21 tomorrow's sun is clean escaped and rushes down** Probably a reference to the legend in which Phaeton, having gained permission to drive the chariot of the sun across the sky, lost control, approaching so close to the earth that he scorched it. Zeus, to save the earth, struck Phaeton with a thunderbolt. **l. 23 Libyan sands** The Libyan desert in North Africa was, between 1940 and 1942, one of the main theatres of action in the Second World War. **l. 25 Narvik** A port on one of the fiords of northern Norway, and the scene of a number of actions in 1940-41. **l. 33 Joshua** See Joshua 10: 12-13. God stopped the sun for a day to aid Joshua and the Children of Israel in battle.

47. I THINK CONTINUALLY

This poem develops through the use of symbols. **l. 3 suns** Source of light and life. **l. 5 touched with fire** As inspired prophets. **l. 10 springs** Waters of life. Compare Moses' rod which brought water from the rock in the wilderness.

Questions: Poems 46 and 47

(a) Contrast Birney's and Spender's handling of imagery.

(b) To what extent has each writer achieved an organic unity for his poem?

48. SONNET XXX: WHEN TO THE SESSIONS OF SWEET SILENT THOUGHT

See the note on poem 33 (p. 367).

l. 1 sessions This introduces a sustained metaphor drawn from courtroom procedure. **l. 7 cancell'd** Paid, as a debt. Note the continuing imagery of business and finance. **l. 9 grievances** Troubles, griefs; legal complaints. **foregone** Long since past. **l. 10 tell** Count; recount.

49. SONNET LX: LIKE AS THE WAVES MAKE TOWARDS THE PEBBLED SHORE

See the note on poem 33 (p. 367).

l. 5 main Ocean. The poet's attention swings from the sea to the sky, and he retains the image of the former as a metaphor for the latter. **ll. 5-7** An instance of Shakespeare's 'packed' imagery. These lines fuse descriptions of the passage from birth to old age, the rise and eclipse of the sun, and a coronation followed by civil war. **l. 10 delves the parallels** Digs furrows, makes lines on the forehead.

50. HERACLITUS

An adaptation of an ancient Greek epigram by Callimachus. **Heraclitus** A native of Caria in Greece, and friend to the poet.

Questions: Poems 48, 49, and 50

(a) How do Shakespeare and Cory keep their tributes to their friends from becoming sentimental?

(b) Is there any similarity in the images these poets have used to suggest the passage of time?

52. WHAT THE DEVIL SAID

This apparently simple poem raises several theological issues.

God's slowness in contracting His attention from the magnificent energy of creation to the suffering woman in a ditch suggests aloofness from human misery; yet there is no doubt about the depth of His concern. Also, God Himself seems to be bound by the inexorable law, 'What is done, is done.' Satan is sudden, vocal, and at hand, and he taunts God's position.

53. ST YVES' POOR

St Yves, a monk, lived in Brittany in the thirteenth century. As a lawyer he was reputed to be a zealous defender of widows and orphans. **Yves** Pronounced 'Eves'. **l. 5 rheumed** With running eyes; here, probably, rheumatic. **l. 27 Michael** St Michael commanded the heavenly army in the war against Satan. The story can be found in Books V and VI of *Paradise Lost*. **ll. 30-45** Cf. Matthew 25: 31-46. **l. 51 rapt** Oblivious to the outer world, consumed in a trance or vision.

54. THE TYGER

This is an early draft of poem 55. The controlling image in the first version is of heating metal in a furnace and forging it into a durable form. Notice the extent to which this image has been retained in the final version. Consider the significance of the alternative in line 4 and suggest the reason for the final wording.

55. THE TYGER

The rich symbolism of the poem is discussed on page 488. **l. 1** See the note on metaphor (p. 486). **ll. 17-18** Probably a reference to the story of the insurrection of Lucifer and his forces, which resulted in their expulsion from heaven and the first presence of evil on earth. Lucifer was the name sometimes given to the morning star. The description of the glinting rays of light and the morning dew becomes part of the symbolism of good and evil which permeates the poem.

56. THEN THE LORD ANSWERED JOB OUT OF THE WHIRLWIND

Job 38: 1-11, 31-35

The Authorized Version of the Bible, published in 1611 at the direction of King James I, was the work of a committee of eminent scholars and theologians. As the most widely read and memorized book in English, it had a penetrating influence on the language of subsequent poetry and prose from Donne and Milton to Edith Sitwell and Dylan Thomas. Rolling, dignified rhythms, parallelism, and pure, natural imagery formed its literary style.

Struck by a series of catastrophes, Job has asked God to show just cause for his suffering. When he rejects the oversimplified view of three friends, who claim that the Lord always rewards the good and punishes the wicked, Job is given an overwhelming experience of the presence of God. This brings, not an explanation for the existence of evil, but confidence in God's power and concern. The author conveys the overwhelming experience of God's presence by the press of unanswered questions which the Lord asks Job. l. 23 **Pleiades** A group of stars named after the seven daughters of Atlas. l. 24 **Orion** One of the most conspicuous constellations in the heavens, identified by the three bright stars which form Orion's belt. l. 25 **Mazzaroth** The signs of the Zodiac. l. 26 **Arcturus** A giant star in the constellation Boötes; the name sometimes given to the Great Bear.

Questions: Poems 51, 52, 53, 54, 55, 56 and 57

(a) Discuss the presentation of evil in 'Eight O'Clock', 'What the Devil Said', and 'The Tyger'.

(b) In 'What the Devil Said' and 'St Yves' Poor', how does the physical point of view adopted affect the portrayal of suffering? How does it indicate the philosophy of the poem?

(c) What is the effect of the unanswered questions in 'St Yves' Poor', 'The Tyger', and 'Then the Lord Answered Job Out of the Whirlwind'?

(d) What attitude on the part of the Almighty to his creations is shown in 'St Yves' Poor', 'Then the Lord Answered Job Out of the Whirlwind', and 'Apparently with No Surprise'?

59. WITHIN MY GARDEN RIDES A BIRD

See the notes on consonance and near-rhyme (p. 514).

The following poem, 'A Route of Evanescence', evolved from this poem by a process of revision. **ll. 13-16** An extreme ellipsis. The poetess and her dog wonder whether they actually saw the bird, or whether it was merely an apparition in 'the garden in the brain'.

60. A ROUTE OF EVANESCENCE

A revision of poem 59. What elements have been retained from the earlier poem? In this version, the bird whirs so quickly through the garden that the poet has time to record only her immediate visual impressions of its flight. Notice the effect of the more relaxed, whimsical tone of the last couplet. **l. 4 cochineal** A scarlet dye.

Questions: Poems 57, 58, 59, 60, and 61

(a) What characteristics of Emily Dickinson's style do you find in each of these poems?

(b) Can you find any superfluous details, or words that seem limp or unnecessary?

62. DRINKING

A development of a drinking song by the Greek poet Anacreon, who celebrated the joys of wine and love.

63. A DRUNKEN MAN'S PRAISE OF SOBRIETY

l. 1 punk Slut.

64. A GLASS OF BEER

The fine art of invective is also displayed in poem 36 (p. 57). **l. 3 whey** In the making of cheese, that part of the milk which remains liquid when the rest forms curd. **l. 10 gill** A quarter-pint (in some areas, a half-pint).

Question: Poems 61, 62, 63, 64, and 65
What range of treatment do these poems display?

68. ZIMRI

See the note on irony (p. 490).

In *Absalom and Achitophel* Dryden satirizes the events and great men of his day. Absalom is King Charles II's rebellious son Monmouth; Achitophel represents Lord Shaftesbury; and Zimri, here described, is the Duke of Buckingham, who after 1670 was chief minister under Charles II.

69. THE RAPE OF THE LOCK, CANTO THIRD

See the note on the epic (p. 481).

This is the third of the five cantos of this 'heroi-comical poem' – Pope's own term for it. Pope first wrote the poem in 1711 in the hope of inducing young Lord Petre and Miss Arabella Fermor, the principals in the original incident, to laugh themselves out of the serious estrangement which had followed the situation he recounts. He expanded it to its present form and published it in 1712.

Cantos I and II describe the elaborate care with which the beautiful heroine prepares for her afternoon social engagement in the 'beau-monde', presents the plan of the romantic young baron to secure a lock of the admired tresses, and introduces the 'machinery' of omens and spirits. Cantos IV and V describe the dire effects of the deed, the efforts at revenge, and the happy resolution. The poem is mock-heroic; that is, although it employs the characteristic features of the great epics, the relative triviality of the subject matter and the incongruous application of the grand style result in humorous satire. **l. 1 meads** Meadows. **ll. 3-4 structure . . . name** Hampton Court, a palace on the Thames about fifteen miles above

London. **l. 7 Anna . . . three realms obey** Anne, Queen of England, Scotland, and Ireland, 1702-1714. **l. 8 tea** Rhymes with obey. **l. 17 supply** Fill in. **l. 22** Dinner was commonly at 4 p.m. **l. 23 th' Exchange** The Royal Exchange where the merchants, bankers, and brokers met to do business. **l. 25 Belinda** The heroine. The motto of the poem is Epigram xii, 84, by Martial, a Latin poet of the first century A.D.:

I did not wish, Belinda, to profane thy locks;
But I am glad to have granted this much to thy prayers.

ll. 27 ff. ombre Ombre was a game of cards, Spanish in origin and very popular in Queen Anne's time. The detailed description of the game which follows is both a parody of the great battles described in epics and of the game of chess in *Yacchia Ludus,* a poem by Vida, an Italian poet of the sixteenth century. Belinda plays against two opponents, one of whom is the baron. Pope describes the kings, queens, and jacks of the four suits as they are pictured on the playing cards. **l. 30 sacred nine** Each player holds nine cards. In early heroic poetry nine was considered a mystic number. **l. 31 aërial guard** The sylphs; that is, the spirits assigned to protect Belinda. **l. 33 Ariel** The chief sylph. **Matadore** The three highest cards were called Matadores – from the Spanish word meaning slayer. **l. 41 succinct** Girt up. **l. 42 halberts** Long-handled axe-like weapons. **l. 44 velvet plain** Here, the card table; the counterpart of the field of battle in epic poetry. **l. 46** Belinda, as the challenger, or ombre, had the right to declare the trumps. **l. 47 sable** Heraldic term for the colour black. **ll. 49-64** Belinda took the first four tricks. She led in turn the three matadores: Spadillio, the ace of spades; Manillio, the deuce of spades; Basto, the ace of clubs. Her king of spades then took the baron's Pam – the jack of clubs – which was the highest card in another card game called loo. **l. 52 verdant field** See the note on l. 44. **ll. 65-88** At this point the baron trumped Belinda's king of clubs with his queen of spades, and proceeded to win three more rounds with king, queen, and jack of diamonds. **l. 67 Amazon** In classical literature, the Amazons were female warriors. l. 71 **What boots . . . head** The fact that he is a crowned king is of no help in this situation. l. 74 Even today the orb appears only on the king of clubs. l. 76 Only the king of diamonds is shown in profile. l. 80 **level green** See the note on l. 44. l. 92 **codille** The name for defeat in ombre. l. 94 **nice** Fine, delicate. ll. 95-98 **An Ace of Hearts . . . Ace** Since the king of hearts ranked above the ace, Belinda won the ninth and tie-breaking trick l. 100 **long canals** A feature of the formal gardens of the period, introduced by William III in imitation of the Dutch landscape. l. 106 **the berries crackle, and the mill turns round** The coffee beans are roasted, then ground in a coffee mill. What further implication is there in the phrase? l. 107 **altars of Japan** Trays or tables of Japanese lacquer. l. 113 **airy band** The protecting sylphs. ll. 122-124 **Scylla's fate** Scylla betrayed her father Nisus, King of Megara, into the hands of Minos, King of Crete, by cutting from Nisus' head the lock of hair on which his special powers depended. Minos, despite the favour done him, drowned Scylla, at which time she was transformed into a sea-bird. l. 135 **sprites** Spirits, the protecting sylphs. l. 147 **forfex** A pair of shears. l. 148 What is the effect of the paradox used at the climax? l. 152 Pope's note reads, 'See Milton Book vi (Paradise Lost), of Satan cut asunder by the Angel Michael.' ll. 157-160 Note the use of anti-climax. l. 165 **Atalantis** The *New Atalantis,* 1709, by Mrs Mary Manley, contained very thinly disguised accounts of scandals in the upper circles of society. l. 169 **assignations give** Make arrangements to meet lovers. l. 171 **receives its date** Is brought to an end. l. 173 **the labour of the gods** Troy was supposed to have been built by Apollo and Poseidon.

70. THE WIF OF BATHE from the Prologue to the *Canterbury Tales*

See the note to poem 128 (p. 406).

This portrait from the Prologue is one of Chaucer's lively and good-humoured observations of contemporary life. **Bathe** The town of Bath. l. 4 **Ypres . . . Gaunt** Yypres and Ghent were centres of the thriving Flemish wool trade. **l. 6 offrynge** People went to make their church offering in order of social standing. **l. 15 worthy** Having some social standing; of good reputation. Chaucer uses this word in many ways, sometimes ironically, sometimes seriously. **l. 16 at chirchè dore** The marriage service proper was conducted outside the church; afterwards the mass was celebrated at the altar. **ll. 19-22** Pilgrims visited shrines in Boulogne, Galicia, and Cologne, often with no deeper religious motives than those of many tourists today. The cathedral in Santiago de Compostela, formerly the capital of Galicia, exhibited the relics of St. James. **l. 24 Gat-tothèd** With teeth set wide apart – variously thought to indicate gluttonous or amorous tendencies, or a desire to travel. **l. 25 amblere** An ambling horse, the most comfortable and the easiest to ride. **l. 26 Y-wympled wel** Well-protected with a hood.

Questions: Poems 66, 67, 68, 69, and 70

(a) In most satirical writing, the satirist assumes that there are acceptable mores or social standards by which to judge other men. To what extent in these poems does the poet accept the standards of the majority, speaking as an average man and satirizing an outsider? To what extent is he an outsider mocking a representative of the social norm? (Compare 'Carol' (p. 132) and 'The Hollow Men' (p. 133), where the speaker is himself the object of satire.)

(b) Compare the tones of satire in these poems.

72. SILENCE

Marianne Moore has built up an impression of a highly unusual personality by subtly welding together several apparently disparate ideas. In their context, the simple concrete details take on a new significance and the simple form of the statements adds further comment. **ll. 2-4** What implication is being made? **ll. 5-7** What is the effect of the expanding of the simile?

73. GREAT THINGS

l. 3 Spinning Cycling. **Weymouth** A seaport in Dorset, the county in which Hardy was born.

Questions: Poems 70, 71, 72, and 73
What details in each poem suggest enjoyment of life?

74. SELECTIONS from *Song of Myself*

Song of Myself consists of a series of 52 poems embodying a wide range of sensuous and spiritual experience. By revealing the most personal details, real and imagined, of his life, Whitman intended to become the voice of American man.

[Poem 1] In this manifesto of his aims and assumptions Whitman declares that he has the breadth of vision and the disinterested concern for all things, good and bad alike, necessary to a great poet. The declaration is reinforced by his cumulative rhetoric with its appositional phrases (in lines 7, 8, 9, and 11) and its use of what is known as the nominative absolute (in lines 6 and 10).

[From Poem 6] **l. 11 Kanuck** A French-Canadian. **Tuckahoe** A Virginian. **Cuff** A Negro.

[From Poem 33] Whitman has already declared that he is qualified as a poet, not by his ability to make metaphors, but by his capacity for identifying with all humanity. Here, in the white heat of imagination, he takes upon himself the sufferings of the martyred slave and fireman. **l. 18 inspired** Inhaled.

[Poem 52] The last poem in the series. Whitman evaluates himself and his poetry, convinced that both will continue to exist. **l. 8 jags** Shreds.

75. SONNET: WHEN I HAVE FEARS

Written in 1818, three years before the poet's death. Keats already feared that he would not live long enough to articulate his poetic vision.

76. THE BIRTH OF TRAGEDY

The title is taken from *The Birth of Tragedy out of the Spirit of Music,* a book by the German philosopher Nietzsche, who suggested a theory of the origin of Greek tragedy. The tragic vision of life, he argued, seizes the person whose self-sufficient contemplation of an ideal world is challenged by the delirious experience of irrational powers beyond himself. His resulting awareness of death makes life appear meaningless. Nietzsche declared that pessimism was decadent, that optimism was superficial, and that the spirit of 'tragic joy' was the only adequate response. Layton believes that the poet must be a passionate man with keen and hungry senses, which are temporarily appeased in the self-expression of poetry. He surpasses the man of action by an awareness of the unity in his observations and by his broad understanding of the cycles of life and death. **l. 15 shadows** Cf. 'When I have fears' (p. 115), l. 7. **l. 18 the perfect gods** Probably Apollo and Dionysus, who preside respectively over the rationally ordered and the delirious, chaotic processes of life. **ll. 19-22** Layton asserts that men, especially poets, who strive to become superhuman, commit acts of rebellious passion which the gods forgive. **l. 27 inflammable air** The poet, in his extreme sensitivity to all life, is constantly receiving sensations from the very atmosphere about him. **ll. 32-33** This evocative sentence gives an unexpected turn to the imagery of fire.

77. SONNET LV: NOT MARBLE, NOR THE GILDED MONUMENTS

See the note on poem 33 (p. 367).

Shakespeare's triumphant boast that he will achieve immortality in his verse echoes the Latin poets Ovid and Horace. **l. 4 Than unswept stone** Supply the word 'in' before 'unswept'. **sluttish** Dirty and unkempt. **l. 6 broils** Embroilments, tumults. **l. 7 Mars** The god of war. **l. 13 the judgment that** The day of judgement when; or, the decree on judgement day that.

Questions: Poems 74, 75, 76, 77, and 78

(a) Discuss the concept of the poet's role in each poem.

(b) A poet frequently adopts a 'persona' or poetic personality, which may or may not resemble his everyday character. Discuss the persona presented by each poet.

79. TO A POET A THOUSAND YEARS HENCE

l. 15 Maeonides Homer, so called because he is thought to have been born in Maeonia, a district in Asia Minor later known as Lydia.

80. JESSE JAMES

See the note on the ballad (p. 474).

This is one of several versions of the ballad of Jesse James. The original composer, whose name in one version is given as Billy Gashade, remains unidentified. It is probable that he wished to remain anonymous for fear of reprisal.

Jesse and Frank James and their gang of Missouri outlaws perfected a technique for robbing banks and trains and were able to pillage the countryside successfully for more than ten years. On the several occasions when the James boys were brought to trial, the influence of some of the southern Democrats, who sympathized with attacks on 'northern enterprises', and the presence of armed James supporters in the court, effected the dismissal of the case.

On 3 April 1882, Robert Ford, a member of the gang, shot Jesse, who had been living in the little town of St Joseph under the alias of Howard. By this act Ford had his revenge, earned $10,000 that had been offered him by the governor of Missouri, and was allowed to leave the state. Jesse's brutality was soon dismissed from popular memory, and romanticized accounts of his exploits portray him as a heroic figure. **l. 31 County of Clay** In Missouri.

81. JOHN HENRY

See the note on the ballad (p. 474).

The Chesapeake and Ohio Railroad was laid in West Virginia between 1870 and 1873. Power-operated machinery was being introduced at this time. The Big Bend Tunnel, the longest tunnel on the line, was drilled through the face of a mountain. **l. 7 steam drill** John Henry has been hammering the steel drill by hand. **l. 36 shaker** The man who holds the drill and turns it after each blow.

Question: Poems 79, 80, and 81

It is characteristic of both the lyric and the ballad forms to illuminate certain basic aspects of human nature. To what extent has this been achieved in these poems?

82. THE ICEBERG

The *Titanic*, the largest ship of her day, was considered unsinkable. On April 15, 1912, she collided with an iceberg on her maiden voyage from Southampton to New York. The ship sank and over 1,500 lives were lost. This excerpt from Pratt's long narrative poem *The Titanic* describes the fatal iceberg. While appreciating with ironic precision its form and movement, the poet traces the emergence of a mindless destructiveness from the iceberg's massive beauty. **l. 1 Godhaven** A settlement on the south end of Disco Island, which lies in the Davis Strait between Greenland and Baffin Island. **l. 4 Behring floe** Ice from the Bering Sea between Alaska and the U.S.S.R. **l. 16 the Labrador** The cold current flowing south from the Greenland coast and meeting the warm Gulf Stream off Newfoundland. **l. 23 parallels** Parallels of latitude. **l. 37 plantigrade** An animal, such as a polar bear, which walks on the flat soles of its feet. **l. 41 forty-four** Forty-four minutes. **l. 44 Corundum** A crystalline mineral, almost as hard as a diamond.

83. EROSION

See the note on juxtaposition (p. 492).

l. 4 scarp The steep face of a cliff; an escarpment.

Question: Poems 82 and 83
Is there any ambivalence in Pratt's attitude to nature?

84. IN A STATION OF THE METRO

See the note on modernist juxtaposition (p. 492).
Metro The Paris subway or underground.

85. EPISTLE TO BE LEFT IN THE EARTH

MacLeish contemplates the destruction (possibly symbolic) of the whole of life; no longer guided by the laws of the universe, the earth has drifted out of orbit into the vast reaches of space. One of the last survivors attempts, with desperate urgency, to set down the truth about human life. **l. 1** Cf. l. 45. The earth moves farther and farther from the life-giving sun. **l. 4 the Great Bear** The constellation also known as the Big Dipper or the Plough from which the North Star, valuable in navigation, may be located. **l. 12 Orion** One of the most conspicuous constellations in the heavens, identified by the three bright stars in Orion's Belt. **l. 42 one tree** Either, a tree which men can worship as the home of a nature deity; or, the Cross. **l. 46 Arcturus** A giant star in the constellation Boötes; sometimes, the name given to the Great Bear. **l. 47** What are the possible meanings of this deliberately ambiguous line?

86. DOMINATION OF BLACK

Stevens' poem assumes a dream-like quality of vivid impression and indefinable statement. Colours, shapes, and sounds interweave, accumulating emotional impact as a pattern evolves. The final domination of black is the expression of a deep despairing anxiety. **l. 8 hemlocks** North American evergreens, commonly used as firewood. **l. 10 peacocks** Eastern birds noted for their gorgeously coloured tail plumage, and their startling and incongruously raucous voices. The peacock is traditionally associated with pride and ostentatious display.

87. CAROL

See the note on modernist irony (p. 491).

The traditional carol, 'The Twelve Days of Christmas', may be a starting point for this poem. The simple story, the lovers' emotions, and the speaker's ironic view of her love affair are conveyed entirely by the connotations of concrete images. **l. 15 laily** Hideous – a deliberate archaism.

88. THE HOLLOW MEN

See the notes on modernist poetry (pp. 495-499), and on juxtaposition (p. 492), allusion (p. 471), and irony (p. 490).

Lamenting the loss of ideals and initiative by the civilization which survived the First World War, Eliot expresses complete despair. In juxtaposed images the poem conveys the condition of men who are spiritually dead, unable to understand the significance of their lives, and incapable of finding any meaning in a transcendant revelation.

Influenced by those liturgical forms of public worship in which some parts of the service are spoken by the congregation and other parts by the priest, the poem begins and ends with a chorus of hollow creatures, huddled together in lamentation. The second section of the poem continues with the terrible cry of a single voice, recoiling from this waking nightmare and confessing cowardice and impotence. The third and fourth sections go on to describe the wasteland and river bank which the hollow men inhabit, tormented by religious intimations in which they cannot believe. The poem concludes with a pathetic mixture of nursery rhyme and liturgy, spoken by men in the grip of total spiritual paralysis.

The epigraphs amplify the suggestion of the poem by allusion: – **Mistah Kurtz – he dead** An expression of hopelessness. The phrase is taken from Conrad's novel, *Heart of Darkness*. **A Penny for the Old Guy** In 1605, Guy Fawkes attempted to blow up the House of

Commons in London, but was caught and executed. (See the final stanza.) On November 5 each year, English children make a stuffed dummy to represent Guy Fawkes and burn it on a bonfire to the accompaniment of fireworks. For weeks beforehand, the children ask for a 'penny for the guy', with which they buy fireworks. The expression here reinforces the allusion to stuffed men.

l.14 death's other Kingdom Eliot refers to his conviction that there are two kingdoms of death – one for those who have already died, one for those who are spiritually dead while physically alive. 'Death's other Kingdom' is probably the eternal life after death which awaits those who have led a deep and courageous spiritual life on earth. It is opposed to 'death's dream kingdom' (l. 20) which is presumably the death in life of the hollow men, those who are without faith and without the ability to act. They are tormented by intimations of a truth which might save them, if only they had the courage to face it. **l. 19 Eyes I dare not meet in dreams** The eyes of those who have gained eternal life. They are the 'direct eyes' of line 14, which challenge the pretences of the hollow men. **ll. 22-28** The interpretation of these lines is uncertain. The difficulty is created by the word 'there' in lines 22 and 24; does it refer to the world of the hollow men (l. 20) or to the world of those who have faced death triumphantly (l. 14)? In either case, the vision is tantalizingly oblique and incomplete. **l. 23 column** The column is often an expression of man's spiritual aspiration. **l. 28 star** A symbol of eternal life. The phrase 'fading star' indicates the remoteness of such reality from the hollow men. Compare the later references to the star. **l. 32 Such deliberate disguises** The rat's coat (tailcoat?), crowskin (tall black hat?), and crossed staves make up a scarecrow's clothing, recalling the image of the stuffed men. The crossed staves also suggest the emblem of Christ's crucifixion, implying that, for the hollow men, religious observance is a 'deliberate disguise', an evasion of the truth. **l. 38 twilight kingdom** A third kingdom, probably a place of transition from life to death, where men must finally face reality. The twilight kingdom is probably the valley (of the shadow of death) of lines 54 and 55. **l. 39 the dead land** Death's dream kingdom. **ll. 39-51** The hollow men erect stone images, idols for worship. In their few moments of authentic spiritual activity, they might be able to express real tenderness to one another, but each is isolated and alone. Hence they continue to utter prayers in fear to the stone images, even though the images are now broken. **l. 54 this valley** The valley of the shadow of death. See Psalm 23. **l. 60 tumid** Swollen; here the impression is one of foulness. The river is often pictured as separating life from death, as the Styx and the Jordan. **l. 61 Sightless** Without vision of truth or of what lies beyond death. **l. 63 perpetual star** Cf. the fading star of line 28 and the dying star of line 54. **l. 64 Multifoliate** Here, many-petalled. **rose** A traditional symbol; here, for the transcendent realities of religion. **ll. 68-98** These lines portray the struggle in the hollow men between religious affirmation and a deliberately mindless despair. **l. 68 Here we go round . . .** This parody of a nursery rhyme, juxtaposed with the fragment of the Lord's Prayer, suggests the utter desperation of men without beliefs. See the discussion of these lines under modernist juxtaposition (p. 493) and allusion (p. 472). **l. 76 the Shadow** The shadow of death. The fear of purposelessness in life and oblivion in death paralyses every response of the hollow men. **l. 98** Even in their last hour the hollow men achieve, not tragic dignity, but pathetic weakness.

89. THE INFERNO, CANTO THIRD

See the notes on the epic (p. 481), terza rima (p. 516), and allegory (p. 489).

The Divine Comedy, written in three parts entitled *The Inferno* (Hell), *Purgatory,* and *Paradise,* is a visionary representation of a spiritual crisis in Dante's own life. He is conducted through Hell and Purgatory by the poet Vergil, the representative of unaided human reason; in Paradise he meets and is guided by Beatrice, a young woman, now dead, whom he had adored and idealized in his youth. She is an emissary of Divine Love.

The Inferno envisages Hell as a great vortex of graduated circles where each sinner is punished according to his crime. Cantos I and II describe Dante's meeting with Vergil and Vergil's explanation of the journey which Dante is to take and its ultimate joyous outcome. At the beginning of Canto III the two poets pass through the Gate of Hell.

Although Ciardi has not found it expedient to follow Dante's terza rima exactly, the suitability of the general form for Dante's purpose is quite apparent. **l. 1 City of Woe** Hell is often described as a city. **ll. 4-6** God's attributes are inscribed above the gates. **l. 7 Only those elements . . . wear** The angels, the heavens, and matter in its elemental form. **l. 9 Abandon . . . here** The warning is for the souls of the damned, not for Dante and Vergil. **l. 11 Master** Vergil, Dante's guide. **l. 18** These souls have not lost their intelligence and understanding, but failed to benefit from them by apprehending God and the truth. **ll. 32-48** The two poets are passing through a limbo occupied by those souls who never acted positively for good or evil. Cf. Revelation 3: 15-16. **ll. 56-57 that soul . . . Denial** Probably Celestine V, who became Pope in 1294 at the age of eighty, but resigned after five months, convinced that his soul was endangered by the worldly preoccupations of the papacy. He was succeeded by Boniface VIII, whom Dante considered to be a symbol of the corruption of the church. Dante's fearlessness can be appreciated from his practice of describing great men of his time, whom he frequently mentioned by name, as damned souls. **l. 68 a wide river** The Acheron, one of the four rivers separating the land of the living from Hell. **l. 80 old man** Charon, the ferryman who, in classical mythology, transported shades of the dead across the Acheron. **ll. 85-90** Charon recognizes that Dante is a living man and cannot enter the land of the dead. Cf. ll. 124-126. **ll. 122-123** These souls have been condemned by divine justice, which they accept to such an extent that they long for punishment. **ll. 133-134** Dante's swoon shows him susceptible to the grief of Hell. As the poem progresses, it reveals also his strong indignation against evil, especially in the politics and the church of his day, and his proud, visionary zeal for a spiritual reawakening to the divine order governing the universe as he understood it.

Questions: Poems 84, 85, 86, 87, 88, and 89

(a) In poems 85, 86, and 88 how does the individual react when faced with the inhumanity of the universe?

(b) Does a poet have the right to give a pessimistic view of human society or human life?

(c) What technique do poems 84, 85, 87, and 88 have in common? Discuss its effectiveness.

(d) Many poems, plays, or novels have a hero who possesses such characteristics as courage, dignity, or self-respect. What characteristics do you find in the 'anti-heroes' of 'Carol' and 'The Hollow Men'?

(e) Compare 'The Hollow Men' and Canto III of *The Inferno* with respect to (i) the affliction of the people amongst whom the speaker in each poem finds himself, (ii) the position of the speaker in each poem in relation to his environment.

90. ULYSSES

This poem has many features of the dramatic monologue (see p. 479).

The speaker is the Greek hero of *The Odyssey*. He has returned to his kingdom of Ithaca and his faithful wife Penelope after ten years of fighting in the Trojan War and ten further years of adventurous wandering. Now in old age, he has been ruling his kingdom for three years. **l. 10 Hyades** A V-shaped cluster of stars which were supposed to indicate rainy weather when they rose with the sun. **ll. 19-21** A sustained metaphor which crystallizes the philosophy of Ulysses. **l. 23 unburnish'd** A reference to his sword, which is dull-coloured from disuse. The image is used to represent Ulysses' inaction. **l. 53 men that strove with Gods** The gods had taken sides and joined in actual combat during the Trojan War. **l. 63 the**

Happy Isles According to ancient belief, a land where warriors who had died honourably and received proper burial rites assumed the form they had in the prime of life. **l. 64 Achilles** The greatest Greek fighter in the Trojan War, killed by an arrow which struck him in the heel. After his death, his armour was awarded to Ulysses.

91. THE DEATH OF THE HIRED MAN

A dramatic idyll set in New England, the poem presents the elemental conflict of love and logic in human relationships. The conversational blank verse, which combines successfully the vernacular and the language of literature, moves simultaneously on two levels. The worlds of both actuality and spiritual values are presented in lines rich in observation and implication. The cleverly contrived combinations of sounds, the varying rhythms of the lines, and the symbols woven into the fabric of both narrative and lyrical passages, allow the reader to experience the poem, as Frost himself says, 'as remembering something I didn't know I knew'. **ll. 83-84** A reference to the practice of water-divining. A forked hazel wand held by a diviner would dip towards the ground indicating the presence of water. **ll. 103-110 and 161-165** The lyrical passages add a softer texture and may be related symbolically to the narrative development.

92. STOPPING BY WOODS ON A SNOWY EVENING

See the detailed discussion by John Ciardi (pp. 323-333).

Questions: Poems 90, 91, and 92

(a) Contrast the attitudes and ways of life of Ulysses and Silas.
(b) Compare the style of Tennyson and Frost in 'Ulysses' and 'The Death of the Hired Man'.
(c) What theme do 'Ulysses' and 'Stopping by Woods on a Snowy Evening' have in common?
(d) Point out examples of Frost's warm, whimsical presentation of nature in 'The Death of the Hired Man' and 'Stopping by Woods on a Snowy Evening'.

93. SNOW

An attempt to understand with the senses and feelings a fundamental truth about our experience of the world. The element of surprise is used effectively, both in diction and in choice of detail. **l. 3 collateral** Situated side by side.

95. LOW TIDE ON GRAND PRE

The village of Grand Pré (Great Meadow) on the Minas Basin in Nova Scotia is one of the oldest French settlements in that province; Longfellow made it the home of his heroine in *Evangeline*. The village gave its name to the surrounding lowlands.

Would the poem be equally effective if it were shorter? If so, how could it be shortened?

96. TINTERN ABBEY

Wordsworth composed this poem and held it in his mind while enjoying a four-day ramble through the Wye Valley with his sister Dorothy. On reaching Bristol, he wrote it down exactly as it stands. One of Wordsworth's recurrent themes was the growth of the individual spirit under the influence of Nature. Natural scenes often aroused in him a visionary power, and he recorded such scenes, not simply for themselves, but because of the effects they had induced in him. **l. 21 some Hermit's cave** The hermit in eighteenth and early nineteenth century literature conventionally suggested solitude in a natural setting. **ll. 28-29 blood . . . heart . . . mind** For Wordsworth, images of natural beauty affect the feelings and emotions more immediately than they do the intellect. But they are impressed into the depth of the poet's being, to the extent that later recollection restores him, as did the experience itself, in times of despair over the degradation of the world that men create. **l. 49** In stillness of body, while the poet contemplates his deep memories of natural beauty, he attains a mystical insight into the spirit which animates the natural world. **ll. 65-111** Wordsworth distinguishes three stages in his relationship with nature. In boyhood (ll. 73-74), he had shown an unreflecting delight in outdoor physical activity. As a young man (ll. 65-72, 75-83), he had turned from the city to the natural landscape, with a hungry longing for something as yet dimly apprehended. At the time of writing this poem (ll. 83-111), maturity has brought a deeper, more satisfying communion. **l. 74 animal movements** Instinctive, unreflecting physical activity. **ll. 106-7** For Wordsworth, half our experience of the world is derived from external nature and half from the senses and imagination, which shape and animate what they perceive.

97. IN EXILE

See the note on the haiku (p. 483).

98. HURRAHING IN HARVEST

See the note on sprung rhythm (p. 510).

'The *Hurrahing* sonnet was the outcome of half an hour of extreme enthusiasm as I walked home alone one day from fishing in the Elwy', wrote Hopkins in a letter of 1878. Some of his most joyous poems were composed in 1877, the year of his ordination as a Jesuit. **l. 4 Meal-drift** The drifting clouds are compared to grain ground into meal. The image continues the parallel between field and sky. **l. 5** An allusion to Psalm 121. **l. 6 glean our Saviour** Search for and gather some indication of the presence of Christ. **ll. 7-8** An overwhelming response comes, more wonderful than any afforded by human love. **l. 9 world-wielding shoulder** In this very complex metaphor, the hills which surround the field are likened to the shoulder of Christ. The myth of Atlas supporting the burden of the world on his shoulders is transferred to Christ, with the added connotation of His bearing the sins of the world. **l. 13** Hopkins scanned this line as follows: 'The heárt reárs wíngs bóld and bólder.' **l. 14 half hurls earth for him** The beholder, dizzied with emotion, feels released from the earth; or, Christ's burden (l. 9) is taken away by the joy of the beholder.

Questions: Poems 93, 94, 95, 96, 97, 98, and 99

(a) Which poets are content to describe natural scenery? Which try to relate it to man or God?

(b) Wordsworth said that poetry 'takes its origin from emotion recollected in tranquillity.' Hopkins declared that 'Hurrahing in Harvest' was written at a peak of direct emotional experience. How is this contrast reflected in the style of poems 96 and 98?

100. THE SHEPHEARDES LAMENT from *The Shepheardes Calender*: December

(Several stanzas of the original have been omitted from this excerpt.) See the note on pastoral poetry (p. 501).

In order to create the pastoral atmosphere, Spenser deliberately used language which was already archaic when the poem was published in 1579. The twelve eclogues or pastoral poems in the *Calender* take their titles from the twelve months. Against the background of the countryside at different times of the year, shepherds discuss such themes as love, poetry, religion, or allegiance to Queen Elizabeth. The December poem is, appropriately, a lament of one shepherd, Colin Clout (often identified with Spenser), over the waste of his life. **l. 11 in the fan be fynd** Be driven off in threshing. **l. 26 stounde** Noise; also, time of trial or pain.

101. BRANWELL'S LAMENT from *A Suit of Nettles:* June

See the note on pastoral poetry (p. 501).

A Suit of Nettles, like *The Shepheardes Calender,* comprises twelve poems. The speakers in the modern poem, however, are geese in an Ontario farmyard. This lament is spoken by Branwell, whom Reaney describes as 'the slightly ridiculous figure of melancholy itself, wrapped up in a suit of nettles he has put on in order to emphasize his sorrow at a fair goose's inattention'. In his morbid state, Branwell has been haunted by visions of a weasel, and of an owl, here thought of as the bird of melancholy. **l. 1 I am like a hol-**

low tree To what extent is this simile developed throughout the rest of the poem? Note the two related elements in the imagery of the containing and that which is contained. Many contemporary Canadian poets develop this motif in their imagery. **l. 22** At the June solstice, sunset occurs at its most northerly point on the horizon; then the days grow shorter. **ll. 24-25** The owl and weasel that plague him are the emanations of a sick mind. It is possible, in the light of Reaney's interest in recreating the imaginative traditions of the past in terms of Canadian experience, that he has in mind a parallel with the harpies of classical mythology. **l. 26 fair** Perhaps a country fair where animals are exhibited. **l. 27 bittern** A small heron that frequents marshy land and makes a curious pumping sound.

Questions: Poems 100 and 101

(a) What elements of the pastoral convention are common to these poems? How has Reaney attempted to treat the convention in modern terms?

(b) In 'Branwell's Lament' Reaney makes special use of the image of the tree. What elements in 'The Shepheardes Lament' are used in a similar way?

102. TEARS, IDLE TEARS

A song from the long poem *The Princess,* Part IV. The song was written at Tintern Abbey (cf. poem 96, p. 157), which held many memories for Tennyson.

103. IN MEMORIAM: SELECTIONS

In Memoriam, which Tennyson wrote over a period of seventeen years, expresses his despair after the death of his friend Arthur Hallam, and the conflict of his doubt with his religious faith as he considers the suffering and waste in nature and the survival of the species rather than the individual. The sequence of 133 poems of varying lengths is unified by developing imagery and themes; the recurring celebration of Christmas, New Year's Day, and Easter, over a period of three years, affords Tennyson a series of vantage points from which to consider his grief and the progress of his meditation. Why is the metre unusual for an elegiac poem? Explain its success.

[VII] The house is Hallam's former residence.

[LIV] Theories of evolution were much disputed in Tennyson's day. Here he tries to assure himself that the struggle and suffering in nature have some ultimate purpose. **l. 7 void** Here, space containing no ordered matter and hence devoid of God's active presence. **l. 8** A deliberately vague image for the creative process.

[CXV] **l. 2 quick** Living plants considered collectively; often, a hawthorn hedge.

[CXVIII] The poet sees a purpose working itself out in the slow processes which produced man, and he concludes that man must continue by his own moral effort the labour of evolving a higher form of life. **l. 26 Faun** In Roman mythology, a pleasure-loving, minor deity of nature, part man, part goat.

[CXXIII] Despair and faith are in precarious balance throughout the first hundred poems of *In Memoriam*. Here Tennyson realizes that, in the perspective of geological time, nature is shadowy and transient. It is therefore partly on the basis of evolution, not in contradiction of it, that he comes to rely on his intuition of the universe as fundamentally spiritual. Hallam has died; but Tennyson is able to affirm that in some higher sphere the friends will be reunited. **l. 12** This line can be understood in at least three ways: I cannot, by mere thought, rid myself of what I have been thinking; I cannot think that Hallam's friendship will never be present again; I cannot conceive the thought, 'Farewell'.

104. COLD STONE

l. 11 The leap The inexplicable gap between living and non-living matter. For the poet, the stone is an inert unordered shape;

the human form, by contrast, maintains the intricate and complex order of living flesh, bone and blood.

Questions: Poems 103 and 104

(a) What differing views of nature does Tennyson present in *In Memoriam* CXVIII and CXXIII?

(b) Contrast Jay Macpherson's view of nature in 'Cold Stone' with Tennyson's in *In Memoriam,* CXXIII.

105. BRAHMA

Brahma In the Hindu religion, the supreme, timeless, and illimitable Reality underlying all things. It is manifested in a trinity of gods: Brahmā the creator (to be distinguished from Brahma, the supreme reality), depicted as a red, four-headed deity; Vishnu the preserver; and Siva the destroyer. The universe created by Brahmā endures for 2,160,000,000 years; it is then destroyed, to be recreated after a like period of time. Every new universe has its own Brahmā. Each period of creation and destruction constitutes a day and a night of Brahma. To Brahma, all oppositions are only apparent; just as, although opposites, the darkness and the light combine to form a day. **l. 1 the red slayer** Probably a fusion of Brahmā, the red creator, and Siva, the destroyer. **l. 14 the sacred Seven** Probably the seven major Vedic gods whom the Hindu trinity superseded.

106. THE TRIUMPH OF BACCHUS

Taken from Canto II of Pound's epic work, *The Cantos,* which describes the false and genuine attempts that have been made throughout history to create a fully human civilization. In this passage, based on lines in Book III of Ovid's *Metamorphoses,* Pound demonstrates that men must be prepared to recognize the divine within the flux of human affairs. Acoetes, trying to persuade King Pentheus of Thebes that he should honour the rituals of Bacchus, recounts the experience of his conversion. **l. 1 Scios Chios,** a large Ionian island off the coast of Asia Minor, famous for its wine. **l. 3 vine-must** Here, the juice of grapes during fermentation. **l. 4 Naxos** A large island in the Aegean Sea. **l. 9 fore-stays** The rigging running from the mast forward to the bow of the ship. **l. 10 Tuscany** A province of Italy. **l. 18 god-sleight** A feat of dexterity characteristic of the god. **ll. 18-79** To describe the miracle performed by Bacchus, Pound adopts the technique of juxtaposing single impressions which convey, in flexible, staccato style, the effect of the miracle on Acoetes. Notice the subtle progression of details in the description of the beasts' appearance. **l. 22 scupper-hole** An opening which allows water to drain from the deck of a ship. **l. 26** The waves are running in the same direction as the ship, but with slightly greater speed. They break forwards, running along the ship's side. **l. 29 cordage** The ropes in a ship's rigging. **ll. 32-53** Notice the musical technique, in which two major themes are woven together (the materialization of the animals, and the metamorphosis of the ship to a vineyard), while minor themes are cross-woven into the ongoing description (e.g. at line 40). **l. 36 Lynx-purr** Among the animals sacred to Bacchus were the lynx, the panther, and the leopard. **l. 44 aether** An immaterial medium which was once believed to permeate all space and account for the transmission of light. Pound ransacked the language for words to convey the insubstantial yet precise effects of light and shade, which he depicted with remarkable virtuosity. **ll. 45-48** Modelled closely on Ovid's description. **l. 48 pin-rack** A rack on a ship's deck, holding the belaying-pins used in making ropes fast. **l. 56 Lyaeus** Bacchus. **l. 61 Olibanum** Frankincense, an aromatic resin, used as incense. **l. 65 Lycabs** The ex-convict mentioned in line 8. **l. 74 Medon** Another sailor. **l. 76 Tiresias** The blind prophet, who had urged King Pentheus to respect the worshippers of Bacchus. **Cadmus** The legendary founder of Thebes.

Questions: Poems 105 and 106

(a) Both Emerson and Pound are writing of an approach to divinity with which their society is not familiar. To what extent do their poems convey what the deity means to one who worships it?

(b) To what extent do they convey what it feels like to be such a worshipper?

107. I HAD A DUCK-BILLED PLATYPUS

The platypus is a peculiar duck-billed, brown-furred mammal of Australia and Tasmania. The poem turns on a pun, for the platypus does lay eggs. Any diplomat who 'laid an egg' would suffer a similar demotion. **l. 1 Trinity** Trinity College.

108. HYMN TO ROVER

See the notes on bathos (p. 475) and parody (p. 501).

The best poetry of Sarah Binks, the Sweet Songstress of Saskatchewan, is marked by an unerring sense of anticlimax – the gift for including the perfect detail at the wrong moment – and an absolute command of lame metre. Her stanzas are brilliantly reminiscent of much inferior nature poetry. She is in fact – life, poems, and critical evaluation – the creation of Paul Hiebert, Professor Emeritus of Chemistry, University of Manitoba.

109. HAWK ROOSTING

ll. 2-4 The hawk is content to be momentarily inactive, not in order to day-dream or to falsify his experience by wishful imagining, but simply as an expression of impulse. Similarly, his dreams are a direct and practical function of his instincts, not an escape.

The contrast between man and hawk remains implicit as the poem develops. What is the attitude of the poet to the bird?

110. KINGFISHERS IN BRITISH COLUMBIA

Kingfishers are predominantly sky-blue in colour; they perch on branches over the water and then, calling dissonantly, dart out and dive to catch a fish close below the surface. **ll. 8-13** The poem shifts cleverly from the flight pattern of the bird to a memory of football games in the poet's youth. **l. 13 halcyon days** The week before and the week after December 21, supposed to have calm clear weather; the kingfishers (also called halcyons) brood at this time. There is a second reference to the 'halcyon days' of the poet's youth, with its rewarding achievement and high promise.

Questions: Poems 107, 108, 109, and 110

(a) In these poems does the poet attribute human feelings to the animal or bird? If so how does this serve his purpose in the poem?

(b) What might be the reason for the marked difference in the form and level of diction in 'Hawk Roosting' and 'Kingfishers in British Columbia'?

111. TO A SKYLARK

See the note on the ode (p. 500).

This ode and the following are examples of the Romantic poetry of the early nineteenth century. Although Shelley by implication criticizes the world of the senses as frustrating and incomplete, he has no other source from which to draw imagery for the supersensible beauty of the bird's song. His poetic strategy, therefore, is to create a series of negative comparisons (ll. 31-60); he describes many sensuous phenomena, only to say that they are far surpassed by the music of the skylark. **l. 66 Chorus Hymeneal** Wedding song.

112. ODE ON A GRECIAN URN

See the notes on pastoral poetry (p. 501), the ode (p. 500) and apostrophe (p. 473).

Keats' imagination was fired by the display of Grecian urns and friezes from the Parthenon, which he saw in the British Museum. With these in mind, he traces the scenes depicted around the curved surface of an antique urn. **ll. 3-4** The essence of history is conveyed more truthfully by the scenes on the urn than by a mere written description. **l. 7 Tempe** A Thessalonian valley celebrated for its rustic beauty, cool shade, and birdsong. **Arcady** A mountainous district in Greece idealized as a place of pastoral contentment. **l. 41 Attic** Here, referring to the purity and simplicity of classical Greek art. **brede** An old form of 'braid'. The effect is of an interwoven design.

Questions: Poems 111 and 112

In these odes compare (i) the philosophic and (ii) the artistic treatment of the poets' sources of inspiration.

113. SONNET CXVI: LET ME NOT TO THE MARRIAGE OF TRUE MINDS

See the note on poem 33 (p. 367).

l. 4 remover One who ceases to love; literally, one who moves away. **l. 8 worth's . . . height** Mariners determine a star's distance above the horizon for purposes of navigation; however, they can never calculate its mystical or occult value.

114. SONNET: HOW DO I LOVE THEE?

This poem is number 43 in the sequence *Sonnets from the Portuguese,* written by Elizabeth Barrett and dedicated to Robert Browning before their marriage.

115. PORPHYRIA'S LOVER

See the note on the dramatic monologue (p. 479).

116. MY LAST DUCHESS

See the notes on the dramatic monologue (p. 479) and juxtaposition (p. 492).

The speaker is almost certainly modelled upon Duke Alfonso II (b. 1533) of the aristocratic Este family in Italy. He married Lucrezia de Medici of Florence when he was twenty-five and she was fourteen. Three years later she was dead, many people suspecting that she had been poisoned. Shortly thereafter the duke began negotiations for the hand of Barbara, niece of the Count of Tyrol. The incident takes place in a picture gallery of the duke's palace at Ferrara, a city in northern Italy. This poem illustrates Browning's effective use of all the resources of the dramatic monologue. **l. 3 Frà** *Frater,* a brother; that is, a member of a religious order. Frà Pandolf and Claus of Innsbruck (l. 56) are imaginary artists. **l. 56 Innsbruck** A town in the Austrian Tyrol near the Italian border. **ll. 54-56** What innuendoes make the Duke's remark more revealing than he intends?

117. A SUBALTERN'S LOVE-SONG

l. 2 Aldershot A town and large military training centre in south-east England. **ll. 3-5 singles** A game of tennis between two opponents. **Love-thirty, love-forty** Tennis scores in which the server has scored no points, and the opponent has won two and three exchanges respectively. **l. 13 euonymus** A shrub whose flowering was once considered an omen of disaster. **l. 29 roads 'not adopted'** Private roads, frequently in a well-to-do area, the upkeep of which has not been undertaken by the local authorities.

118. THE BRAW WOOER

l. 13 keen'd Longed for. The word 'kenned' meaning 'knew' appears in other versions. **l. 18 Gate-slack** The name of a road through the glen. **l. 21 petted** Felt ill-humoured. **l. 22 the tryst o' Dalgarnock** The meeting place at the fair of Dalgarnock, a seventeenth century village in the border country of Scotland. Ordinarily a tryst is a pre-arranged meeting of lovers; here, however, the meeting is unplanned.

119. PLUCKING THE RUSHES

Waley's version captures the quality, characteristic of Chinese poetry, of relying as much upon omission as upon what is said.

120. THE RIVER MERCHANT'S WIFE: A LETTER

Translated from a Japanese version by Rihaku of the original Chinese. Chinese poetry frequently evokes the emotional overtones of a concrete situation by means of suggestion and understatement. **l. 5 Chokan** A village in China near Nanking.

121. A BIRTHDAY

Christina Rossetti was a member of the 'Pre-Raphaelite' group of artists and poets who wished to revive a natural, realistic style such as they imagined to have existed in painting before Raphael's time. This poem represents the poet in her most joyful mood, in which she uses bright pictorial imagery to convey her spiritual state. **l. 6 halcyon** Calm; the halcyon or kingfisher is believed to bring peaceful weather at its breeding time. **l. 10 vair** The fur of a type of squirrel, used to trim garments in medieval times; the word may also be used here in its heraldic sense of parti-coloured.

Questions: Poems 113, 114, 115, 116, 117, 118, 119, 120, 121, 122, and 123

(a) These are all love poems, but no two treat love in the same way. What is the particular situation and atmosphere presented in each?

(b) In each poem, is your strongest impression of the beloved, the lover, or the nature of their love?

(c) Do any of these poems fail to appeal to you? Would you be willing to say, nevertheless, that they are imaginative or well-written?

124. AN IRISH MONK ON LINDISFARNE, ABOUT 650 A.D.

Lindisfarne is a peninsula on the northeast coast of England. At high water it becomes an island, but at ebb-tide it is connected again with the mainland. Its monastery, founded in 635 by Irish monks from Iona, was destroyed by the invading Danes in 793. **l. 3**

Iona An island of the Inner Hebrides off the coast of Scotland. St. Columba and his disciples from Ireland founded a religious community there in 563 A.D. **l. 48 Pict** The Picts were former inhabitants of northern Scotland, noted for their frequent and successful attacks on the defences of Roman Britain.

125. DOVER BEACH

See the note on the dramatic monologue (p. 479).

Arnold evokes the loneliness and despair of his time, which accompanied, he says, a loss of faith in the certainty of religion. Personal constancy in love remains as his last hope. **ll. 3-8** The chalk cliffs of Dover and the coast of France are only twenty-one miles apart. **l. 15 Sophocles** A Greek tragedian of the fifth century B.C. His writing depicts the tragic suffering of noble characters who have encountered the impersonal laws which order the universe. He dwells on the value and the transience of all human achievement. **l. 16 Aegaean** The arm of the Mediterranean to the east of Greece.

126. GREEN FLOWS THE RIVER OF LETHE—O

See the notes on free verse (p. 482) and the symbol (p. 487).

Biblical and classical imagery support the structure of this lament over the transience of life. Dame Edith has made use of a complex colour symbolism in which green, normally the symbol of pastoral contentment, suggests the peace-bringing forgetfulnes and oblivion of death; red (except in line 24) is the symbol of the fiery, often destructive activity of the blood and of all life; and white is the colour of drained vitality and earthly desolation, perhaps after the judgement of God. The poem elaborates the image of the prophetess, contemplating the passage of all living things from vitality to oblivion.

Much of the difficulty of the poem springs from the poet's use of private symbols, which have a personal meaning for her; the reader must interpret these for himself. This technique is probably the most severely criticized in modern poetry. Do you feel that it justifies itself here? **Lethe** In Greek mythology the river of forgetfulness from which people drank to obliterate all memory of their past lives, before taking up their abode in Hades. **l. 1 Lethe—O** In her recorded reading of this poem, Dame Edith lengthens the 'O', making it a link with the second line. **l. 6 Cities of the Plains** Sodom and Gomorrah, two cities of Abraham's time, destroyed by fire from Heaven as a judgement on their sinful worship of pleasure. See Genesis 19: 24-25. **l. 9 evanescent** Short-lived; possibly with a pun on 'vanessa', a genus of butterfly. **l. 12** A pillar of fire led the Israelites by night on their wanderings through the wilderness to the promised land. See Genesis 13: 21. **l. 13 incarnadine** Bright red. **l. 15 white as the Dead Sea** The excessive salt content of the Dead Sea in Israel gives the shore a whitish cast.

127. REMEMBER NOW THY CREATOR

See the note on poem 56 (p. 375).

Ecclesiastes urges a sceptical view of the achievements and pleasures which are commonly valued by the world. We are to think of God and enjoy his gifts before we are old. This passage uses the symbol of the house to depict, with dignity and restraint, the coming of old age. Some commentaries on the Bible interpret each detail as symbolic of the ageing of one part of the body — the 'keepers of the house' as the arms, the 'grinders' (women grinding meal) as the teeth. **l. 12 daughters of musick** Lovers of pleasure; the image can be interpreted as a reference to the voice. **l. 15 almond tree** The bitter almond; the image can be interpreted as a reference to the hair, because of this tree's white blossom. **l. 16 the grasshopper shall be a burden** Plague and pestilence will be visited on the old (see Exodus 10: 4); the line can also be interpreted 'any triviality will become disproportionately burdensome'. **l. 17 his long home** The grave. **l. 19 silver cord . . . golden bowl** The lamp, in Old Testament times, consisted of a bowl which held burning oil. It was suspended by a cord from the ceiling. The silver cord may be the thread that connects life and death, and the golden bowl the vessel that holds life. **ll. 19-21** Light and water are traditional symbols of life.

128. LINES from the Prologue to the *Canterbury Tales*

The Canterbury Tales, Chaucer's most ambitious work, concerns a party of pilgrims travelling to the shrine of St Thomas à Becket at Canterbury. To make the journey more amusing they tell stories. Chaucer wrote a general prologue to introduce the situation and characters, then linked their stories by passages of lively narrative. **l. 8 Ram** The zodiacal sign of Aries, the ram. According to the astrological system of the time, Aries was dominant in the month following March 12. **l. 13 palmeres** Palmers; originally, pilgrims who wore crossed palm leaves after a journey to the Holy Land. The word was extended to include any religious votary or pilgrim. **l. 17 martir** Becket was martyred in 1170. His shrine soon became popular for pilgrimages. **l. 18 seeke** Sick. The identical rhyme, here between 'seke' and 'seeke', was an acceptable convention in Chaucer's day.

129. CHURCH GOING

The speaker sees the religious observances of today as gradually dying and being forgotten even though the need which gave rise to them persists. **l. 17 Irish sixpence** Irish money does not, of course, circulate in the United Kingdom. **l. 25 pyx** A vessel in which consecrated bread is held. **l. 30 simples** An archaic word for herbs used as medicine. **l. 41 rood-lofts** The galleries at the head of the screen separating the nave from the choir. The screen is usually surmounted by a cross. **l. 42 ruin-bibber** Formed by analogy with wine-bibber, a guzzler of wine. **randy** Here, excited and greedy. **l. 47 cross of ground** The church is cruciform.

130. THE LAST HOUR OF FAUSTUS

The legend of Faust has fascinated such great writers as Marlowe,

Goethe, and Thomas Mann. Marlowe's play, *The Tragical History of Doctor Faustus,* was written about 1590 in London. The scholar Faustus sold his soul to Mephistopheles, an emissary of Lucifer (Satan), in return for twenty-four years of unlimited power. Now, in the last scene of Marlowe's tragedy, comes the hour of reckoning. **l. 4 ever-moving spheres** The Pythagoreans taught that the earth stood at the centre of nine transparent spheres, one inside another, which rotated ceaselessly carrying the planets and stars. **l. 10** From Ovid: 'Run slowly, slowly, horses of the night.' How does the pace of the Latin line affect the meaning of the words? **ll. 13-21** Faustus becomes more and more remote from God. He is facing the fact of his imminent damnation: he has made his unholy pact with Lucifer and is incapable of accepting God's mercy. His half-prideful conviction of his own damnation is much stronger than his awareness of grace. Notice that at line 15 Faustus addresses Christ directly. Yet to whom is line 16 addressed? **l. 42 metempsychosis** Transmigration of souls, a doctrine taught by Pythagoras. At death, the soul of one creature passed into the body of another, not necessarily of the same species. In each successive life on earth the soul earned a higher or lower position in the scale of creation. **l. 58 books** Books of black magic.

131. REASON HAS MOONS

What is it that delights and gives wisdom to the poet, while confusing the calculations of the rationalist?

Questions: Poems 124, 125, 126, 127, 128, 129, 130, and 131

(a) In 'Dover Beach' and 'An Irish Monk on Lindisfarne', compare the attitude of each speaker toward his faith, the role of the companion mentioned, and the significance of the sea.

(b) In 'Dover Beach' and 'The Last Hour of Faustus', what is the attitude of each speaker to the absence of religious hope?

(c) What do 'Green Flows the River of Lethe–O' and 'Remember Now Thy Creator' say about youth and age? Compare the imagery and the rhythm of these two selections.

(d) A poet frequently adopts a 'persona' or poetic personality, which may or may not resemble his everyday character. What persona do you find in each of 'Dover Beach', 'Green Flows the River of Lethe—O', 'Church Going', and 'The Last Hour of Faustus'?

132. LUCIFER IN STARLIGHT

See the note on the sonnet (p. 511).

According to Milton's *Paradise Lost,* when Lucifer (Satan) revolted against God, he fell from Heaven through Chaos to Hell. Later he made his way up to earth where he tempted Adam and Eve. This poem depicts Lucifer attempting to approach Heaven once more.

133. IN THE WIDE AWE AND WISDOM OF THE NIGHT

See the note on the sonnet (p. 511).

Contrast the mood and conclusion here with those of the preceding poem. **l. 7 laws** Compare poem 132, l. 14 (p. 221).

134. WELSH NIGHT from *Under Milk Wood*

See the note on cadence (p. 507).

A play for voices, first broadcast in its final form by the BBC on January 25, 1954. This selection is the opening, spoken very gently by a narrator. The evocative language and cadence of the prose make it scarcely distinguishable from poetry. **Milk Wood** An imaginary Welsh seaside town. **ll. 4-5 sloeback** The blue-black colour of the sloe, a small wild plum. **l. 7 dingle** A narrow valley or shady glen. **Captain Cat** An inhabitant of Milk Wood. **l. 14 Llaregyb** Pronounce with a voiceless 'l', stress the middle syllable, and pronounce 'gyb' as in Gibbon. **l. 17 bombazine** A fine fabric used for mourning clothes. **ll. 18-19 mintoes** Mints. **l. 19 four-ale** A cheap mild ale; here, probably, a public house or tavern. **l. 20 domino** As quiet as one of the pieces in a game of dominoes in the bar.

ll. 20-21 Ocky Milkman . . . Dai Bread Ocky, the milkman, and Dai (David) the baker. Pronounce Dai as 'die'. **ll. 25-26 neddying . . . snuggeries** Neddy is commonly a child's name for a donkey; a snuggery is a small cosy place, especially a parlour in a public house. What effects are achieved by the juxtaposition here?

135. HYMN TO DIANA

Diana The chaste goddess of the moon and the hunt. **l. 4 wonted** Accustomed. **l. 5 Hesperus** The evening star. **l. 9 Cynthia** Another name for Diana.

Questions: Poems 132, 133, 134, 135, and 136

(a) What do the moon or stars suggest to each poet?

(b) Night is a favourite subject for poets. Can you suggest why this might be?

139. THE SICK ROSE

See the note on the symbol (p. 487).

As in poems 55 (p. 85) and 185 (p. 293), this poem presents a symbol to the reader, leaving him to decide its meaning.

Question: Poems 138 and 139

What is the force of the image of the rose in each of these poems? Comment also on the images of the snail and the worm.

140. FARMERS

l. 11 gazetted Publicly listed as a bankrupt.

Question: Poems 140 and 141

Why, and to what extent may poetry be less suitable than prose for descriptions of family life?

143. THE PRIZE CAT

Pratt has said that there is no intentional reference in this poem to a specific international situation. But since Italy had attacked Abyssinia (Ethiopia) in 1935, shortly before the poem was written, many choose to read it as a powerful comment on this act of aggression. The reference of the poem is multiple: it speaks directly about the blood-lust latent in domestic cats, as well as referring to the behaviour of human animals and of nations. **l. 5 gads** Spurs; here, claws. **l. 12 optic parallels** The fixed gaze of the cat's eyes. **l. 20 whitethroat** A species of North American sparrow; the bird which the cat has trapped.

145. CHEERIO MY DEARIO

Archy the cockroach used Don Marquis' typewriter at night to relate his adventures with Mehitabel, an alley-cat who claimed to be a reincarnation of Cleopatra. Archy typed by leaping off the carriage and striking a key with his head: unfortunately, he could not work the shift key. His poem should be read aloud. Would you consider it a dramatic monologue? **l. 1 boss** i.e. Don Marquis. **ll. 12-15 king tutankhamen** An Egyptian Pharaoh who lived some thirteen centuries before Cleopatra. **l. 49 sisters of uncharity** An unflattering reference to the uncharitable gossips who have made life difficult for Mehitabel. The Sisters of Charity are an order of nuns founded by St Vincent de Paul; they devote themselves largely to charitable work in nursing and education. **l. 73 anvil chorus** A rhythmic, hammering chorus from Verdi's opera *Il Trovatore;* in Mehitabel's vivid slang, the 'sisters of uncharity' of lines 45-49. **ll. 77-80** The sisters of uncharity have had local groups meeting all through history.

Question: Poems 143, 144, and 145
Explain the particular fascination of the cat for each poet.

Question: Poems 142 and 145
How is incongruity used to effect in 'Birds, Bags, Bears and Buns and 'Cheerio My Deario'?

146. THE BISHOP ORDERS HIS TOMB AT SAINT PRAXED'S CHURCH

See the note on the dramatic monologue (p. 479).

The church referred to is San Prassede, named in honour of the daughter of a Roman senator in the second century who gave freely of her wealth to help poor Christians. Beyond its name, however, and its ornate decoration, the poet does not describe the actual church. Both the bishop and his rival, Gandolf, are imaginary. Ruskin says of the insight displayed into the spirit of the Italian Renaissance: 'I know no other piece of modern English, prose or poetry, in which there is so much told, as in these lines, of the Renaissance spirit, – its worldliness, inconsistency, pride, hypocrisy, ignorance of itself, love of art, of luxury, and of good Latin.' (*Modern Painters*) **l. 1 Vanity** Compare Ecclesiastes 1:2. An ironically appropriate beginning. **ll. 3-5** Characteristically gnarled Browning lines. As the bishop lies dying, his mind moves restlessly from topic to topic. **l. 21 epistle-side** The right side of the altar as one faces it. The gospel-side is to the left. **l. 25 basalt** Very hard black rock. **l. 26 tabernacle** The canopy of the tomb. **l. 31 onion-stone** An inferior greenish-yellow marble that peels in layers. **l. 41 olive-frail** A basket for olives. **l. 42 lapis lazuli** A semi-precious blue stone. **l. 46 Frascati** A beautiful town in the Alban Hills near Rome. **l. 49 Jesu Church** The Jesuit church of Rome. **l. 51 Swift as a weaver's shuttle** Job 7: 6 – 'My days are swifter than a weaver's shuttle, and are spent without hope.' **ll. 53-54** The bishop now decides on a more costly marble. **l. 57 Pans and Nymphs** Minor nature deities of classical mythology. The figure of Pan is frequently depicted in pursuit of a nymph. Notice the source to which the bishop turns for subjects. **l. 58 tripod** A three-legged stool upon which the priestess of Apollo sat at Delphi as she answered questions put to the Oracle. **thyrsus** A staff associated with the celebrations of Bacchus, the god of wine and sensual ecstasy. It was usually surmounted by a pine-cone or ivy leaves. **l. 62 the tables** The tablets on which the Ten Commandments were engraved. **l. 66 travertine** A porous light-yellow rock, used for ordinary buildings in Italy. **l. 67** Gandolf has had his effigy carved for the top of his tomb, as the bishop intends to do. **l. 68 jasper** A semi-precious stone, the most esteemed colour being green. **l. 73-75** The bishop expects the saint to grant his every wish after death. **l. 77 Tully** Marcus Tullius Cicero (106-43 B.C.) whose prose style is the accepted classical model. **l. 79 Ulpian** Domitius Ulpianus (170-228 A.D.), a learned Roman jurist, whose style had lost some of the purity of the classical period. **l. 82 God made and eaten** A reference to the sacrament of the mass. **l. 89 mortcloth** Funeral pall. **l. 93** The bishop appears to hold the pagan belief in reincarnation. **l. 95 Saint Praxed at his sermon on the mount** The bishop becomes momentarily incoherent. Compare ll. 59-60. **l. 99 Elucescebat** Ulpian's florid form of the Latin *elucebat* – 'he was illustrious.' **l. 101** See Genesis, 47:9. **l. 108 vizor** A mask. **Term** A bust on its pedestal. **l. 116 Gritstone** A coarse sandstone which deteriorates quickly.

Question: Poem 146

Compare the characters of the speakers in 'The Bishop Orders His Tomb at Saint Praxed's Church' and 'My Last Duchess' (p. 195). How is the interview used in each poem?

147. PASSING BY

l. 10 Similarly, my beloved changes her dwelling place.

149. A SWEET DISORDER

Herrick was one of the best of the Cavalier lyricists; his poetry is characterized by a civilized neatness and grace. Note the difference in style from the contemporary metaphysicals, Donne and Herbert (poems 156-161, pp. 254-260). **l. 3 lawn** A shawl made of lawn, a fine linen. **l. 6 stomacher** An ornamental cloth, like a cummerbund, worn under the lacing of a bodice.

150. TO HIS COY MISTRESS

Andrew Marvell united the elegant grace of the Cavalier poets with the wittier, more closely-packed style of the metaphysicals. Here he echoes a recurrent theme of Greek and Latin lyrics: *carpe diem,* seize the pleasures of the day, **l. 7 complain** Sing a love lament. **l. 10** A popular cliché of Marvell's time: endlessly. **l. 40 his slow-chapt power** The power of time's slow-moving jaws.

151. SHE DWELT AMONG THE UNTRODDEN WAYS

l. 2 Dove A tiny stream in a part of northern England which Wordsworth had explored. It runs through the narrow valley of Dovedale.

152. SHE WALKS IN BEAUTY

Composed after Byron's first meeting with his cousin Mrs Robert Wilmot.

Questions: Poems 147, 148, 149, 150, 151, 152, and 153

(a) Account for the appeal of each of these love lyrics.

(b) How much do they have in common?

154. HYND HORN

See the note on the ballad (p. 474).

l. 4 birk Birch tree. **l. 10 auger-bore** Small hole made by an auger, a sharp grooved instrument. **l. 16 laverocks** Larks. **l. 35 weed** Clothes. **l. 48 gowd** Gold. **l. 68 cloutie** Patched, made of pieces of cloth. **l. 71 stown** Stolen.

155. TRUE LOVE

See the note on the ballad (p. 474).

Auden frequently uses the image of the industrial town to suggest the unsatisfactory quality of the social life which men create for themselves. Here, the clocks of the town speak a far more sombre message than does the lover. The style is typical of Auden, with its sardonic wit and cryptic descriptions which demand great agility from the reader. **ll. 41-56** Auden, like many modern poets, makes amusing and ironic use of nursery rhymes and well-known children's stories. **l. 45 raffle** Sell by raffle; or, riffle through, as with the pages of a book. **l. 47 Lily-white Boy is a Roarer** A reference to the ancient number-song, 'Green Grow the Rushes—O': 'Two, two, the lily-white boys, clothèd all in green—O.' In a very early version of the song, the lily-white boys were young assistants to a Druid priest; in the later Christian version, they were taken to be Jesus Christ and John the Baptist. A roarer is a street rowdy.

Questions: Poems 154 and 155

Compare the traditional ballad and the literary ballad, referring to 'Hynd Horn' and 'True Love' and to others with which you are familiar.

156. A VALEDICTION FORBIDDING MOURNING

See the note on metaphysical poetry (p. 494).

Note the effect of Donne's association of divine love with physical love.

Donne wrote this poem to his wife just before departing from England on a diplomatic mission to France. In the first six stanzas a series of images evokes an emotional response to changes in the physical world. The last three stanzas develop a single conceit, which has become one of the most famous in English poetry. **Valediction** A farewell address. **ll. 1-8** Donne draws a comparison between the gentle parting of a godly man from life on earth to a higher life beyond, and the peaceful severance of the physical companionship of the husband and wife, which will enable their relationship to enter a more exalted state. **l. 8 laity** Church members as distinct from the clergy. **ll. 9-12** A contrast between earthquakes (equated with physical love) which bring harm and fear, and the vibration of the spheres (equated with the communion of a higher love) which produces heavenly harmony. In the Ptolemaic system the universe is conceived of as a series of rotating spheres, one inside another, with the earth at the centre. **ll. 13-16** Earthly love cannot survive separation because its very life depends on physical presence. **ll. 17-20** An image based on the refinement of metals by the removal of impure elements. **ll. 21-24** When gold is beaten into gold leaf the surface is extended but the metal is nowhere broken. **ll. 25-36** This conceit presents the image of a pair of compasses, of which one foot remains in a central position while the other maintains a fixed relation to it in tracing out a circle.

157. A HYMN TO GOD THE FATHER

See the note on metaphysical poetry (p. 494).

Note the pun on the name of the poet. The seriousness of the poem is intensified by Donne's self-mockery. **l. 1 that sin where I begun** Original sin. **ll. 15-16** In a feat typical of the metaphysical poets, Donne unites Greek and Christian theology with a serious pun on the word 'sun'. Plato writes of the sun as the supreme manifestation of the Good; for Christians the Son is the supreme manifestation of God.

158. DEATH

Donne harnessed the concentrated power of the sonnet, traditionally used for love poetry, to express the complexities and the emotional impact of his religious convictions. **ll. 1-2** See I Corinthians, 15: 51-55. **l. 11 poppy** The poppy as the source of opium.

159. CHARITY

See the note on poem 56 (p. 375).

Notice the extensive use of concrete images and of symbols. It is interesting to compare the 1611 translation of this passage with modern translations. **Charity** Christian love.

160. LOVE

See the note on metaphysical poetry (p. 494).

This poem was written after Herbert's agonized decision to take orders in the Anglican Church. God's forgiving love is personified as a beautiful woman who entices him in to a feast.

161. VIRTUE

l. 11 closes A multiple pun. The box of spring must eventually be closed; its sweets – the 'sweet days and roses' – must be locked away in death. With reference to music, 'closes' also meant concluding cadences. **ll. 13-16** This elaborated comparison is a metaphysical conceit. Seasoned wood does not warp or bend, but actually improves with age. Similarly the soul matured by virtuous living does not die but achieves a greater vitality when freed from the body. The poet elaborates the simile further. Living plants and trees may finally die and decompose to form coal; the soul, however, attains its fullest life after death.

Questions: Poems 156, 157, 158, 159, 160, and 161

(a) 'I have a sin of fear.' What does Donne fear? How do his religious beliefs affect his fears?
(b) Compare Donne's and Herbert's attitudes to sin and divine grace.
(c) What elements are typical of the metaphysical style?
(d) The translation from St Paul and the poems by Donne and Herbert are roughly contemporary. Compare the styles, mentioning the differences you see in imagery, pace, idiom, and pattern of development.

162. HAIL, HOLY LIGHT

The first two books of *Paradise Lost* have described Satan and his cohorts in the darkness of Hell. At the end of Book II Satan, on a mission to earth, has re-passed the boundaries of Hades and caught a distant glimpse of the celestial light. This passage, the opening of Book III, serves to translate the reader to the radiant glory of God's world. It is also a great lyrical statement, in the midst of the narrative, concerning Milton's physical blindness and the inner light he has been granted. **l. 6 effluence** A flowing out. **l. 14 Stygian Pool** See *Paradise Lost* II, ll. 575-81. The River Styx was one of the four rivers of the underworld. The shades of the departed were ferried across it to Hades. **ll. 17-21 Orpheus** A legendary Greek poet and musician, who descended to Hades when his wife Eurydice died, and so pleased the god Pluto by his music that he was allowed to lead Eurydice back to life. Because she looked back during their ascent from Hades, contrary to the condition imposed by Pluto, she was lost to Orpheus forever. **l. 30 Sion** Zion, the holy mountain of Israel; for Milton, the home of the Muse which inspired the prophets and writers in the Judaeo-Christian tradition, and which he identified with the Holy Spirit. **ll. 35-36 Thamyris** A poet whom the Muses blinded. **Maeonides** Homer, the blind Greek epic poet. **Tiresias** A Theban who was granted the gift of prophecy when he lost his sight. **Phineus** A blind prophet whom Jason and the Argonauts met.

Scan lines 1-6. How has Milton adapted the iambic pentameter? (See the notes on syncopation, p. 506 and cadence, p. 507.)

163. LAST CHORUS FROM SAMSON AGONISTES

In the Greek tragedies, on which Milton modelled *Samson Agonistes,* dialogue and soliloquies are interspersed with the lyrical reflections of a chorus, which usually represented a group of interested spectators. This is the final choral passage from Milton's poetic drama.

The Biblical record is in Judges 16: 23-31. After his infatuation with Delilah, Samson had been captured and blinded by the Philistines. At a great public gathering in the temple of Gaza where he was to be mocked, he toppled the two massive pillars that supported the roof, destroying himself and the Philistines in the temple. In this chorus, his fellow Israelites find in his revenge a vindication of Jehovah. It is almost impossible not to draw an analogy between the blind, suffering hero Samson, and Milton, blind and despairing, living in a kind of exile in Restoration England.

The form of this chorus is derived from that of the sonnet. What has Milton changed in the metre? (See the notes on syncopation, p. 506 and cadence, p. 507.) **Agonistes** A Greek word meaning 'competitor at public games'. Milton appears to have used the word with the further connotation of suffering or agony. **l. 11 acquist** Acquisition.

164. ON HIS BLINDNESS

See the notes on the sonnet (p. 511) and on Milton's life (p. 456).

The poem gains richness and depth through its use of multiple meanings. In line 2, for example, the world is dark both to the blind poet and in its ignorance. **ll. 3-8** See Matthew 25: 14-30. **l. 7 day-labour** See John 9: 4. **l. 8 fondly** foolishly. **l. 11 His mild yoke** See Matthew 11: 30.

Questions: Poems 162, 163, and 164

(a) What is Milton's final attitude to affliction in the 'Last Chorus from Samson Agonistes', and 'On His Blindness'?

(b) In 'Hail, Holy Light', and 'On His Blindness', what levels of significance are given to darkness and to light?

165. THE UNSLEEPING

The endless activity of nature follows a cyclical pattern of birth and death, creation and disintegration. God does not interrupt it; man cannot. Notice that the 'I' works within nature, time and space, but endures after they have crumbled away. While there is no single 'correct' interpretation of the poem, it is illuminating to compare it with the first four verses of St John's gospel.

166. DECEMBER 29, 1170

At the opening of Part II of *Murder in the Cathedral,* a poetic tragedy, the women of Canterbury chant this chorus. Mourning the desolation of winter, and mistrusting the coming of spring, they create an atmosphere of foreboding and suspense before the murder of Thomas à Becket, Archbishop of Canterbury.

The questions and answers have the effect of a litany in the church service, where the clergy and congregation alternately offer invocations and responses. The play was written to be performed in Canterbury Cathedral. **l. 7 a wind is stored up in the East** The women are referring both to the breeze of spring and to the return of Archbishop Thomas from France. **l. 15 death in the Lord** A dramatic irony. The sacrifice to the prosperity of spring will be the martyred Thomas. **l. 21 elder and may** Flowering trees: elder, a low tree with white flowers and black berries; may, the flowering hawthorn.

167. THE SWIMMER'S MOMENT

The whirlpool, a highly dramatic symbol with a wide range of meaning, tests the courage and the quality of a person's life. What kinds of defeat and spiritual death can be undergone by those at the edge of the whirlpool, and by those within its vortex? Who are the people who reach the estuary? From which side of the vortex does the poet speak?

168. THE COLD GREEN ELEMENT

See the notes on archetype (p. 474), and allusion (p. 471).

Layton, as often in his best work, muses on the fate of the poet who seeks the full experience of life. The poem shows the influence of Nietzsche (see the note to poem 76, p. 382) and D. H. Lawrence. It is interesting to compare its theme with that of 'The Birth of Tragedy' (p. 116).

The dominant image, nowhere specifically mentioned, is of the poet as a god of death and rebirth. The allusion is possibly to Apollo, not only the god of poets and prophecy, but the sun-god as well, who, in his cycle of setting and rising, represents rebirth.

Shifting and unusual images merge one into another in dream-like sequence to create an image of the poet as the god-like centre of vitality and dissolution; the god is seen as a heart beating in the grass, as a drowned poet, as a crucified figure, as a mutilated and multiple figure hanging from various trees, as fruit drooping from a tree, as a spot of red sunlight on a leaf, as a swimmer. **ll. 1-7** Both the figure of life and the figure of death are attended by the inscrutable 'wind and its satellite', which are always near but never comprehended. **ll. 16-20** A deliberate ambiguity. Does the 'one' refer to the tree or the poet? **l. 27 catalpa** A small tree native to North America and Asia. It has large simple leaves and trumpet-like flowers. **ll. 31-37** Life can be seen and recognized as emerging through death, or living within death. The conception of the cycle is emphasized with the worm, usually associated with death, held within the throat of the robin whose song is proclaiming life. **ll. 38-40** Although the poet recognizes the inevitable failures and anguish of life, he ironically maintains a kind of optimism and chooses to undergo the shocks of experience.

169. ANYONE LIVED IN A PRETTY HOW TOWN

The anonymity of Cummings' hero is expressed in his name, 'anyone'. The cycle of his life is traced in fancifully generalized terms. Anyone's early life is anonymous; he wins the respect and love of 'noone' whom he takes in marriage; the joys and griefs of his married life go unremarked by the world around him; when he dies, life carries on its cycle, and anyone and noone lie side by side 'dreaming their sleep'. **l. 4** This line is typical of Cummings' writing, both in its unconventional syntax and in its ability to communicate an abstract idea. The use of verb forms where nouns would be expected stimulates close attention to what is being said. The negative form, balanced immediately by the positive, suggests anyone's unreflecting passage through the negative and positive experiences of life.

170. THE APPRENTICE PRIESTLING

See the note on the haiku (p. 483).

171. SONG OF THE HORSEMAN

l. 1 Córdoba The capital city of the province of Córdoba in southern Spain.

172. HOME AFTER THREE MONTHS AWAY

The poem is from the collection entitled *Life Studies.*

The speaker, who has been undergoing treatment for mental illness, tries to take up the threads of his life again. **l. 13 levee** The morning ceremony at which a sovereign received select visitors as he prepared to rise from bed. **l. 28** A self-mocking allusion to Mathew 6: 28.

173. IN TIME OF 'THE BREAKING OF NATIONS'

This poem was written in 1915, during the First World War, although the incidents are recalled from forty years earlier. **l. 9 wight** Young man. The archaic word stresses the timelessness of love.

Questions: Poems 165, 166, 167, 168, 169, 170, 171, 172, and 173

(a) Describe the element of despair in each of these poems.

(b) When the poet considers the passage of time and the cycles of nature, does he find anything that enables human life to transcend its natural surroundings?

174. GOD'S GRANDEUR

See the notes on sprung rhythm (p. 510), assonance and consonance, and internal rhyme (p. 514).

Hopkins blends emotional and intellectual perception in his forceful imagery, unorthodox, highly compressed syntax, and in the suggestive power of his phrases. He wrote elsewhere of 'the contemplation of the Holy Ghost sent to us through creatures.... All things therefore are charged with love, are charged with God and if we know how to touch them give off sparks and take fire, yield drops and flow, ring and tell of Him.' As in the poem, Hopkins describes the immanence of the Holy Spirit in terms of both fire and liquid. **l. 1 charged** In the sense of electrically charged; also, given the responsibility of. There is the further connotation of surging force. **l. 2 shook foil** Hopkins wrote to the poet Robert Bridges: 'I mean foil in its sense of leaf or tinsel . . . Shaken gold foil gives off broad flares like sheet lightning and also, and this is true of nothing else, owing to its zigzag dints and creasings and network of small many cornered facets, a sort of fork lightning too.' **ll. 3-4** The reference is to the emergence of gleaming oil from olives crushed in a press (many religious uses for this oil are described in the Old Testament); or, to the crushing of oil from oil-bearing shale, by the weight of the rock above it. **l. 4 reck** Take heed of, modify one's behaviour on account of. **rod** The symbol of God's authority, with a secondary reference to the miraculous rod of Moses which brought forth the spring of water from the rock. Cf. ll. 10 and 12. **ll. 7-8** An intensely compressed statement of an ironic situation. What has unnaturally bared the soil? When man is no longer in his natural barefoot state, what changes in his relation to nature? **l. 9 spent** Used up completely; exhausted, without further energy. **l. 10** The compression of the line suggests the new life that is ready to surge forth. **ll. 13-14** For the image of the Holy Spirit as a gently brooding dove, see Matthew 3: 16-17. Compare also *Paradise Lost* I, ll. 20-22.

175. THIS LIME-TREE BOWER MY PRISON

Coleridge wrote this poem while living in the Quantock Hills. It commemorates a visit of William Wordsworth and his sister Dorothy, Charles Lamb and his sister Mary. Coleridge was prevented by a scalded foot from accompanying them on a walk. **Lime-Tree** The linden, an ornamental tree with heart-shaped flowers.

Question: Poems 174 and 175

Contrast the religious significance which nature has for Hopkins and for Coleridge.

176. NO DOCTORS TODAY, THANK YOU

l. 6 welkin Poetic term for the vault of the sky. The play is upon the expression 'To make the welkin ring'. **l. 8 marabou** The under-tail feathers of a stork, used in millinery. **l. 17 Wurlitzer** The 'mighty organ' of the movie theatre or sports arena. **l. 18 Berlitzer** One who studies at a Berlitz School of Languages.

177. BIRTHDAY

l. 4 Yevtushenko's first marriage ended in divorce. **l. 12 the Revolution** The Russian Revolution of 1917, in which the Tsarist regime was overthown and the Bolsheviks seized power. Although he demands the right to criticize Communist failures, Yevtushenko believes passionately in fundamental Communist principles.

178. THE COCKY WALKERS

Peake depicts the street-corner existence of boys who are neither criminals nor accepted members of society. The recurring natural imagery of trees and green vegetation is ironic in this city poem, for the boys are shown as 'rootless'. The slang is British. **l. 2** In certain areas of some British cities, gaslight is still in use. It casts a yellowish pallor of the shade of a Rembrandt etching. **l. 3** Rembrandt frequently chose the disreputable for the subjects of his etchings. In etching, lines are scratched with a needle on a wax-covered copper plate, which is then dipped into acid to prepare it for printing. **l. 9 Hummock** Here, hunch. Literally, a small mound of earth. **ll. 15-16** An ironic reference to Olympic runners passing on the torch. **l. 18 sprig** A contemptuous word for a young man. **flash boy** A showy dresser; also, a 'sharpie', on the verge of lawlessness. **l. 23 unthought conspiracy** Following their unreflecting instinct to herd together the boys are not huddled in premeditated conspiracy to cheat others, but are themselves the victims of a pattern of behaviour which cheats them of any richness in life.

179. ON THE MOVE

Gunn has drawn on the philosophy of the French existentialist philosophers, who argue that one cannot find a set of values unless one creates them from moment to moment through whole-hearted action. **l. 5 their** The birds'. **l. 7 baffled sense** Human beings have confused, obscure instincts and cannot express them exactly in words. The following stanzas describe the attempt to express them in violent movement. **l. 24 the taken routes** Men choose the routes they will take without knowledge of where they lead, and stake their futures on the choice. **l. 30 valueless** Without defined values.

180. THE FIGHTS

l. 5 slues Turns forcibly aside. **l. 6** What is the source of this image? What effect is gained by using it in this way? **l. 31 long count** A trick used by a dishonest referee. When the boxer whom he favours is knocked down, he counts more slowly than is legitimate.

181. THE TOP HAT

l. 3 Bay Street The financial centre of Toronto, and of much of Canada.

Question: Poems 177, 178, 179, 180, 181, and 182

These poems portray social rebels. To what extent are they presented sympathetically? To what extent are we intended to censure their weaknesses?

183. SELECTIONS from the *Rubáiyát of Omar Khayyám*

Omar Khayyám (Omar the Tentmaker), a Persian mathematician and poet of the eleventh century, wrote some five hundred rubais or quatrains. Although most were self-contained epigrams, they were held together by a philosophy of pleasure and a melancholy awareness of death's finality. These stanzas are excerpts from the first edition of Fitzgerald's free translation, made in 1859. **l. 20 Sultán Máhmúd** Sultan of Ghazni (971?-1029), in what is now Afghanistan.

184. THE DARKLING THRUSH

l. 5 bine-stems The climbing, twisting stems of the honeysuckle and similar plants. **l. 10 outleant** Stretched out, reclining.

185. AH! SUN-FLOWER

See the note to poem 139 (p. 409).

The entire poem is an apostrophe with no main verb. The sunflower turns to face the sun directly, following its progress from east to west.

Question: Poems 183, 184, 185, and 186

By what methods do these poets represent human joy? How do they relate it to sorrow?

187. ON WENLOCK EDGE

l. 1 Edge The crest of a steep, narrow ridge of land. Wenlock Edge is in Shropshire, England. **l. 2 Wrekin** A hill in Shropshire, some 1300 feet in height. **l. 4 Severn** One of the principal rivers of England, flowing into the Bristol Channel. **l. 5 holt and hanger** Copse and sloping woodland. **l. 6 Uricon** A fortified Roman town in Shropshire, now called Wroxeter.

188. HER STRONG ENCHANTMENTS FAILING

The details of this poem artfully suggest a background of supernatural intrigue. **l. 3 limbecks** Vessels used in alchemy and early chemistry; alembics.

189. FISHES' HEAVEN

A witty reversal of the point of view represented in Tennyson's *In Memoriam,* LIV (p. 170). The poem can be read as a whimsical addendum to the prophetic tradition. In the Bible the end of the world is described in visionary terms, including references to 'the worm that dieth not' (Isaiah 66: 24 and Mark 9: 44) and to a heaven where 'there shall be no more sea' (Revelation 21: 1). **l. 22 Squamous** Scaly.

Questions: Poems 187, 188 and 189

(a) What traditional elements can you distinguish in these poems?

(b) What are the distinctive characteristics of Housman and Rupert Brooke?

190. THE FISHERMAN

Yeats tried for years to establish an Irish national literature. But the intrigues of Dublin public life and the riots of 1907 that greeted John Synge's play, *The Playboy of the Western World,* convinced him that the general public was not a deserving audience. Here he explains his resolve to write more directly and candidly, with a new kind of reader in mind. **l. 4 Connemara** A rugged district in County Galway, Ireland. **l. 12 reality** Parallel to 'What I had hoped' in line 10. **ll. 13-24** Most of the references in these lines are to local personalities; in the heat of Yeats' invective, they become types of the philistine and the rogue. **l. 14 the dead man** The playwright John Synge, who had died five years before. **ll. 33-34** A reference to fly-fishing.

191. THE CHOICE

This excerpt from 'A Dialogue of Self and Soul' is the second part of a debate within the poet's mind, in which he balances the implications of reincarnation against those of an afterlife. Reincarnation would mean accepting the conditions of earthly life, which Yeats found increasingly bitter: violent hatreds, physical prostration, and a frustrated love affair seemed ample cause for giving up this life with relief. Yet after bitterly enumerating his trials, Yeats decides that he would 'live it all again'. **ll. 22-24** For fifteen years Yeats had loved Maud Gonne, a prominent Irish actress and revolutionary. She married a man whom Yeats despised, but wanted to keep the poet as a friend. **ll. 25-27** Yeats thought it possible, from his studies in the occult, that the soul relived its past life immediately after death; when the soul had 'followed to its source' its entire life, it could achieve forgiveness and consequent reincarnation.

192. DEATH

The poem was written in 1927 after the assassination of Kevin O'Higgins, an outstanding statesman in the Irish Free State. Noted for his justice and ruthless integrity in dealing with republican extremism, he had said proudly to his wife, 'Nobody can expect to live who has done what I have done.' **ll. 2-5** Cf. *Julius Caesar,* Act II, scene 2, ll. 32-37. **l. 10 Supersession** Replacement. **l. 12** Death is only imagined by men (see note to ll. 25-27 of the preceding poem, 'The Choice'); or, the importance of death is created by men's own sense of the value of life—they can be tragic victors even as they die.

Questions: Poems 190, 191, and 192

(a) These poems contrast strongly with such early lyrics as 'The Lake Isle of Innisfree' and 'The Fiddler of Dooney'. In 'The Fisherman', why has Yeats become disillusioned? For what kind of reader does he resolve to write?

(b) How do the language, imagery, and rhythms of these poems reflect this new temper?

194. AND DEATH SHALL HAVE NO DOMINION

See the notes on consonance and near-rhyme (p. 514), and transferred epithet (p. 516).

The prose sense of this poem is simple: though men die they will be raised at the end of time. This theme, which Thomas states in the first line of the poem, is developed in rich and powerful variations through to the last line. It is a reaffirmation of the general resurrection prophesied in the Book of Revelation; in fact, the poem can be read as an expansion of Revelation 20: 13: 'And the sea gave up the dead which were in it; and death and hell delivered up the dead which were in them.' Thomas's imagination was steeped in the Bible; his prophetic tone and many of his cadences derive from the same source.

The tone and mood of the poem progress from the explosive harshness of the first stanza, through the brutal imagery of torture in the second verse, to the more mellow affirmation of the final stanza. The title is drawn from Romans 6: 9: 'Knowing that Christ being raised from the dead dieth no more; death hath no more dominion over him.' **ll. 5-8** What parallels can you find with poem 159 (p. 258)? **l. 6 go mad** Become insane; leave this existence while insane. **l. 12 windily** A serious pun. The word refers back to the 'winding of the sea', suggesting both the movement of the sea and the shroud in which the dead are buried at sea. **l. 16 unicorn evils** The unicorn is often symbolic of Christ. Note the force of the paradox.

Questions: Poems 192, 193, and 194

(a) Contrast the attitudes and moods of these poets as they contemplate death.

(b) How is the form of each poem suited to the approach taken by the poet?

195. THE ISLES OF GREECE

See the note on ottava rima (p. 500).

Byron wrote the sixteen-canto poetic fantasy *Don Juan* before the war in which Greece gained her independence from Turkey. This selection from Canto III displays his deep admiration for

Greece, an admiration which led him to join in the struggle for freedom. These stanzas are presented as being in the manner of a Greek poet. They convey a strong sense of the countryside and traditions of Greece. **l. 2 Sappho** A lyric poetess, from the Greek island of Lesbos, who wrote about 600 B.C. **l. 4 Delos** A small island in the Aegean, supposed to have been summoned from the sea by Neptune. It was said to have been the birthplace of Phoebus Apollo, the god of the sun and of music, poetry, and prophecy. **l. 7 Marathon** A plain about 22 miles from Athens and the scene of a victory of the Athenians over the Persians in 490 B.C. Before the victory, a messenger ran the 150 miles from Athens to Sparta in 48 hours to convey a request for help; the modern marathon race perpetuates the memory of the feat. **l. 13 A king** Xerxes (c. 519-465 B.C.), king of the Persians. **l. 14 Salamis** The Greeks defeated Xerxes in 480 B.C. in a naval battle just off the island of Salamis near Attica. **ll. 22-24 A remnant . . . Thermopylae** In 480 B.C. Leonidas and three hundred Spartans heroically held off the forces of Xerxes at the pass of Thermopylae between Thessaly and Greece.

196. ALL THAT'S PAST

Contrast the philosophy and tone of this poem with those of poem 194 (p. 302). Observe de la Mare's control of vowels and consonants, particularly in the first stanza. **l. 24 amaranth** An imaginary flower that never fades.

197. ECHO

An example of de la Mare's ability to evoke the mysterious, fearful world of the troubled mind.

198. TO S. R. CROCKETT

Written by Stevenson when S. R. Crockett, a Scottish author, had dedicated a book of stories to him. **ll. 3-4** Lines from the dedication. Stevenson, an exile in Samoa because of his health, had expressed a desire to see Scotland once again before he died. **whaup** A large curlew.

Questions: Poems 195, 196, 197, 198, and 199

(a) Which of these poets discuss the passage of time in purely personal terms? Which discuss it in larger terms?

(b) Do the poets who are making abstract statements succeed in holding your interest? Why, or why not?

200. DEATH THE LEVELLER

See the note on metonymy (p. 494).

This is a song from Shirley's play, *The Contention of Ajax and Ulysses* (1659). In the early and middle seventeenth century, many writers gave voice to the disillusionment and sense of transience which had replaced the heroic self-confidence of the Elizabethans.

201. SONG from *Cymbeline*

From Act IV, scene 2, ll. 258-281.

A lament at the supposed death of Imogen, the heroine of the play, who had disguised herself as a boy. **l. 11 Physic** Medical knowledge. **l. 14 thunder-stone** Thunderbolt. **l. 18 Consign to thee** Submit to the same terms as you do; sign, together with you, a contract. **l. 19 exorciser** Here, one who conjures up evil spirits. **l. 21 unlaid** Not set at rest **l. 23 consummation** Completion of life.

202. SONG

A song in the comedy, *Summer's Last Will and Testament* (1600). The plagues at the end of the sixteenth century killed great numbers of people. Here the anxiety of men confronted by death is intensified for us by the sophisticated, elusive rhythms, and by liturgical and popular phrases expressing resignation. **l. 10 Phisick** The art of medicine. **l. 19 Helens** Helen of Troy. In the classical revival of the Renaissance, Helen of Troy became a conventional symbol of secular beauty. **l. 23 Hector** The most valiant Trojan leader in the battle for Troy. **l. 26** Bells were rung in the streets of London to warn people to stay indoors as the bodies of the dead were taken to burial during a plague. **l. 29** What is the effect of the change of rhythm? **l. 36 degree** Social rank.

204. I GIVE YOU THE END OF A GOLDEN STRING

l. 4 Jerusalem New Jerusalem, the heavenly city of God (Revelation 21: 2, 10).

Questions: Poems 200, 201, 202, and 204

(a) How has each poet used concrete images to realize his theme?
(b) It has been said that a lyric poem cannot achieve an effect akin to catharsis in tragedy. On the basis of these poems would you support or oppose this statement?

Biographies

ACORN
Milton
b. 1923

Milton Acorn has worked as a carpenter and factory hand in his native province, Prince Edward Island, and in Toronto, where he led a campaign for poetry readings in city parks. Always vigorous, sometimes brutal, his poetry reflects a passionate concern for the welfare of his fellow human beings.

THE FIGHTS p. 286

ARMSTRONG
Martin
b. 1882

Armstrong studied science and architecture at Cambridge University. Except for his army service in World War I, however, he has devoted his life largely to writing. In much of his poetry he expresses the humour and pathos in the lives of ordinary people.

MRS REECE LAUGHS p. 107

ARNOLD
Matthew
1822-88

For most of his life Arnold was an inspector of secondary schools; for ten years he was also Professor of Poetry at Oxford. An idealist, he wrote to pass on his conviction that the pursuit of a broad enlightened life of the mind was the highest form of human endeavour. His deep philosophic melancholy resulted from religious doubts and disillusionment with what he saw as the low calibre of national life. His active social conscience led him in later years to devote more of his energies to literary, religious, and social criticism than to poetry.

DOVER BEACH p. 211

AUDEN
Wystan Hugh
b. 1907

Auden was one of a group of English poets who became interested in Marxism during the depression of the 1930s. He has since become an American citizen, less radical politically, and an adherent of the Anglo-Catholic faith. In addition to his experiments with form, he is noted for daring wit and verbal skill.

LOOK, STRANGER p. 4
THE AVERAGE p. 39
THE UNKNOWN CITIZEN p. 40
TRUE LOVE p. 251

AVISON
Margaret
b. 1918

Miss Avison was born in Galt, Ontario, and graduated from the University of Toronto. Although she has been publishing her poems in various periodicals since 1939, her first collection of verse did not appear until 1960, and it contains only a fraction of her work. She combines visual and conceptual impressions in poetry that moves with detachment between immediate detail and the cosmic order.

THE SWIMMER'S MOMENT p. 268

BARRINGTON
Patrick William
Daines
(11th Viscount)
b. 1908

At various times a barrister, a second Lieutenant, a civil servant in the Foreign Office, and a contributor to *Punch,* Barrington is best known for his comic verse.

I HAD A DUCK-BILLED PLATYPUS p. 179

BELLOC
Hilaire
1870-1953

Born in France but educated in England, Belloc was a prolific writer of essays, travel books, and children's stories. His wit and zest for life won attention for his controversial opinions and his defence of Roman Catholicism.
ON HIS BOOKS p. 118

BETJEMAN
John
b. 1906

Betjeman's light verse recalls with whimsical affection the heyday of the upper middle class in England. His guides to several English counties are well known for their knowledgeable appreciation of English architecture and Victoriana.
A SUBALTERN'S LOVE SONG p. 197

BINKS
Sarah

See HIEBERT, Paul G.

BIRNEY
Alfred Earle
b. 1904

Earle Birney, a professor of English at the University of British Columbia, has won acclaim both as a humorist, for his army novel *Turvey*, and as a poet. A strong sense of irony permeates much of his work.
DUSK ON ENGLISH BAY p. 73

BLAKE
William
1757-1827

Blake, apprenticed as a child to a London engraver, later illustrated his poetry with his own distinctive engravings. He moved from clear, apparently simple lyrics to darker satirical poems and complex symbolic prophecies. A revolutionary thinker, he believed that divine love pervaded the world but could be known only in the human imagination, that the usual

contrast between good and evil was inadequate, and that external authority should be disregarded.
THE TYGER p. 83 and p. 85
THE SICK ROSE p. 227
AH! SUN-FLOWER p. 293
HE WHO BINDS TO HIMSELF p. 293
I GIVE YOU THE END OF A GOLDEN STRING p. 313

BRIDGES
Robert
1844-1930

Originally a physician, Bridges became Poet Laureate in 1913. His lyrical poems are distinguished by their exquisite and scholarly classicism and their controlled metre. He writes particularly of classical mythology and English landscape.
I LOVE ALL BEAUTEOUS THINGS p. 313

BRONTË
Emily
1818-48

Emily Brontë is best known as author of the novel *Wuthering Heights*. She lived with her talented but turbulent family on the edge of the lonely Yorkshire moors which set the mood for much of her writing. The form of her poems was often influenced by Methodist hymns.
FALL, LEAVES, FALL p. 29

BROOKE
Rupert
1887-1915

Brooke began writing poetry while at school, continuing at Cambridge University and during his travels in the United States, Canada, and the South Seas. Some of his most moving patriotic poems were written during World War I.
THE HILL p. 56
FISHES' HEAVEN p. 296

BROWNING
Elizabeth Barrett
1806-61

Elizabeth Barrett led the retired life of a semi-invalid until her romantic elopement from London to Italy with Robert Browning. Her literary reputation depends largely upon her letters and her love sonnets to her husband.

SONNET: 'How do I love thee?' p. 192

BROWNING
Robert
1812-89

As a believer in progress, liberty, and the individual's struggle for self-fulfilment, Browning appealed to the optimistic spirit of Victorian England. He wrote large-scale poetic dramas, short lyrics, and the remarkable dramatic monologues for which he perfected the poetic form. His frequently gnarled style is both vigorous and compressed. After his elopement with Elizabeth Barrett he lived for a long time in Italy, and the influence of the Renaissance on his work is quite evident. Browning societies were formed in England where he read and explained his own poetry to fashionable audiences.

HOME THOUGHTS FROM ABROAD p. 11
PORPHYRIA'S LOVER p. 193
MY LAST DUCHESS p. 195
THE BISHOP ORDERS HIS TOMB AT SAINT PRAXED'S CHURCH p. 237

BURNS
Robert
1759-96

Burns, a Scottish farmer burdened by poverty, had a great capacity for enjoying life. His aim was to fix in writing the sung and spoken tradition of the people and to return it to them as living literature. His poetry, which won him acceptance in Edinburgh at the height of its glory as an intellectual centre, reflected the robust humour, tenderness, and love of liberty of the Scottish people.

THE BRAW WOOER p. 199

BYRON
George Gordon
(6th Baron)
1788-1824

Wealthy, handsome, and unconventional, Lord Byron became a notorious romantic hero in England and finally escaped gossip by living in Europe. Passionately dedicated to the concept of freedom, he died in the Greek struggle for independence from Turkey. Although he wrote serious love lyrics, satirical poems, and reflective cantos on historical subjects, it was his brooding disillusioned hero, typified in Childe Harold, that had a profound influence on European literary thought.

SHE WALKS IN BEAUTY p. 246
THE ISLES OF GREECE from *Don Juan* p. 303

CAMPBELL
Roy
1901-57

After a stormy boyhood in South Africa, Campbell studied at Oxford University. He later lived in Spain where he became an amateur bull-fighter. His poems and translations show great verve and finesse in their handling of language.

SONG OF THE HORSEMAN, a version from García Lorca p. 273

CARMAN
Bliss
1861-1929

Born in New Brunswick of Loyalist stock, Carman gave up law studies and school-teaching for a life of wandering and poetry. At his best, he combined the lyrical celebration of nature with an elegiac melancholy at the passing of love. At times, however, his melodic lines fall into a glib lyricism.

LOW TIDE ON GRAND PRÉ p. 155

CHAUCER
Geoffrey
1340?-1400

Chaucer spent his life in the King's service, appointed to such various posts as sheriff and diplomatic agent. Since the Norman Conquest, the aristocracy in England had written and spoken in French. Chaucer wrote his long narrative poems in the London dialect, thereby establishing English as a literary language. Shrewd and loving in his insight into human nature, possessing a rich and varied humour, he ranks with the great authors of the world.

THE WIF OF BATHE, from the Prologue to the *Canterbury Tales* p. 105
LINES from the Prologue to the *Canterbury Tales* p. 215

CIARDI
John
b. 1916

A Bostonian who served as an air-gunner in the Pacific during World War II, Ciardi has become well known as a critic, professor of English, editor, and poet. His characteristically relaxed but incisive style is illustrated by the title of the essay *How Does A Poem Mean?* which has been included in this anthology. His version of Dante's *Divine Comedy* is one of the major translations of modern times.

CANTO III from *The Inferno,* a version from Dante p. 137
HOW DOES A POEM MEAN? p. 314

COHEN
Leonard
b. 1934

A native of Montreal, Cohen lives on the Mediterranean island of Hydra. He writes poetry and novels in which Jewish lore, secular cynicism, religious aspiration, and the celebration of physical love are combined.

GO BY BROOKS p. 247

COLERIDGE
Samuel Taylor
1772-1834

Although Coleridge's life was marred by poverty, poor health, and an addiction to opium, his mind teemed with ideas and projects. His contributions to poetry, philosophy, and literary criticism were original and stimulating, though the variety of his interests frequently prevented him from finishing projects. He wrote his greatest poetry – unique for its mysterious charged atmosphere – during the period of his friendship with Wordsworth.

THIS LIME-TREE BOWER MY PRISON p. 278

CORNFORD
Frances
1886-1960

Frances Cornford, the grand-daughter of Charles Darwin, lived in Cambridge, England, where she befriended many young poets including Rupert Brooke and Thom Gunn. She wrote unaffectedly on simple themes, imparting to them a pleasingly original flavour.

TO A FAT LADY SEEN FROM A TRAIN p. 7

CORY
William
1823-92

A naturally gifted teacher, William Cory spent most of his life as a classics master at Eton. His best poems are adaptations of Greek and Latin lyrics.

HERACLITUS p. 78

COWLEY
Abraham
1618-67

Cowley, a spy for the Royalists during the Cromwellian regime, wrote metaphysical lyrics, epics, and satirical comedies. He made fashionable the irregular ode, a variation of the classical ode, later imitated and refined upon by Dryden.

DRINKING p. 93

CRABBE
George
1754-1832

Crabbe practised medicine in Suffolk, England, before becoming a curate. He met the ugliness and unpleasantness of life squarely, with a grim sense of humour. In his stories and poetry he criticizes human foibles realistically and with biting wit. His long poem *The Village* is particularly memorable as an effective answer to Goldsmith's *The Deserted Village*.

THE NEWSPAPER p. 44

CUMMINGS
E. E.
1894-1962

Cummings, who was born in Massachusetts, won attention as a painter and draughtsman while living in Paris. His experiments with unusual typography and his unpredictable words and syntax give an amusing eccentricity to his otherwise simple satirical and romantic poetry.

ANYONE LIVED IN A PRETTY HOW TOWN p. 271

DANTE
Alighieri
1265-1321

Dante was involved in the bitter political feuds of medieval Florence; as a result of antagonizing the Pope in one such feud, he was banished to spend the last twenty years of his life in relative obscurity in Northern Italy and Paris. The penalty, if he returned, was to be death by burning. His most famous work, *The Divine Comedy*, was written during this exile. Sublime, brilliant, gracious, and grim in turns, it is both personal and topical. It is one of the great works of European literature.

CANTO III from *The Inferno* p. 137

DEKKER
Thomas
1570?-1632?

Dekker's many plays, poems, and tracts present a vivid picture of contemporary London. Although he suffered from poverty and was im-

prisoned for debt, his works, which express his sympathy for the poor and oppressed, are marked by a sunny simplicity.
GOLDEN SLUMBERS p. 226

DE LA MARE
Walter John
1873-1956

Walter de la Mare, a poet, novelist, and writer of short stories, is chiefly noted for his unique blend of reality and fantasy, and the whimsical haunting effects created by the musical quality of his writing. He is one of the comparatively few twentieth-century poets of note who adopted the traditional techniques of the previous century.
THE SONG OF THE MAD PRINCE p. 61
ALL THAT'S PAST p. 305
ECHO p. 306

DICKINSON
Emily
1830-86

Emily Dickinson lived a secluded life in her father's home in Massachusetts. Her poetry, in which profound thoughts are masked by apparent simplicity, was first published after her death. Her innovations in diction and rhyme make many of her poems miniature *tours de force.*
APPARENTLY WITH NO SURPRISE p. 88
THE LAST NIGHT THAT SHE LIVED p. 89
WITHIN MY GARDEN RIDES A BIRD p. 90
A ROUTE OF EVANESCENCE p. 91
I TASTE A LIQUOR NEVER BREWED p. 92

DOBSON
Henry Austin
1840-1921

Dobson, an English poet and man of letters, was educated in France and England. He is best known for his biographies of eighteenth-cen-

tury literary figures, and his light verse, characterized by the use of French verse forms.
A KISS p. 53

DONNE
John
1573-1631

Donne forfeited his career as secretary to Sir Thomas Egerton, Keeper of the Great Seal, by secretly marrying Anne More, Lady Egerton's niece. For this indiscretion he was dismissed from his position and imprisoned. After his wife's death, he entered the Church and won fame for the passionate, rhetorical sermons he preached as Dean of St Paul's. He created the metaphysical style in poetry, which influenced many writers in the seventeenth and twentieth centuries. Donne wrote most frequently about love; his early poems were written in praise of woman, the later ones in praise of God.
A VALEDICTION FORBIDDING MOURNING p. 254
A HYMN TO GOD THE FATHER p. 256
DEATH p. 257

DRYDEN
John
1631-1700

A versatile man of letters, Dryden became Poet Laureate under Charles II. After joining the Roman Catholic Church, however, he lost his public honours and lived his later years in poverty. His occasional and satirical poetry, poetic dramas, translations, and literary criticism had a wide influence among eighteenth-century writers. He made the heroic couplet a vehicle for witty and urbane comment.
SONG FOR ST CECILIA'S DAY, 1687 p. 63
ZIMRI from *Absalom and Achitophel* p. 98

ELIOT
Thomas Stearns
1888-1965

T. S. Eliot, born in St Louis, became a British subject in 1927. In the poems written before 1930, when his *Ash Wednesday* appeared, he expressed frustration with what he saw as a hypocritical, sterile society. The term 'Ash-Can School' has been applied to this poetry by his detractors. After his conversion to Anglo-Catholicism, his beliefs grew less pessimistic. He wrote perhaps his greatest poetry, the *Four Quartets,* on the transfiguration of ordinary life by the experience of the eternal. His revolutionary techniques, substantially derived from those of Ezra Pound, had a far-reaching influence on contemporary poets.

EMERSON
Ralph Waldo
1803-82

Emerson resigned from a promising career in the Unitarian ministry to develop a philosophy in which spiritual experience superseded formal religion. His competent, didactic poetry supplements the stimulating essays and lectures. He was one of the first American writers to gain international recognition.

EVTUSHENKO
Evgeny

See YEVTUSHENKO, Yevgeny.

FITZGERALD
Edward
1809-83

Fitzgerald, a friend of Tennyson and many other Victorian writers, is remembered chiefly for his poetic version of the *Rubáiyát* which he composed from existing translations in several languages.

SELECTIONS from the *Rubáiyát of Omar Khayyám* p. 289

FLECKER
James Elroy
1884-1915

Flecker served briefly as a British vice-consul before his early death from tuberculosis. He strove for the perfection of form which he found in French poetry. His optimism and boyish simplicity appeal to most readers.

TO A POET A THOUSAND YEARS HENCE p. 119

FROST
Robert
1875-1963

Although Frost's poetry has a basically American flavour, reflecting the years he spent in teaching, editing a newspaper, and running a farm in New England, the first recognition of his poetry came from Britain. He grew to be accepted as the quiet voice of rural and peaceable America, although he retained an individualist's approach to life. Geniality, rural speech patterns, and wry humour mark most of his poetry.

DEPARTMENTAL p. 42
THE DEATH OF THE HIRED MAN p. 145
STOPPING BY WOODS ON A SNOWY EVENING p. 152

GOLDSMITH
Oliver
1728-74

Author of a well-loved novel, *The Vicar of Wakefield,* and the amusing comedy *She Stoops to Conquer,* Goldsmith was a member of an important group of eighteenth-century writers and artists which included the famous Dr Johnson. Shy and undemonstrative as a person, he expressed in his writing a warmth and gentle charm.

THE VILLAGE MASTER from *The Deserted Village* p. 25

GRAVES
Robert
b. 1895

Graves served as a captain in World War I, and went on to become Professor of English at the Egyptian University in Cairo, before settling down to make his home on the island of Majorca, and establishing himself as a professional writer. He has written on Greek mythology, Roman history, and primitive Christianity. His poetry, prose, translations, and criticism have established him as one of the eminent men of letters of our time. Since 1961 he has been Professor of Poetry at Oxford.

MODERNIST POETRY AND THE PLAIN READER'S RIGHTS p. 335

GUNN
Thomson
b. 1929

Educated at Cambridge University, Thom Gunn has since emigrated to California. His poetry reveals his intuitive understanding of the primitive and the violent aspects of life. He has created in some of his poems a personal myth of the black-jacketed motorcycle rider as a kind of modern hero, rootless, but constantly pushing into the unknown in search of values.

ON THE MOVE p. 284

HARDY
Thomas
1840-1928

Hardy was a promising architect before he discovered his talent for writing. Relatively traditional in form, his novels are set in 'Wessex' – his native Dorsetshire. They reveal his belief that fate pursues its course relentlessly, indifferent to human suffering. His poems also reveal his human sympathy and deep awareness of the ironies of life, but they break away from Victorian diction and methods of poetic organization.

GREAT THINGS p. 109
IN TIME OF 'THE BREAKING OF NATIONS' p. 276
THE DARKLING THRUSH p. 291

HENDERSON
Harold G.
b. 1889

Born in New York City, and a chemical engineer by training, Henderson became interested in Oriental culture. He spent three years in Japan, and then taught the history of Japanese art at Columbia University. In 1960 the Japanese government awarded him the Order of the Sacred Treasure.

IN EXILE, a version from the Japanese p. 162
THE APPRENTICE PRIESTLING, a version from Shiki p. 272

HERBERT
George
1593-1633

Herbert renounced an academic career at Cambridge University to become a parson in rural England. His metaphysical poems, concerned chiefly with his personal faith, are noted for their unusual form and elaborate, ingenious metaphors.

LOVE p. 259
VIRTUE p. 260

HERRICK
Robert
1591-1674

Herrick wrote bright lyrics celebrating the joys of simple pastoral life, adopting the classical theme of *carpe diem* – taste the pleasures of life before they fade. After his appointment as

a clergyman in Devonshire he turned to religious subjects.
WHENAS IN SILKS p. 241
A SWEET DISORDER p. 242

HIEBERT
Paul G.
b. 1892

Paul Hiebert, a retired professor of chemistry, created Sarah Binks, her poetry, and her biography from his own quizzical imagination. The 'Sweet Songstress of Saskatchewan' produces poetry of monumental ineptitude, while the critical commentary devised by Hiebert spoofs all that was ever misguided and provincial in the appreciation of poetry.
HYMN TO ROVER p. 182

HODGSON
Ralph
1871-1962

An English poet who moved to the United States, Hodgson wrote simple melodic poetry which often expressed his feeling of comradeship with the inarticulate and oppressed. Many of his poems take animals as their subject.
REASON HAS MOONS p. 221

HOPKINS
Gerard Manley
1844-89

Hopkins became a Jesuit novice at the age of twenty-two. He suppressed his desire to write poetry and learn the Welsh language: to him they were forms of self-indulgence. An understanding superior, however, advised him to cultivate his aesthetic talents. Influenced by Welsh and Anglo-Saxon poetry, Hopkins developed an energetic vocabulary which drew upon alliteration, coined words, and rich sound patterns. The study of classical and Welsh metres led to the development of sprung rhythm. Modern poets have applied these techniques with interesting variations. Many of Hopkins' poems

reflect his ecstatic response to nature as a manifestation of God's love.
HURRAHING IN HARVEST p. 163
GOD'S GRANDEUR p. 277

HOUSMAN
Alfred Edward
1859-1936

A. E. Housman produced four volumes of lyrics, only two of which were published during his lifetime. He created a simplified style suitable for his melancholy, philosophical reminiscences of Shropshire, his boyhood home.
EIGHT O'CLOCK p. 79
ON WENLOCK EDGE p. 294
HER STRONG ENCHANTMENTS FAILING p. 295

HUGHES
Langston
b. 1902

Langston Hughes, whose first volume of poems was hailed as a revival of Negro art in America, writes mainly of the sufferings of his people. He writes essentially as a city poet; his rhythms are those of jazz and the blues.
LITTLE GREEN TREE p. 32
SNAIL p. 227

HUGHES
Ted
b. 1930

Although Hughes is a graduate of Cambridge and a former university teacher, his poetry still has the brooding wildness of the Yorkshire moors. Many of his poems contrast the defiance and independence of animals, or of men who live by their immediate instincts, with the more effete representatives of civilization.
HAWK ROOSTING p. 183

JARRELL
Randall
b. 1914

Randall Jarrell, poet, professor, critic, and editor, was born in Nashville, Tennessee. His experiences in the Second World War are responsible for many of his best known poems, although he is by no means a war poet. His unacademic approach to poetry is indicated by his statement: 'A good poet is someone who manages in a lifetime of standing out in thunderstorms, to be struck by lightning five or six times; a dozen or two dozen times and he is great.'

THE TRUTH p. 70

JOHNSTON
George
b. 1913

George Johnston writes mainly of the suburban lives of ordinary people in light verse that is whimsical but by no means superficial. He is a professor of English at Carleton University, Ottawa, and is popular for his colourful recitations of poetry.

WAR ON THE PERIPHERY p. 72

JONSON
Benjamin
1572-1637

Jonson's brawling masculine spirit, which led to his imprisonment on two occasions, made such plays as *The Alchemist* exuberant masterpieces. Paradoxically, the civilized grace of his lyrics made them models for the Cavalier poets at court. His rigorous scholarship and painstaking approach to writing are often contrasted with the more freewheeling genius of Shakespeare.

HYMN TO DIANA p. 225

JOYCE
James
1882-1941

Joyce passed most of his life as a voluntary exile from his native Dublin, for he believed that Ireland could not forget its religious prejudices sufficiently to appreciate art. His originality emerges most strongly in the coined language and stream-of-consciousness technique that he uses to portray character in his novels. Many contemporary writers have been greatly influenced by his techniques.

I HEAR AN ARMY CHARGING UPON THE LAND p. 30
THE HITHERANDTHITHERING WATERS OF from *Finnegan's Wake* p. 31

KEATS
John
1795-1821

Keats abandoned the study of medicine in order to devote his life to poetry, becoming one of the great figures of the English Romantic movement. His poems are characterized by an intense yearning for beauty and an imaginative evocation of the sensuous. Never physically robust, he became seriously ill with tuberculosis in 1820, and died the following year.

SONNET: 'Bright Star!' p. 55
SONNET: 'When I have fears' p. 115
ODE ON A GRECIAN URN p. 189

KIPLING
Rudyard
1865-1936

Born in Bombay, Kipling wrote short stories and novels, many of which gave a colourful, dramatic picture of India. His verse celebrates the qualities of bravery, self-sufficiency and patriotism. His writing has survived a reaction against the jingoism of his time.

CITIES AND THRONES AND POWERS p. 308

KLEIN
Abraham M.
b. 1909

Klein, a resident of Montreal, reflected in his early poetry his absorption in Jewish history, philosophy, social conditions, and religious rites. In his later works the emphasis shifts to French-Canadian themes.

AUTOBIOGRAPHICAL p. 8

LAMPMAN
Archibald
1861-99

Lampman, an Ottawa civil servant, cultivated his deep appreciation of nature on canoe trips and walking excursions. His reading of Keats and Wordsworth influenced his poetic style.
IN NOVEMBER p. 154

LARKIN
Philip
b. 1922

Larkin is an English university librarian and an authority on jazz. In poems which deliberately avoid a heroic style he frequently explores the 'quiet desperation' beneath the surface of ordinary people's lives.
CHURCH GOING p. 216

LAWRENCE
David Herbert
1885-1930

Born and raised in an English coal-mining family, Lawrence became acutely sensitive to brutality and vitally concerned with human relationships. He travelled widely in Europe and America, hoping to find a society that did not shackle the elemental drives in human nature. His poetry and novels, which reflect his deep response to his experiences, explore the psychology of love and hate.
SNAKE p. 12
GIORNO DEI MORTI p. 34

LAYTON
Irving
b. 1912

The gifted, rambunctious poetry of this Montreal writer has always aroused controversy in Canada. He celebrates the sensual life, sees the poet as a prophetic hero, and pours scorn on all who would limit his absolute freedom. His vigorous imagery and speech cadences are frequently controlled by a painstaking craftsmanship.
THE BIRTH OF TRAGEDY p. 116
THE COLD GREEN ELEMENT p. 269

LEAR
Edward
1812-88

Lear wrote and illustrated accounts of his travels, but is best known for his *Book of Nonsense* and his popularization of the limerick.
SELF PORTRAIT p. 35

LEVI
Peter
b. 1931

Peter Levi is a graduate of Oxford and a member of the Society of Jesus. His poetry is spare and controlled, and frequently takes the form of meditation on images from nature. He translated Yevtushenko's 'Birthday' in collaboration with Professor Milner-Gulland, who first provided a literal translation of the Russian.
BIRTHDAY, a version from Yevtushenko p. 282

LI PO
701-762

A Chinese poet whose verses are among the finest known, Li Po combined a love of adventure with a light-hearted disregard of honours and rewards. In his youth, he and five companions were known as 'The Six Idlers of the Bamboo Streams'. He was highly favoured by the emperor, but petitioned to be allowed to leave the court to lead the life he preferred. He is said to have been drowned while attempting to kiss the moonlit water on which his boat was sailing. Some two thousand poems are accepted as his work, though this may be only about a tenth of the number he wrote.
THE RIVER-MERCHANT'S WIFE: A LETTER, a version by Ezra Pound p. 202

LORCA
Federico García
1898-1936

Born and raised on a farm in the province of Granada in southern Spain, Lorca began the study of law but soon abandoned it for poetry and drama, becoming one of his country's greatest playwrights. Though he took little part in politics, he was shot by Fascist soldiers during the Spanish Civil War. His great poetic themes were love and death and their ritual expression in birth, marriage, and funeral. He fused sophisticated techniques with a style drawn from gypsy ballads, folk songs, and even children's lyrics.

SONG OF THE HORSEMAN, a version by Roy Campbell p. 273

LOWELL
Robert
b. 1917

Robert Lowell, probably the most talented poet of the Lowell family, has lectured on poetry and creative writing. His early poetry relies on complex metaphors fused under great emotional pressure; in his later work he has developed a simpler, more direct form of expression. Whether religious or autobiographical, his poems issue from a tragic sense of life.

HOME AFTER THREE MONTHS AWAY p. 274

LOWRY
Malcolm
1909-57

Born in England, Lowry left university to go to sea. For many years he lived in a shack on the beach near Vancouver; the stories of his unsettled life have made him a minor legend in North American literature. His vigorous tormented writing includes poetry and several autobiographical novels, which explore the guilt and agony of the alcoholic.

KINGFISHERS IN BRITISH COLUMBIA p. 184

MACKAY
Louis
b. 1901

A native of Hansall, Ontario, Mackay was educated at the University of Toronto. A professor of classics, at present in California, Mackay writes robustly satiric poetry.

THE ILL-TEMPERED LOVER p. 57

MAC LEISH
Archibald
b. 1892

MacLeish, an American lawyer, has taken part in the Spanish Civil War, edited *Fortune* magazine, helped to plan UNESCO, and lectured at Harvard. His poetry, plays, and essays depict man's attempt to find himself in the vastness of the universe.

EPISTLE TO BE LEFT IN THE EARTH p. 128

MAC NEICE
Louis
1907-63

Irish by birth, MacNeice lectured in classics at Oxford University and then became an author-producer with the British Broadcasting Corporation. He wrote of the contemporary scene, transforming colloquial speech into poetry by the skilful use of pauses, changed rhythms, and word order.

SNOW p. 153

MACPHERSON
Jay
b. 1932

Born in England and educated at Carleton University, Ottawa, Miss Macpherson now lectures at Victoria College in Toronto. Drawing on traditional literature from nursery rhymes and riddles to the Bible and the songs of William Blake, her witty poems achieve a highly sophisticated simplicity.

COLD STONE p. 174

MARLOWE
Christopher
1564-93

Marlowe epitomizes the man of the Renaissance in his intoxication with the physical universe, his search for the extremes of sensual and spiritual experience, and the mixture of scorn and deep fascination in his attitude to religion. He contributed to the development of Elizabethan drama by the rhetorical power of his blank verse and the arrogant sweep of his

imagination. His unsolved murder in a tavern brawl cut short a career that might have rivalled Shakespeare's.
THE SHEPHERD TO HIS LOVE p. 21
THE LAST HOUR OF FAUSTUS from *The Tragical History of Dr Faustus* p. 218

MARQUIS
Don
1878-1937

Marquis's columns in New York newspapers and his books such as *archy and mehitabel* made him popular as a satirist. In archy the cockroach he created a voice for his raffish opinions on contemporary life.
CHEERIO MY DEARIO p. 233

MARVELL
Andrew
1621-78

Marvell, employed as a tutor to Lord Fairfax's daughter during Cromwell's regime, later entered politics and wrote violent satires against Charles II. His witty humane lyrics were influenced by metaphysical poetry.
TO HIS COY MISTRESS p. 243

MC GINLEY
Phyllis
b. 1905

An author of light humorous essays, verse, and children's books, Phyllis McGinley lives in New York. Her poems appear in *The New Yorker* and other well-known magazines.
GIRL'S-EYE VIEW OF RELATIVES p. 229

MEREDITH
George
1828-1909

An Englishman, aristocratic in outlook and iconoclastic in opinion, Meredith wrote poems, novels, and an outstanding essay on comedy. His style in poetry is complex, sometimes obscure.
LUCIFER IN STARLIGHT p. 221

MILLAY
Edna St Vincent
1892-1950

Edna St Vincent Millay became popular in America during the 1920s as a high-spirited rebel. Her lyrics are direct emotional statements, often tinged with a grave disillusionment. Among her best work are the love sonnets, which draw extensively on the resources of the great Elizabethan sequences.

DIRGE WITHOUT MUSIC p. 301

MILTON
John
1608-74

Milton was a renowned scholar, polemicist, and poet in seventeeth-century England. Much of his work reveals his impassioned belief in individual, religious, and civil liberty. He experimented in the use of classical and medieval poetic forms – odes, elegies, pastorals, sonnets, epics, and poetic drama. He interrupted his writing to become Secretary of Foreign Tongues to Oliver Cromwell, continuing for several years in this position despite his failing eyesight. His epic *Paradise Lost*, composed, and dictated to his daughter, after he became totally blind, takes its place with Homer's *Iliad*, Vergil's *Aeneid*, and Dante's *Divine Comedy* among the great poetic achievements of mankind.

HAIL, HOLY LIGHT from *Paradise Lost*, Book III p. 261
LAST CHORUS from *Samson Agonistes* p. 263
ON HIS BLINDNESS p. 264

MOORE
Marianne
b. 1887

Miss Moore, an American, was successively a teacher, a librarian, and a literary editor. Her verse, which is highly experimental, has had a distinct influence on many of the recent American writers. She developed a particular

quality in her poetry which is described by Kenneth Burke: 'If she were discussing the newest model of automobile I think she would somehow contrive to suggest an antiquarian interest.'
SILENCE p. 108

MORTON
John Bingham
b. 1893

J. B. Morton is best known for his satirical column written under the name 'Beachcomber' in a London newspaper. His publications include several biographies of famous Frenchmen, humorous stories, satire, and poetry.
THE DANCING CABMAN p. 96

NASH
Ogden
b. 1902

Ogden Nash, besides working on scenarios for Hollywood, writes light poetry characterized by an absurd twisting of words and rhymes. His bantering style gives piquancy to his mild social criticism. The first collected edition of his poems was called *The Golden Trashery of Ogden Nashery.*
REFLECTIONS ON ICE-BREAKING p. 95
NO DOCTORS TODAY, THANK YOU p. 281

NASHE
Thomas
1567-1601

A writer of pamphlets, plays, and novels, Nashe took an active part against the Puritans in the ardent religious controversy of Elizabethan England.
SONG from *Summer's Last Will and Testament* p. 311

OWEN
Wilfred
1893-1918

Owen was born in Shropshire and died in France one week before the armistice which ended World War I. A precocious poet, he wrote angrily about the tragedy and waste of war.

ANTHEM FOR DOOMED YOUTH p. 67
STRANGE MEETING p. 68

PEAKE
Mervyn Laurence
b. 1911

Peake, born in China of English parents, now lives in England. In addition to his poetry, he has published novels and plays; he is also well-known for his work as a painter and illustrator.

THE COCKY WALKERS p. 283

PICKTHALL
Marjorie Lowrey Christie
1883-1922

Marjorie Pickthall was born in England, but lived much of her life in Toronto. Her poems and short stories are often concerned with mystical Christianity, death, and haunting dreams of medieval times.

ST YVES' POOR p. 81

POPE
Alexander
1688-1744

During his childhood Pope contracted a crippling disease. This handicap and the discrimination he suffered as a Roman Catholic in eighteenth-century England contributed to the bitterness with which he conducted his literary feuds. He brought the poetry of satire to a new level of brilliance and elegant irony. Through his verbal dexterity and his great skill in the use of balance and antithesis he perfected the heroic couplet.

EPIGRAM p. 97
CANTO III from *The Rape of the Lock* p. 99

POUND
Ezra Loomis
b. 1885

After a stormy career in American universities Pound emigrated to England and finally to Italy. He has always aroused controversy, whether as a poetic innovator or in his heroic, often ingenuous attempts to renew Western civilization single-handed. The erratic violence of his political views led him to broadcast Fascist propaganda for Italy during World War II. He was committed to an asylum by an American federal court from 1945 to 1958. His poetry is marked by great sensitivity and flexible control in both cadence and language, and his translations are among the finest in English literature.

IN A STATION OF THE METRO p. 127

THE TRIUMPH OF BACCHUS from *The Cantos* p. 176

THE RIVER MERCHANT'S WIFE: A LETTER, a version from Li Po p. 202

PRATT
Edwin John
1883-1964

E. J. Pratt left his native Newfoundland to study and teach at the University of Toronto, but never forgot the rugged coast and sea of his youth. His narrative poems frequently contrast the mindless, sometimes destructive, energies of nature with the hard-won triumphs of human ingenuity and courage. Pratt's ability to spin a tale and his exuberant use of technical language combine to place him in a distinctive, personal niche in the literature of his time.

THE ICEBERG from *The Titantic* p. 125

EROSION p. 127

THE PRIZE CAT p. 231

RALEGH
Sir Walter
1552-1618

Sir Walter Ralegh is popularly known for his position of favour in the court of Queen Elizabeth and his expeditions to the Americas. It is thought that he wrote his graceful lyrics

in the Tower of London where he was imprisoned and finally executed on a charge of conspiring against James I. Only about thirty of these lyrics have survived.
THE NYMPH'S REPLY p. 22

RALEIGH
Sir Walter
Alexander
1861-1922

Sir Walter was a distinguished professor of English at various British universities. He is best known for his essays and literary criticism.
WISHES OF AN ELDERLY MAN AT A GARDEN PARTY p. 288

REANEY
James
b. 1926

Reaney is one of the leading experimental poets in Canada, combining a scholarly knowledge of literature with a freewheeling, witty gift of invention. Many of his poems and plays depict life in and around Stratford, Ontario, his birthplace. He is currently a professor of English at the University of Western Ontario.
BRANWELL'S LAMENT from *A Suit of Nettles: June* p. 167

ROBERTS
Sir Charles G. D.
1860-1943

Roberts led the Canadian poets who, in the 1890s, were discovering the aesthetic potential of the landscape of northern Ontario and the Maritimes. Less familiar than his nature poetry and animal stories are the 'transcendental' poems in which he places man face to face with the universe or with God.
THE MOWING p. 164
IN THE WIDE AWE AND WISDOM OF THE NIGHT p. 222
THE UNSLEEPING p. 265

ROBINSON
Edwin
Arlington
1869-1935

Living entirely for his poetry, Robinson supported himself by a succession of jobs until President Theodore Roosevelt created a sinecure for him. His poetry includes many portraits of small-town characters sketched in clear outline. His style combines precision and economy with unexpected irony and wry humour.
RICHARD CORY p. 37

ROETHKE
Theodore
1908-63

Roethke lectured in English at a succession of American universities. He wrote sensitive lyrics which drew on his detailed observation of nature to describe man's kinship with all forms of life. Many of his poems trace a progression from despair to ecstatic joy.
A FIELD OF LIGHT p. 16

ROSSETTI
Christina
1830-94

Born in England of Italian parentage, Christina Rossetti is known for her allegories, children's verse, and religious poetry. Clearly conceived and vividly expressed, often pictorial, her poetry has a spiritual melancholy cast.
A BIRTHDAY p. 204

SACKVILLE-WEST
Victoria
1892-1962

Besides two long pastoral poems, Victoria Sackville-West has written novels, a history of the famous Sackville family, and books on gardening.
SHEPHERDS AND STARS from *The Land* p. 20

SANDBURG
Carl
1878-1964

Sandburg is famous for his great biography of Abraham Lincoln. As a poet, he has become a spokesman for industrial America. In championing the common man, he developed a tough, powerful idiom to depict both the vitality and the brutal injustices of the society in which he lives.

NIGHT BELLS p. 226

SHAKESPEARE
William
1564-1616

Shakespeare grew up in Stratford, married at eighteen, and later joined an acting company in London. His early plays were relatively awkward attempts to follow the accepted pattern of his predecessors and of contemporaries such as Marlowe, but within two decades he had created the greatest body of drama ever written. His 154 sonnets, which for ten years he showed only to friends, trace the course of an intimate friendship, the poet's discovery of his own genius, and his musings on time, death, and love.

SONNET XVIII: 'Shall I compare thee to a summer's day?' p. 54
SONNET XXX: 'When to the sessions of sweet silent thought' p. 76
SONNET LX: 'Like as the waves make towards the pebbled shore' p. 77
SONNET LV: 'Not marble, nor the gilded momuments' p. 118
SONNET CXVI: 'Let me not to the marriage of true minds' p. 191
SONG from *Cymbeline* p. 310

SHELLEY
Percy Bysshe
1792-1822

Shelley was expelled from Oxford for his pamphlet *The Necessity of Atheism*, and later left England to avoid public censure of his radical convictions in politics, morality, and religion. While living in Switzerland and Italy he wrote pantheistic lyrics of great beauty, portraying

God and the natural universe as synonymous. He tried to sustain a tone of ecstatic elevation by deliberate imprecision of imagery, vowel music, and the repeated use of such words as 'soaring' and 'ethereal'. His lyrical drama, *Prometheus Unbound*, sums up his vision of freedom in which the human spirit is to triumph over all who would restrain it by force.

ODE TO THE WEST WIND p. 26
TO A SKYLARK p. 185

SHIKI
Masaoka
1867-1902

Shiki, a precocious young Japanese poet who suffered from tuberculosis, dedicated his whole life to developing a more natural style in the writing of haikus. He shocked his contemporaries by disparaging the artificiality of much of the work of his revered seventeenth-century predecessor, Matsuo Basho.

THE APPRENTICE PRIESTLING, a version by Harold Henderson p. 272

SHIRLEY
James
1596-1666

Originally a priest in the Church of England, Shirley later joined the Roman Catholic Church and became a teacher. He was also a popular playwright. His best known poems are lyrics from his plays.

DEATH THE LEVELLER p. 309

SITWELL
Dame Edith
1887-1964

The poetry of Edith Sitwell communicates a strange intensity by combining apparently alien images, and by making use of private symbols and modern dance rhythms. She once said that her hobbies were 'listening to music and silence'.

GREEN FLOWS THE RIVER OF LETHE—O p. 212

SMITH
A. J. M.
b. 1902

A native of Montreal, Smith has spent his life in university teaching. His trenchant criticism during the thirties and forties set far more rigorous standards than Canadian poetry was attaining at the time. His own writing is disciplined and austere.

THE LONELY LAND p. 18

SOUSTER
Raymond
b. 1921

A bank clerk, Souster writes terse, slangy poems, each based on a single everyday incident, which together form a multiple image of life in the city of Toronto. Many of his poems champion the victims of impersonality and injustice.

THE TOP HAT p. 288

SPENDER
Stephen
b. 1909

Spender was one of a group of politically radical English poets headed by W. H. Auden in the 1930s. His sense of urgency, sustained rhythms, and use of machine-age images frequently produce poetry which is vivid and exciting. In 1953 he became co-editor of the important English journal of opinion, *Encounter.*

I THINK CONTINUALLY p. 75

SPENSER
Edmund
1552-99

One of the early Elizabethans who created English poetry, Spenser wrote his major work, the allegory of *The Faerie Queene,* while serving eighteen years as a political appointee in Ireland. His pictorial imagery and masterly handling of sound and rhythm give a rich texture to his serious themes of religion, love, and morality.

THE SHEPHEARDES LAMENT from *The Shepheardes Calender: December* p. 165

STEPHENS
James
1882-1950

Stephens was born in the slums of Dublin, and became an authority on Gaelic literature and art. In his prose fantasy, *The Crock of Gold,* he contributed to a new mythology for Ireland. He delighted in incongruities, ranging from high-spirited shenanigans to gentle solemnity or impassioned prophecy.

WHAT THE DEVIL SAID p. 80
A GLASS OF BEER p. 95

STEVENS
Wallace
1879-1955

An American insurance executive, Stevens published his first volume of poetry at the age of forty-four. He wrote frequently of the longing, anguish, and consolations of the religious skeptic, preferring to work through suggestive detail rather than by explicit statement. His extravagant, mannered language and brilliantly sustained cadences make him one of the twentieth-century masters of technique.

DOMINATION OF BLACK p. 130

STEVENSON
Robert Louis
1850-94

Stevenson, a Scot, suffered from tuberculosis for most of his life and travelled widely in search of a favourable climate. His final voyage took him to Samoa in the South Seas, where he spent his last days. A sedulous craftsman with words, he found expression for his humour and vigorous imagination chiefly in adventure stories and children's verse.

TO S. R. CROCKETT p. 307

SUCKLING
Sir John
1609-42

Suckling, a gallant, witty Cavalier poet, fought for the King in the Civil Wars and then fled to France where, in fear of poverty, he is said to have committed suicide. His songs, many of which were incorporated into his plays, display a flippant cynicism which masks his melancholy spirit.

THE CONSTANT LOVER p. 205

LOVE TURNED TO HATRED p. 206

SWINBURNE
Algernon Charles
1837-1909

Because Swinburne repudiated the moral and religious conventions of Victorian England he was both scorned and venerated by his generation. His rich melodious verse recreates the pagan spirit of classical literature and mythology.

LINES from 'The Garden of Proserpine' p. 33

SYNGE
John Millington
1871-1909

Synge depicts in his plays the realistic, comical, and mystical elements of the Irish character. He developed a lyrical, earthy style based on the dialect of the Aran Islands off the Irish coast.

AN OLD WOMAN'S LAMENTATIONS, a version from François Villon p. 47

TENNYSON
Alfred Lord
1809-92

Tennyson's skill with imitative harmony, melodious language and vivid phrasing made him a much-quoted poet during his lifetime. In 1833 the death of his friend, Arthur Hallam, precipitated a period of religious doubt in his life. *In Memoriam* traces the gradual resolution of that doubt and the achievement of a mystical faith. While he was Poet Laureate, Tennyson described the legendary exploits of King Arthur as statesman and religious leader,

using them to mirror the conflicts of Victorian England.
ULYSSES p. 143
TEARS, IDLE TEARS from *The Princess* p. 169
SELECTIONS from *In Memoriam* p. 170

TESSIMOND
A. S. J.
1902-62

At the age of 16, Tessimond ran away to London from his home in Birkenhead. Failing to make a living there, he resumed his studies, took a university degree, and eventually became a writer of advertising copy. Much of his poetry dealt with modern urban life in England.
CATS p. 232

THOMAS
Dylan
1914-53

The energetic, wayward life of this Welsh poet has become a modern legend. His rich, commanding voice won him a wide audience as he read his poetry and sketches for the BBC and on tours in the United States. Using in English the rich idiom of Welsh speech, he developed rhetorical rhythms and explosive, sensuous language. Artfully ambiguous diction and traditional symbols charged with private significance may at first obscure his meaning, but render his feelings with precision.
FERN HILL p. 1
WELSH NIGHT from *Under Milk Wood* p. 223
AND DEATH SHALL HAVE NO DOMINION p. 302

THOMAS
R. S.
b. 1902

A vicar in West Wales, Thomas writes of the poverty and dignity of the people he serves. His cadences suggest something of the bleakness of his native country.
A PEASANT p. 38

TURNBULL
Gael
b. 1928

Born in Edinburgh, Gael Turnbull spent his boyhood not far from Lindisfarne, and has lived in England, Canada, and the United States. During his three years as a logging camp doctor in northern Ontario he was one of the first translators of French-Canadian poetry into English. Many of his own poems, written while he was an anaesthetist in California, have been published under the name of 'Migrant'; his restlessness has now taken him, together with his wife and family, back to England. It is appropriate that his work and his attitude of mind should be represented here by 'An Irish Monk on Lindisfarne'.

AN IRISH MONK ON LINDISFARNE, ABOUT 650 A.D. p. 207

WALEY
Arthur
b. 1889

Waley is an English authority on Chinese and Japanese literature; his translations of Chinese lyrics rank as poetry in their own right.

PLUCKING THE RUSHES, a version from an anonymous Chinese poem p. 201

WHITMAN
Walt
1819-92

Whitman's work has been called the beginning of modern poetry; yet its lack of inhibition, its robust spirit of brotherhood, and its aggressive free verse aroused rage and derision. Whitman's great subject was himself, as spokesman of the teeming America that he loved and as archetypal man in harmony with the cosmos. Although he finally achieved recognition, Whitman died in poverty. His influence has persisted in the rhythms and themes of subsequent American poetry.

SELECTIONS from *Song of Myself* p. 110

WILKINSON
Anne
1910-61

Anne Wilkinson was born in Toronto, but received most of her education informally in Europe. Her poetry, with its distinctive combination of romanticism and wit, has not been widely read, probably because the reader must establish each poem's terms of reference in order to perceive its coherence.

CAROL p. 132

WILLIAMS
William Carlos
1883-1963

Williams, a physician in a small New Jersey town, was also an experimental writer. To avoid being 'poetic', in the sense of being artificial, he developed a conversational rhythm and diction, while constantly relating his ideas to the physical world.

RALEIGH WAS RIGHT p. 24

WORDSWORTH
William
1770-1850

Wordsworth was the prime figure of the Romantic movement in English poetry. He and Coleridge expressed their radical beliefs about poetry in the preface to their *Lyrical Ballads.* Rejecting the artificial conventions of eighteenth-century poetry, Wordsworth undertook to write of common life exalted by powerful feeling. Reflecting on his boyhood in the English Lake District he wrote of his belief that the spiritual education of the sensitive individual depended upon the interaction of nature and the imagination. The French Revolution and events in England inspired his stirring political sonnets.

THERE WAS A BOY from *The Prelude* p. 5
SONNET: 'The World is too much with us' p. 6
SONNET: 'It is not to be thought of that the Flood' p. 66

LINES COMPOSED A FEW MILES ABOVE TINTERN ABBEY p. 157
SHE DWELT AMONG THE UNTRODDEN WAYS p. 245

YEATS
William Butler
1865-1939

Yeats' colourful career included a prolonged and unhappy love affair, nationalist activities during the Gaelic revival, assistance in the founding of the famous Abbey Theatre in Dublin, and lifelong experiments with magic and the occult. His lonely childhood was reflected in the languid rhythms and world-weary mood of such early lyrics as 'The Lake Isle of Innisfree'. Gradually, however, he forged a style whose racy, idiomatic language and hard, sometimes brutal, imagery allowed him to move from controlled invective to poignant love poetry or to exalted philosophical reasoning. T. S. Eliot called him the greatest lyric poet of the century.

A DRUNKEN MAN'S PRAISE OF SOBRIETY p. 94
THE FISHERMAN p. 297
THE CHOICE from 'A Dialogue of Self and Soul' p. 299
DEATH p. 300

YEVTUSHENKO
Yevgeny
Alexandrovich
b. 1933

The son of Siberian peasants, Yevtushenko has had spectacular success with the Russian public, particularly with the younger generation who find represented in his poetry their special concerns and problems. His poetry often deals with social themes, where his independence of mind has continually provoked hostile government reaction. His poetic style is racy and declamatory.

BIRTHDAY, a version by Peter Levi and Robin Milner-Gulland p. 282

Glossary

OF TERMS
USED IN THE
DISCUSSION
OF POETRY

Although talking about a poem must never be taken for experiencing it, a fuller understanding of the components of poetry clarifies a reader's sense of values and allows what may have been a vague appreciation to become a rich response. It is for this reason that the following comments have been included. Some titles of books useful for further study have been indicated on pages 518-519.

ACCENTUAL VERSE See RHYTHM (p. 509).

ALEXANDRINE A verse line in iambic hexameter; that is, one having six iambic feet. Although its use is limited in English, in French verse the alexandrine has an importance equivalent to that of the iambic pentameter in English.

ALLEGORY See IMAGERY (p. 489).

ALLITERATION See SOUND (p. 514).

ALLUSION Allusion is an undeveloped reference to some figure, place or event outside the immediate framework of the subject discussed. It may be historical, biblical, mythological, or literary. In poetry such as the Homeric epics, where a listening audience may be taxed by the details of an unfolding story, allusions to matters of common background are used to provide a reassuring atmosphere of familiarity. An allusion may also enrich a poem by inducing the reader, at the mention of a proper noun or strategic phrase, to recall an entire story. He is expected to apply its significant features to the subject being discussed, without there being any actual digression at the surface level of the poem.

When Milton mentions the Orphean lyre in 'Hail, Holy Light' (p. 261) from *Paradise Lost,* he invokes the whole story of Orpheus and Eurydice. Allusion may even be used for comic effect. When Ogden Nash in 'No Doctors Today, Thank You' (p. 281) says that he has 'the agility of a Greek god and the appetite of a Victorian' the knowing reader mentally refers to his knowledge of Apollo, Hermes, and Adonis, and of the bounding gusto of the Victorian period; the slightly ludicrous picture that results could only be achieved by comic allusion.

Modernist Allusion. Modernist allusion not only refers to earlier history or literature, but frequently incorporates the actual phrases of earlier writing. Thus a modernist writer may weave into the texture of his poem a fragment from Shakespeare, Dante, or a state document of the Renaissance. The intention is usually to give a double perspective on the subject of the poem, whether by providing an ironic contrast, or by reinforcing some element of that subject, or by suggesting the continuity of human experience.

In 'The Hollow Men' (p. 135), Eliot juxtaposes a re-worded nursery rhyme, 'Here we go round the prickly pear', and a quotation from the Lord's Prayer, 'For Thine is the Kingdom'. The combination of allusions is neither blasphemy nor plagiarism, for Eliot is deliberately taking our minds back to the certainty and hope of the Christian prayer. The effect is like a double exposure on film: the confusion and anguish of the speaker, mouthing fragments of a nursery rhyme, are superimposed upon the 'peace which passeth all understanding' of Christian devotion. The allusions are ironic, for serenity is incongruously suggested amidst great suffering and deprivation.

AMBIGUITY The expression of an idea in such a way that more than one meaning may be attributed to it. Although in straightforward exposition this can give rise to undesirable confusion, its deliberate use in literature adds a rich complexity. Poets in particular use words to suggest two or more equally suitable senses in a given context, or to convey a basic meaning accompanied by a variety of overtones. The last two lines of 'Fern Hill' (p. 1) by Dylan Thomas

Time held me green and dying
Though I sang in my chains like the sea.

suggest simultaneously the ideas of youth and decay, freedom and subjection to inexorable laws, enjoyment of new experiences and decline into death.

AMPHIBRACH A foot having one unaccented, one accented, and one unaccented syllable (e.g. stăccátŏ). For a fuller discussion of metre, see RHYTHM (p. 503).

ANAPAEST A foot having two unaccented syllables and one accented (e.g. ă sŭrpríse). For a fuller discussion of metre, see RHYTHM (p. 503).

ANTITHESIS Two adjoining phrases, clauses, or sentences of more or less parallel grammatical structure but of contrasting meaning are said to be in antithesis. The device is often used in couplets, with antithesis occurring either between lines or halves of a line. Pope used it with virtuosity:

Who but must laugh, if such a man there be?
Who would not weep, if Atticus were he?

APOSTROPHE A direct greeting or appeal to a person, usually not present, or to an object or an abstraction, usually personified. The device suggests the close involvement of the poet with the subject apostrophized.

In 'Ode on a Grecian Urn' (p. 189) Keats apostrophizes the urn as 'Thou still unravish'd bride of quietness'.

In the invocation to *Paradise Lost* Milton addresses the heavenly muse:

O Spirit, that dost prefer
Before all temples th' upright heart and pure,
Instruct me.

ARCHETYPE Literally, the original model from which a pattern is formed. The term has been used by many literary critics in the twentieth century to describe any image, plot, or character type which appears and reappears in many forms, particularly in religion, mythology, or literature.

The word was originally adopted in Carl Jung's depth psychology to describe the images which, he believed, are found in the 'collective unconscious' which is common to all men. Such images recur continually, he argued, in the thoughts and dreams of civilized men no less than in the rituals of the savage, generating powerful responses which well up from beneath a person's rational nature. Hence they appear to be one of the fundamental forms, or 'primordial images' through which the unconscious expresses itself.

The work of many writers generates these archetypal responses. A typical example of an archetypal image is the cycle of day and night, the seasons, life and death; of an archetypal character, the hero-saviour; of an archetypal plot, the purifying journey.

ASSONANCE See SOUND (p. 514).

BALLAD The *traditional ballad* is a simple narrative poem composed to be sung. As early as the eleventh or twelfth century, travelling minstrels in Europe were composing and singing stories of romance and tragedy. By the fifteenth century, such tales were being composed in increasing numbers for enthusiastic audiences of people who had a taste for violent tales of love and revenge, tales of war and treachery often described with grimly realistic detail, and tales of the supernatural. Also popular were riddles, and stories of humorous escapades and of practical jokes.

Although some of these ancient ballads became fixed in print over the succeeding centuries, many continued to be passed on from generation to generation by word of mouth and in various dialects. Thus, different versions of ballads exist because of the changes which were inevitably made in the course of these repetitions. Some were collected and adapted by later enthusiasts, such as Sir Walter Scott.

The ancient ballads are simple narratives, fraught with strong emotions or crude humour. Stark imagery, homely detail, alliteration, direct speech, and sudden transitions from one idea, event, or setting to the next make them fast-moving, powerful poems. Frequently so many details have been omitted that the ballad begins near the climax of the plot. Lines and phrases are repeated, often with slight variations.

The usual *ballad stanza* consists of four lines: the first and third lines are in iambic tetrameter, occasionally rhyming, and the second and fourth in iambic trimeter, usually rhyming.

Starting in the eighteenth century, many poets, admiring the simplicity of the traditional ballads, imitated them in a more polished and sophisticated style. Probably the most famous of these *literary ballads* are those of Sir Walter Scott and Wordsworth.

The influence of the ballad form is still strong in the popular songs of North America and the Caribbean. Some modern folk ballads, such as 'Jesse James' (p. 120) or 'John Henry' (p.122), preserve the strong story line and bare emotion of their predecessors, with colloquial speech and slang as the equivalent of dialect. Such literary ballads of the twentieth century as Auden's 'True Love' (p. 251) dispense with conventional phrases and develop only a few of the traditional ballad features, thereby emphasizing the mood and message of the poem rather than its story. By sophisticated means, the literary ballad achieves self-conscious simplicity and power.

BALLAD STANZA See the preceding note.

BATHOS From the Greek word meaning 'depth', bathos is the term used when an effect of elevation or intensity is destroyed by the writer's inept choice or ordering of words or images, giving the reader the sensation of plunging from the heights to the depths:

Ascend, my Muse, on Sorrow's sable plume,
Let the soft number meet the swelling sigh;

With laureated chaplets deck the tomb,
The blood-stained tomb where Smith and comfort lie.

THOMAS CHATTERTON, Elegy on Mr William Smith

Bathos may be used intentionally, of course, for its humorous or satirical effect:

On that great day of the final bark,
Rover (as usual) will beat the lark.

SARAH BINKS, Hymn to Rover (p. 182)

For a contrasting term, see CLIMAX (below).

BLANK VERSE A series of unrhymed lines of poetry, almost always in iambic pentameter. Although there is no conventional division into stanzas, the lines are often grouped in verse paragraphs to mark the development of thought. Elizabethan poets and dramatists used blank verse because of its resemblance to unrhymed classical poetry. It has also great advantages for reproducing normal English speech rhythms. Of all regular metrical patterns, it is the most flexible; in the hands of a master, it can be used to achieve effects of sustained power. See also RHYTHM (p. 503).

CADENCE See RHYTHM (p. 507).

CAESURA A pause in the metre of a verse line. See RHYTHM (p. 509).

CANTO One of the major sections or divisions of a long poem. Dante's *Divine Comedy* is divided into 100 cantos.

CLIMAX The effect of fulfilment that may be achieved at the end of a series when its elements are arranged in a scale of ascending importance. The series may be one of words, images, ideas, incidents, emotional responses, rhythms. Consider the list of infinitives in the last line of 'Ulysses' (p. 145) and the accumulation of ideas in 'Love Turned to Hatred' (p. 206).

COMPARISON See IMAGERY (p. 484).

CONCEIT An ingenious or far-fetched comparison, in which subject[1]

[1] These terms are introduced in the section on comparison (p. 484).

and object[1] often have no apparent similarity. In the *Petrarchan conceit* the subject – frequently the poet's beloved – is compared at length to something more or less appropriate, such as a garden, a star, or a season of the year. See Shakespeare's sonnets XVIII (p. 54) and CXVI (p. 191), and Spenser's 'Shepheardes Lament' (p. 165). In the *metaphysical conceit* the comparison is apparently inappropriate; yet the startling, involved, and often wittily impudent analogies are justified in a successful conceit. See Donne's 'A Valediction Forbidding Mourning' (p. 254), and Herbert's 'Love' (p. 259) and 'Virtue' (p. 260).

CONNOTATION The *denotation* of a word is its specific meaning, independent of its emotional colouring or associations. The word 'cat', for instance, denotes a specific domestic animal.

The *connotation* of a word or phrase is the body of implications that it may carry, the unstated associations which it awakens in the mind. Such associations may be completely personal, or common to a number of people who speak the same language.

It is the writer's task to select a word which will evoke the response he is seeking, not only by its denotation, but by the connotations which it can convey. For example, 'He ran like a weasel' is an apt simile for speed, but it also connotes viciousness in the runner. The connotation might be appropriate if the poet were describing a thief in flight; in most cases, however, he would reject the comparison as evoking an inappropriate response.

CONSONANCE See SOUND (p. 514).

CONVENTION A device, style, or theme which has become familiar, and is, therefore, in spite of its apparent artificiality, recognized and accepted as an instrument of literary expression. To this extent, most of the techniques of language and versification in poetry may be said to be conventions. We accept the soliloquy, for instance, as a stylistic convention by means of which a dramatist can convey the thoughts of one of his characters. In the same way we accept, as a thematic convention, the pastoral with its idealized picture of country life. Thus any convention demands of the reader 'a willing suspension of disbelief'.

COUNTERPOINT See RHYTHM (p. 506).

COUPLET Two consecutive rhyming lines in the same metre. The couplet is a suitable unit for expressing one idea or image concisely, as in the conclusion of a Shakespearean sonnet. It is especially effective for epigrams:

I am His Highness' dog at Kew;
Pray tell me, sir, whose dog are you?

ALEXANDER POPE, Epigram

The *heroic couplet* expresses a self-contained thought in two rhyming lines of iambic pentameter. Relying also on end-stopped lines, parallel structure, and the caesura, Dryden, Pope, and other eighteenth-century poets achieved striking epigrammatic effects:

The hungry judges soon the sentence sign,
And wretches hang that jurymen may dine;

ALEXANDER POPE, *Rape of the Lock, Canto* III (p. 99)

DACTYL A foot having one accented syllable followed by two unaccented syllables (e.g. lázĭlў). For a fuller discussion of metre, see RHYTHM (p. 503).

DENOTATION See CONNOTATION (p. 477).

DIDACTIC POETRY Poetry written to persuade the reader of the rightness of some point of view, usually moral, religious, or political. A good poem can be thoroughly didactic (as in poem 127, p. 214), have a mildly didactic purpose (as poem 106, p. 176), or be apparently without didactic intent (as poem 92, p. 152). Most readers object to inferior didactic poetry, which disregards the artistic demands of the poem in the interest of moralizing.

DIMETER A verse line of two feet. For a fuller discussion of metre, see RHYTHM (p. 503).

DRAMATIC IRONY See IRONY (p. 491).

DRAMATIC MONOLOGUE A form of dramatic poetry in which a situation is presented through the medium of a sustained speech made by one character to a silent audience of one or more persons. The progressive revelation of the nature of the speaker, who may be either an historical or imaginary person, is the major source of interest. This focal character unmasks himself and his past unconsciously by his gestures and manner of speech, and by the implied reactions and comments of the person or persons with him.

The circumstances which bring together the speaker and his audience have an intrinsic interest and tension but they also provide an artistic framework, a setting, and a motivation for psychological analysis. In 'My Last Duchess' (p. 195), for example, Browning has chosen a meeting between the widowed Duke and an envoy sent to negotiate a new marriage. At the beginning of the poem the two men have just entered a gallery in the Duke's home. At the end of the poem they are leaving together.

The poet's beliefs are often implicit in the total situation and are revealed objectively. For example, in 'The Bishop Orders His Tomb' (p. 237) Browning's views on the Renaissance become quite evident, although nowhere in the poem is there an explicit statement made on the subject. The speaker's voice is not the direct voice of the poet.

Eliot's 'The Love Song of J. Alfred Prufrock' (p. 48) uses some of the techniques of the dramatic monologue: tension in the mind of a character, indications of a setting, of a companion, and of gesture. 'Look, Stranger' (p. 4) would not be considered a dramatic monologue: although there is one speaker, a listener, a setting, and an attitude to life, there is no set of circumstances providing dramatic tension; nor is there a revelation of the facets of the speaker's life as a source of major interest.

DRAMATIC POETRY Poetry which presents a situation involving tension or emotional conflict between characters. It employs dialogue extensively or exclusively and is frequently suitable for stage presentation. Creating one or more characters as voices distinct from his own, the poet reveals their nature by means of their individual responses. Such poetry may occur in a poetic drama such as *Murder in the Cathedral* (see p. 266), or it may be an independent poem such as the dramatic monologue 'My Last Duchess' (p. 195), which employs many of the same techniques of characterization and revelation as the drama. The excerpt from the *Book of Job* (p. 86) may be discussed in terms of dramatic poetry, since it represents the words of the Lord revealing His nature, rather than the direct comments of the poet upon the Divine nature.

ELEGY A poem of lament or of sober meditation. The subject is a mournful event (usually the death of a person), regret for the past, or pessimistic fears for the future. The poems of *In Memoriam* (p. 170) deal extensively with these themes. The diction and syntax of an elegy are highly stylized and the expression is grave and controlled rather than passionate. Conventions from the pastoral (p. 501) are sometimes used, as in Milton's *Lycidas*.

ELLIPSIS A figure of speech in which grammatically necessary words or phrases are omitted. The device can produce the effect of witty condensation:

Wife silk and satin,
Boy Greek and Latin,
And you'll soon be gazetted. (p. 228)

or of an energetic bypassing of the normal patterns of language. Hopkins used ellipsis for the latter purpose when he wrote: 'There lives the dearest freshness deep down things.'

END-STOPPED LINE A line of poetry which ends with a pause. See RHYTHM (p. 509).

ENGLISH SONNET See SONNET (p. 512).

ENJAMBEMENT The device of continuing the sense and cadence of one line of poetry into the next, without a pause between the two lines. See RHYTHM (p. 509).

EPIC A long narrative poem with a serious theme of national or universal significance, recounting heroic deeds of the past in a consistently dignified style.

The unifying theme emerges from the culture of a particular period, although the events dealt with may be mythical or historical. Embodying many of the ideals of their society, epic heroes, though fallible, perform deeds requiring great courage and superhuman strength.

Certain conventions are common to most epics. The poet generally opens by stating his theme and invoking a Muse to inspire him. He then plunges *in medias res* (into the middle of the action), allowing the necessary exposition to follow in later portions of the epic. Throughout the poem elements of the supernatural and divine intervention play an important part. The poet includes lists of warriors, ships, armies; puts long stylized speeches into the mouths of his main characters; and makes frequent use of the epic simile (p. 486). Frequently a recurring proper name is associated with a particular adjective. For example, in *The Odyssey* the name Ulysses is usually linked with an adjective meaning 'of many wiles'; such an adjective is often called a *Homeric epithet.*

Examples of the English epic are the Old English *Beowulf,* Spenser's *The Faerie Queene,* and Milton's *Paradise Lost.*

Mock Epic. In the mock epic or *mock heroic* poem the tone and conventions of the epic proper are applied to some trivial incident or theme; the poet's humorous or satirical purposes are served by the deliberately bathetic effect. An example of the mock epic is Pope's *Rape of the Lock* (p. 99); many characteristics of the form are to be found in *The Newspaper* (p. 44).

EPIC SIMILE See IMAGERY (p. 486).

EPIGRAM A brief, memorable, often witty poem. Pope's 'Epigram' (p. 97) is an example. The term has also come to denote a concise and memorable statement in prose: 'Cisterns contain: fountains overflow.' – Blake; 'A little sincerity is a dangerous thing, and a great deal of it is absolutely fatal.' – Wilde.

EXTENDED METAPHOR See IMAGERY (p. 487).

FABLE A brief tale, in prose or verse, which illustrates a moral. The moral is often explicitly stated at the end. In its usual form the fable satirizes some aspects of human nature by attributing them to animals; the slight shock of seeing human foibles in such a setting establishes the author's satirical point. Frost's 'Departmental' (p. 42) is an example.

FALLING FOOT A foot, such as the trochee or the dactyl, which begins with an accented syllable and ends with an unaccented. For a fuller discussion of metre, see RHYTHM (p. 503).

FEMININE ENDING The ending of a line in which the final syllable is unaccented. For a fuller discussion of metre, see RHYTHM (p. 503).

FEMININE RHYME A rhyme in which the final syllables are unaccented. The final accented syllable and all subsequent unaccented syllables must rhyme, as in 'showing – going'. For a fuller discussion of rhyme, see SOUND (p. 513).

FIGURES OF SPEECH A comprehensive term for certain technical devices used in poetry. The term includes various types of metaphorical language such as simile and metaphor (see pp. 485-487), personification (p. 503), metonymy (p. 494), and rhetorical devices such as oxymoron (p. 500), transferred epithet (p. 516), and hyperbole (p. 483).

FOOT See RHYTHM (p. 504).

FREE VERSE Free verse differs from more traditional verse in the methods it uses to establish the pattern for a poem. Without imposing a regular metre, pre-determined lengths for the lines, or a fixed form for each stanza, it develops its pattern of rhythm and cadence in response to the immediate needs of the poem. Its resources, therefore, are as variable as language itself. Free verse is difficult to use well, for it demands a knowledge of regular forms, sensitivity to word values, and a well-developed sense of rhythm from the poet who must, in effect, create a new form for each poem. Although free verse in English is as old as the poetry of the Authorized Version of the Bible, modern poets have seized on its unlimited possibilities for experimentation and complexity:

Green flows the river of Lethe–O
Long Lethe river
Where the fire was in the veins – and grass is growing
Over the fever –
The green grass growing . . . .

EDITH SITWELL, Green Flows the River of Lethe–O (p. 212)

HAIKU (or *hokku*) A Japanese word picture consisting of three unrhymed lines containing five, seven, and five syllables. Whether sombre or merry, it usually refers to a season of the year or to a time of day, and is built around a contrast. The poet presents the source of his inspiration and suggests the nature of his response, leaving the reader to complete his own realization of the moment evoked. (See 'The Apprentice Priestling', p. 272.)

The haiku evolved from the tanka, an earlier thirty-one syllable form of verse. (See pp. 347-348.)

HEROIC COUPLET Two rhyming lines of iambic pentameter which express a self-contained thought. For a fuller note on the COUPLET, see p. 478.

HEXAMETER A verse line of six feet. For a fuller discussion of metre, see RHYTHM (p. 503).

HOMERIC EPITHET See EPIC (p. 481).

HOMERIC SIMILE See IMAGERY (p. 486).

HYPERBOLE Extravagant exaggeration, usually for comic or dramatic effect. Marvell uses hyperbole to describe his lady in 'To His Coy Mistress' (p. 243).

IAMBIC PENTAMETER A verse line of five iambs. See also RHYTHM (p. 503) and BLANK VERSE (p. 476).

IAMBUS OR IAMB A foot having one unaccented syllable and one accented (e.g. tŏ bé). For a fuller discussion of metre, see RHYTHM (p. 503).

IMAGERY This section on imagery will probably be most helpful if read as a unit.

Image. A mental representation, in memory or in imagination, of some aspect of the external world. In the critical discussion of poetry, the term 'image' is often applied to a word or phrase which evokes such a mental representation. Such a word is concrete; it calls up a mental picture, sound, scent, taste, or any of a number of sensations. In Arnold's 'Dover Beach' (p. 211) the phrase 'the grating roar of pebbles' creates an aural, visual, and tactile image.

Imagery. The imagery of a poem is a collective term for the individual images it contains, as well as others it may suggest. 'Dover Beach' includes imagery of the sea and of music.

Comparison. Imagery can be used in two ways: *literally,* for straightforward description of the external world, and *figuratively,* for making the expression of something abstract, vague, or hackneyed as concrete and compelling as possible. A line from 'The Love Song of J. Alfred Prufrock' (p. 48) illustrates the difference in usage. Eliot speaks of 'The yellow fog that rubs its back upon the window-panes'. The first image, 'yellow fog', and the third, 'window-panes', are both used literally; they evoke details of the scene which Eliot is actually describing. The second image, 'rubs its back', is employed figuratively to make vivid the motion of the fog by comparing it to that of a cat. (It is interesting to note the shift in the corresponding figurative image in Eliot's next line, 'The yellow smoke that rubs its muzzle on the window-panes.')

The figurative use of images always occurs in comparisons.[1] Poetry, like good prose and vivid conversation, is so reliant upon

[1] Not to be confused with the simple comparison of degree as in 'He is *taller* than I am.'

comparisons that it is easy to overlook their importance, or even their presence. In fact, it is difficult to complete a sentence without reaching for comparisons with which to flesh out one's thought. The technical study of poetry at its most evocative is, to a great extent, the study of comparison.

There are two elements in every comparison: the *subject* of which the author is speaking and the *object* to which he compares it. (Subject and object are sometimes termed *tenor* and *vehicle* respectively.) A man might say, 'I'm as poor as a church mouse.' The subject of the comparison is the penniless speaker, the object is the underfed church mouse.

In this case the comparison is *explicit,* because the point of similarity, poverty, is openly stated. If the point of similarity or the object of comparison were no more than implied, the comparison would be *implicit.* The metaphor 'He was burning with rage' makes an implicit comparison between subject (a man) and object (a fire).

Simile. A simile is the most straightforward kind of comparison. By means of the words 'like' or 'as' it compares the subject to some object more familiar or more gripping: 'The Assyrian came down like the wolf on the fold.'

A simile often restricts the connotations (p. 477) of its object, selecting the one feature common to subject and object and underlining it. If a person says, 'This house is as cold as an igloo,' he is not suggesting that the house looks like an igloo, or that it will melt in warm weather. He is explicitly pointing out that coldness is the one relevant common feature. Hence the simile is most valuable for clinching a single, striking point about the subject, often with detachment or wit.

There is one instance in which it is difficult to distinguish between simile and metaphor. In some comparisons using the verb 'to be', it is possible to omit the words 'like' or 'as'. 'He was like a whirlwind' can readily be shortened to 'He was a whirlwind'. For practical purposes, it makes little difference whether the resulting comparison be considered an incomplete simile or a metaphor; technically speaking, however, it is a metaphor.

The *Homeric* or *Epic simile* is an elaborate form of simile in which the illustration is worked out in detail, for its own sake, so as to produce a picture complete in itself. The details are added for artistic and emotional effect, and must not be regarded as necessarily corresponding to features in the thing illustrated. In many epic similes the object is introduced by 'as when' or 'just as', and the subject by 'so' or 'thus'.

Clubs, Diamonds, Hearts, in wild disorder seen,
With throngs promiscuous strew the level green.
Thus *when dispersed a routed army runs,*
Of Asia's troops, and Afric's sable sons,
With like *confusion different nations fly,*
Of various habit, and of various dye;
The pierc'd battalions disunited fall,
In heaps on heaps; one fate o'erwhelms them all.

ALEXANDER POPE, *Rape of the Lock, Canto* III (p. 99)

Metaphor. A metaphor compares subject and object implicitly, without using 'like' or 'as'. Either the point of similarity is implied:

I think continually of those who were truly great.
Who, from the womb, remembered the soul's history
Through corridors of light *where* the hours are suns,

STEPHEN SPENDER, I Think Continually (p. 75)

or the object of the comparison is implied:

Tyger! Tyger! burning *bright*

WILLIAM BLAKE, The Tyger (p. 85)

In either case, the effect of the omission is twofold: it involves the reader more closely by leading him to complete the comparison in his own imagination; and it multiplies the connotations of the object.

Consider the metaphor, 'Tyger! Tyger! burning bright'. The

image of a tiger and the image of a burning fire are set side by side in our minds. As we find the readiest connection between the images (the bright colour found in both flames and the tiger's eyes and fur), a flash of insight links the two images. The comparison is etched into our minds, for we have, in a sense, participated in writing the poem. In 'Fern Hill' (p. 1) or in Shakespeare's sonnet, 'Like as the waves' (p. 77) a series of such flashes lights up the poem.

The other source of strength in a metaphor is its refusal to be confined to a single meaning. In Blake's poem the tiger is compared to a flame, 'burning bright', and we see the brightness of the beast in our mind's eye. But at once the word 'burning' suggests more than that; the tiger is not only bright as fire, but menacing as fire, untameable as fire. Blake has found a metaphor so telling that its connotations are as powerful as its primary meaning.

A metaphor, then, begins by insisting on one meaning and concludes by suggesting a great deal more. By making its comparison implicitly, it invites us to complete it for ourselves and so make it more fully our own. The more sensitive a reader is, the richer and more complex his responses will be.

Occasionally a poem is governed by a general metaphor, from which a succession of individual images takes its origin. For example, in Shakespeare's sonnet 'When to the sessions' (p. 76), four or five comparisons are derived from commerce, the object of the governing metaphor. This development of an image is often referred to as *extended metaphor*. Allegory, discussed more fully on p. 489, is a special kind of extended metaphor.

For a discussion of other forms of metaphor, see CONCEIT (p. 476), METONOMY (p. 494), and PERSONIFICATION (p. 503).

Symbol.[1] A symbol is the object of a comparison whose subject is implied but not explicitly defined. This represents a re-

[1] This note employs the terms introduced in the section on comparison (p. 484).

versal of the customary technique of comparison, in which the poet begins with the subject to be discussed and compares it to an object. In a symbol, however, the subject is left unstated, and the object is examined so closely that it comes to suggest a deeper meaning, or a number of deeper meanings, extending beyond its normal range of connotation. A classic example of such a symbol occurs in Blake's 'The Tyger' (p. 85).

There are some subjects which are difficult to discuss directly without sounding either vague or pretentious. Examples are plentiful in poetry about love, patriotism, or the meaning of life, where the poet has striven for profundity but achieved only triteness. A good poet may adopt a different strategy. Instead of trying to make explicit statements about his subject – the conflict of good and evil, for example – he may imagine a concrete object which suggests certain aspects of it. This object can implant a complex idea in the reader's imagination, leaving him to discover its meaning by probing for all the possible connotations. In such a case, the object has become a symbol.

In 'The Tyger', Blake suggests the energy, beauty, and destructiveness of his object – the tiger – so powerfully that the meaning of the image expands, and we begin to understand by it all the forces of evil, or of untamed energy, in the world. Our only approach to these larger meanings, however, is through the image of the tiger, which does not cease to be itself even while it participates in the greater meaning.

By presenting such a vivid physical image, Blake has created a symbol of compelling power, one which enables him to pose a highly metaphysical question in concrete terms. He is able to raise one of the ultimate problems of life by asking, 'Did He who made the Lamb make thee?' Paraphrased, the question may be reduced to such prose as 'How can God be responsible for both good and evil, or for both purity and daemonic energy?' In its symbolic terms, however, the question enters the reader's consciousness at a deeper level than that of rational formulation. (Blake does not, of course, attempt to give an explicit answer to the question. It is with the rich poetic statement of one of the mind's predicaments that he is concerned.)

A lesser poet might have tried to indicate what his symbol 'really means'. But a poet of Blake's genius simply lets the symbol stand, knowing that if we gaze at it and through it long enough, it will reveal infinite reaches opening out behind the literal import of the words.

There are two classes of symbols. One consists of conventional or traditional symbols, which are widely used and immediately understood. Over the centuries a body of traditional symbols has come into being, each of which has acquired great richness of suggestion. Among these are the rose, the star, the eagle, the mountain top, the journey, towers, the colour green. It is inaccurate to say that the star symbolizes man's aspirations alone, perfect beauty alone, or divine guidance alone; yet at various times poets have invested the star with each of these meanings. Like every other symbol, the star is limited to a single interpretation only when it is used mechanically.

The second class consists of private symbols, which have wholly personal meanings derived from the poet's own experience and beliefs. Often the poet succeeds in conveying the wealth of meaning and association which a private symbol has for him; Blake's depiction of the tiger is an example. Sometimes, however, a reader feels that the symbol has remained private even after it has been embodied in a poem; some readers respond in this way to symbols in 'Green Flows the River of Lethe—O' (p. 212) and 'The Hollow Men' (p. 133).

Allegory. A special form of extended metaphor in which abstract ideas are personified and presented in a narrative. Frequently the personifications represent virtues and vices and a journey provides the narrative thread. Thus the allegory moves on two levels of interest, one the superficial story, the other the allegorical revelation of truth. Bunyan's *Pilgrim's Progress,* Melville's *Moby Dick,* Faulkner's *A Fable,* Spenser's *Faerie Queene,* and Golding's *Lord of the Flies,* are all allegories.

Allegory was one of the favourite literary forms of medieval writers, who developed an elaborate system whereby the narrative operated at three levels of meaning other than the literal. Dante's *Divine Comedy* is grounded in this approach.

Allegory and symbolism are occasionally confused with each other. It is important to realize that the one-to-one correspondence of poetic details with elements in the larger scheme, which in a short symbolic poem might be the result of a certain mechanical clumsiness on the poet's part, is a legitimate and essential part of the allegorical method.

IMITATIVE HARMONY See SOUND (p. 515).

IMITATIVE RHYTHM See SOUND (p. 515).

INTERNAL RHYME Rhyme between the final word in a line and an earlier word in the line; in a wider usage, rhyme between any two words in a line. For a fuller discussion of rhyme, see SOUND (p. 513).

INVECTIVE A direct and often overstated denunciation of follies or vices. If handled with a degree of finesse, invective can become a liberating expression of anger for writer and reader alike (see poems 36, p. 57, and 64, p. 95); if the speaker appears heavy-handed or self-righteous, however, his words can degenerate into an irritating, ineffective tirade.

IRONY The presentation of a character, incident, or idea in such a way as to suggest two points of view at one and the same time. Irony may exist in the contrast between the words of a speaker and his actual attitude, between the understanding of a speaker and what observers know to be true, or between what is expected and what is realized in retrospect to have been true.

Dryden, for example, speaks of Zimri (p. 98) as:

A man so various that he seemed to be
Not one, but all mankind's epitome.

Such a description would normally imply a boundless admiration; yet Dryden is speaking ironically, and his words actually condemn Zimri as a pathetic dilettante. In 'I Had a Duck-Billed Platypus' (p. 179), there is an ironic divergence between the speaker's sprightly, matter-of-fact tone and the outlandish subject matter.

The irony of 'The Average' (p. 39) is apparent only in retrospect; the parents, intending to help their son, actually start him on the path to disaster. Irony of this type is inherent in the plots of many novels or plays, where it may achieve tragic stature.

Dramatic Irony. Dramatic irony occurs in a play when the audience perceives some aspect of a speech or situation of which the characters involved are unaware. In *Macbeth,* for example, Duncan speaks these words on his arrival at Cawdor:

> *This castle hath a pleasant seat; the air*
> *Nimbly and sweetly recommends itself*
> *Unto our gentle senses.*

The dramatic irony is intense, for the audience knows that the castle will be the scene of Duncan's murder.

Modernist Irony. Poets of the modernist movement rely heavily on irony to present their disillusionment with society or their concern with the burden of the isolated individual. They may use allusion (p. 471) or juxtaposition (p. 492) to supply a second point of view, often setting the present against the great achievements of the past.

Modernist irony need not be on a grand scale, however. 'Carol' (p. 132) is an ironic lyric in which the double point of view gives the poem its wry flavour: the poetic tradition to which it alludes is contrasted with the misadventures of the metre and rhyme.

Like much of contemporary literature, 'Carol' offers an unheroic view of the speaker. This is a further development of irony, in which it begins to undercut itself. The poetess is like the lady in a medieval love song; she is also like a worn-out Christmas tree ornament. The modernist poet does not merely see from two points of view what lies outside himself; he has begun to see himself in the same double perspective. The effect is the self-deprecation typical of modernist irony.

JUXTAPOSITION The term 'juxtaposition' has been adopted by some critics to describe the device of placing side by side, without comment, elements which would not normally be associated. These may be words, sentences, images, ideas, or quotations; in every case, the elements which have been juxtaposed on the page are to be united by an act of the reader's imagination.

In 'My Last Duchess' (p. 195) the Duke refers to his late wife and her portrait in these words:

I gave commands;
Then all smiles stopped together. There she stands
As if alive.

It is obvious that there is a gap between the first sentence, in which the Duke speaks of his late wife as a person, and the second, where he refers to her as if she were a possession. With ordinary sensitivity, the Duke would have been unable to make such an abrupt transition; Browning uses the juxtaposition to suggest his inhumanity.

Modernist Juxtaposition. As the device appears in most English poetry, it is not too difficult to perceive the context within which the juxtaposed elements are relevant to one another. About the time of the First World War, however, Ezra Pound and T. S. Eliot began to explore a more extreme technique, under the influence of French and Chinese[1] poetry. In modernist juxtaposition the elements tend to be juxtaposed with a greater starkness than previously and are frequently, though not always, drawn from widely separated contexts.

A justly famous example of this starkness is Pound's brilliant poem, 'In a Station of the Metro'. It began as a thirty-line description of several girls glimpsed in a Paris subway station. In the

---

[1] In the Chinese *ideogram* a number of calligraphic symbols are juxtaposed to form a more elaborate symbol, and can thus communicate a complex idea without blurring the relations between the parts of the idea.

final version the two most important images are juxtaposed—and that is the poem:

> *The apparition of these faces in the crowd;*
> *Petals on a wet, black bough.*

The conclusion of 'The Hollow Men' (p. 135) illustrates the distance which can exist between juxtaposed elements. Fragments of nursery rhyme, philosophic exposition, and the Lord's Prayer are placed side by side to convey the complex state of mind in which the speaker finds himself. For a fuller discussion of these lines, see p. 472.

When used responsibly, the technique of juxtaposition makes possible a subtle and exciting form of poetic communication. The influence of the technique can be traced in the work of such poets as Archibald MacLeish (see p. 128) and Theodore Roethke (see p. 16).

LYRIC The word 'lyric' is derived from a Greek term which referred to poetry accompanied by the music of the lyre. The phrase 'lyric poetry' is sometimes used loosely to apply to most if not all short poems, including sonnets, songs, odes, triolets, as well as poems without a conventional form. It is probably more useful, however, to restrict the meaning of the term to a short poem, whether regular or irregular in form, distinguished by its intense personal feeling and unified by the poet's consistent response to an incident or idea. Such a lyric frequently exhibits a graceful, fluid rhythm and an evocative pattern of sound.

Lyrics are sometimes classified by their approach to the subject. The *descriptive lyric,* the most objective of the lyrical forms, describes some natural object or some event without stressing the poet's reaction to it. Sir Charles Roberts' 'The Mowing' (p. 164) is an example.

The *reflective* or *meditative lyric* often starts from some concrete object or situation, moves through the poet's immediate reactions, and attains a conviction or attitude of more universal application. The poems from *In Memoriam* (p. 170) are among the many examples in this book.

MASCULINE ENDING The ending of a line in which the final syllable is accented. For a fuller discussion of metre, see RHYTHM (p. 503).

MASCULINE RHYME A rhyme in which the final or only syllables are accented (e.g. ago – show). For a fuller discussion of rhyme, see SOUND (p. 513).

METAPHOR See IMAGERY (p. 486).

METAPHORICAL LANGUAGE A comprehensive term applied to all the figures of speech in which one idea is presented in terms of another; for example, simile, metaphor, metonymy. See IMAGERY (p. 484).

METAPHYSICAL POETRY A term used to describe the work of the seventeenth-century poets, led by John Donne, who were in revolt against the conventions of Elizabethan poetry. The attempt of these writers to express directly their perception of life as complex and extreme resulted in poetry of intellectual vigour and subtlety, often characterized by daring exploration rather than assurance. They used deliberately unromantic language and drew their imagery from commonplace sources or from the world of science that was opening up to them. Great use was made of the metaphysical conceit (p. 477), with its emphasis on the quality of mind which finds similarities where others perceive only differences. At its best, metaphysical poetry reproduces the direct apprehension of life by a passionate intellect; at less than its best, however, it can deteriorate into a laboured exercise in cleverness.

METONYMY A special kind of metaphor in which a sign is substituted for the thing signified (The *pen* is mightier than the *sword*); a container for the thing contained (The *kettle* is boiling); a cause for an effect ('When I consider how my *light* is spent'). Occasionally the reverse procedure is followed, as in the reference to reading Shakespeare rather than reading the plays of Shakespeare.

Synechdoche. Synechdoche is a form of metonymy in which the significant part is used for the whole, or a genus for a species. Thus sailors are often referred to as 'hands'.

The recent tendency is to allow the term metonymy to assume the function of both terms.

METRE See RHYTHM (p. 505).

METRICAL VERSE See RHYTHM (p. 504).

MILTONIC SONNET See SONNET (p. 513).

MOCK EPIC, MOCK HEROIC See EPIC (p. 481).

MODERNIST ALLUSION, MODERNIST IRONY, MODERNIST JUXTAPOSITION See ALLUSION (p. 471), IRONY (p. 490), JUXTAPOSITION (p. 492).

MODERNIST POETRY A term adopted by some critics to designate much of the poetry written between 1915 and the present. Like 'Elizabethan' or 'Romantic', it is a useful label with which to identify literature of a given period which exhibits certain general characteristics. The term is not synonymous with 'modern'.

Robert Graves' essay (p. 335) is a helpful analysis of a modernist poem. Further discussion may be found in the historical note below, and in the notes on JUXTAPOSITION (p. 492), ALLUSION (p. 471), and IRONY (p. 490).

The Modernist Revolution. The writing of poetry neither improves nor deteriorates with the passage of time; it changes. New habits of speech and thought develop in poetry in the same way as they do in society. But because accepted forms of poetic expression can become stiff and conventionalized, altering them often involves a major revolution.

From one point of view, the history of literature is the history of these successive revolutions. A particular vision of the world and way of expressing it is developed. It gradually loses its hold on men's imaginations, however, and after a great deal of controversy is replaced by a new, more satisfying poetic mode.

Despite initial reaction against it the new mode develops until it too wanes and must be replaced. After any of the half-dozen major revolutions in English writing, poets have invariably gone on to produce triumphs and failures comparable to those of their predecessors.

Sir Philip Sidney and John Donne wrote only thirty years apart; but it is clear, from the following passages, that the poetic revolution from 'Elizabethan' to 'Metaphysical' had taken place in the meantime.

When nature made her chief work, Stella's eyes,
In colour black why wrapt she beams so bright?
Would she in beamy black, like painter wise,
Frame daintiest lustre, mix'd of shades and light?
Or did she else that sober hue devise,
In object best to knit and strength our sight,
Lest, if no evil these brave gleams did disguise,
They, sunlike, should more dazzle than delight?

Astrophel and Stella, VII (c. 1582)

Our two souls therefore, which are one,
Though I must go, endure not yet
A breach, but an expansion,
Like gold to airy thinness beat.

If they be two, they are two so
As stiff twin compasses are two;
Thy soul, the fixed foot, makes no show
To move, but doth, if th' other do.

A Valediction Forbidding Mourning (c. 1612)

Many people were shocked by Donne's innovations. They considered that Sidney's rich, sonorous treatment of conventional Elizabethan subject matter was the only legitimate way to write poetry, and they could point to the achievements of Spenser, Marlowe, and Shakespeare in confirmation. It was easy to scoff at the deliberately unromantic style of Donne, with its complex scientific imagery and far-fetched comparisons.

Others, to whom the metaphysical revolution seemed justified, spoke of the thousands of worthless sonnets writen in the Elizabethan style during the 1590s. The older resources of feeling and imagination had been exhausted, they argued; valid poetry must speak with the new sensibility of seventeenth-century man. Today we can see that neither approach was intrinsically better, although a change of some sort was inevitable.

Obviously not all poets in a revolutionary period adopt the new style. A solid core of writers continues to develop within the tradition which the rebels reject. Hence we recognize the worth of both John Donne and the translators of the Authorized Version of the Bible, who worked in such different modes in the early seventeenth century.

Another such revolution can be dated from 1798, the year in which Wordsworth and Coleridge published their *Lyrical Ballads.* Wordsworth in particular was anxious to re-evaluate eighteenth-century diction and sensibility, which he considered painfully artificial. The opening lines of Collins' 'Ode to Evening' illustrate this style.

> *If ought of oaten stop, or pastoral song,*
> *May hope, chaste Eve, to soothe thy modest ear,*
> *Like thy own solemn springs,*
> *Thy springs, and dying gales,*
> *O Nymph reserv'd, while now the bright-hair'd sun*
> *Sits in yon western tent, whose cloudy skirts,*
> *With brede ethereal wove,*
> *O'erhang his wavy bed.*
>
> (Before 1747)

Readers who considered Collins' style the only proper voice for poetry must have been horrified by Wordsworth's drastic simplification. One of the most bitterly attacked of his early poems was 'The Idiot Boy', which treated the same subject in these words:

'Tis eight o'clock, — a clear March night,
The moon is up, — the sky is blue,
The owlet, in the moonlight air,
Shouts from nobody knows where;
He lengthens out his lonely shout,
Halloo! halloo! a long halloo!

(1798)

Most of Wordsworth's early readers did not understand how he could claim this as poetry. But while no one would defend all Wordsworth's experiments — including, possibly, 'The Idiot Boy' — as successful, they in fact became the foundation of his own superb achievement and of much subsequent poetry. Indeed the revolutionary techniques of the romantics came to tyrannize over nineteenth-century poetry.

The 'modernist' revolution, the most recent poetic upheaval, began in France and spread across most of Europe and North America; in England it occurred roughly between 1914 and 1930. Like earlier revolutions, it seemed to many people at the time to signal the end of real poetry. And like its predecessors, it produced volumes of would-be poetry and a small proportion of magnificent work. One valid reason for making a special study of the modernist revolution is that, even after forty years, some of its techniques and ways of thought have not been assimilated.

After the First World War, the optimistic world-view enshrined in popular thought seemed to be passing away. Einstein was challenging older scientific concepts with his theory of relativity. Freud's research in psychology led some people to distrust the traditional views of human nature. After the brutality of the war, many young writers grew bitterly disillusioned with society.

In England the most adventurous poetic rebels were led by two American expatriates, Ezra Pound and T. S. Eliot. With cherished convictions and ways of life eroding on all sides, they set themselves a Herculean task: to reappraise the traditions and values of Western civilization. They would take stock of contemporary society in Europe and North America, presenting their analysis in a poetry of radical technique.

In 1922 Eliot published *The Waste Land,* a prolonged reverie over the decline of Western civilization in which an intense personal despair rode just below the surface. The poem was an instantaneous scandal, for its philosophy grated on open nerve-ends while its technique was so revolutionary that Eliot was accused of playing an elaborate joke. Both he and Pound continued to write, however, and their 'modernist' techniques were taken up by other young poets.

Their revolution had been reinforced when the poetry of Gerard Manley Hopkins was finally published in 1918. Hopkins had died forty years earlier, and his writing survived only in the manuscripts which he entrusted to the poet Robert Bridges. Hopkins could never have been appreciated in his own time, for the daring of his language and metaphors was the exact opposite of current fashion. After the war, however, his innovations became another major source of power for young poets.

We can now see that the course of English poetry was changed once again. Without too great a simplification we can distinguish two streams of poetry written since the twenties, the division being largely one of technique. Neither is more 'correct' than the other; in each it is possible to write excellent poetry, or pretentious and incompetent poetry.

Poets of one group use the more traditional methods which Pound and Eliot rejected. Robert Frost and Walter de la Mare are outstanding examples. Poets of the other group have taken up the modernist innovations, adding to them, modifying them, or using them in poetry quite different from Hopkins' or Eliot's. W. B. Yeats and E. E. Cummings, for example, both profited immensely from the modernist revolution.

A brief discussion of typical modernist innovations can be found under ALLUSION (p. 471), IRONY (p. 490), and JUXTAPOSITION (p. 492).

MONOMETER A rare verse line of only one foot. For a fuller discussion of metre, see RHYTHM (p. 503).

NARRATIVE POETRY Poetry which is primarily concerned with the relating of events and experiences rather than with the dramatic interplay of character or the poet's individual response.

NEAR-RHYME See SOUND (p. 514).

OBJECT See IMAGERY (p. 485).

OCTAVE That part of a sonnet consisting of the first eight lines. See SONNET (p. 511).

ODE An elaborate lyric which celebrates a serious theme. The original Greek ode developed by Pindar followed a strict form. In English literature, however, the term is used more loosely to describe any poem, often inspired by an important occasion, expressing lofty ideas and exalted feelings. Some conventions of the original form may be retained. Keats' 'Ode on a Grecian Urn' (p. 189), and Shelley's 'Ode to the West Wind' (p. 26) are well-known examples of the English ode.

ONOMATOPOEIA See SOUND (p. 514).

OTTAVA RIMA A stanza pattern having eight iambic pentameter lines rhyming *abababcc*. It has been credited to Boccaccio and used effectively by Spenser, Milton, Keats, and Byron. See 'The Isles of Greece' (p. 303).

OXYMORON A condensed form of PARADOX in which a writer combines two terms (usually noun and adjective, or verb and adverb) which are opposed in sense, but which in his usage have a legitimate meaning together because the shock value of the juxtaposition of opposites lends intensity to the idea. Thus in 'To a Skylark' (p. 185) Shelley wishes to speak 'harmonious madness' to the world.

PARADOX A statement that at first sight appears to be self-contradictory, but on further examination proves to be justified. For example, John Donne, in his poem 'Death' (p. 257), reversing the point usually made, says that death is the 'slave to fate, chance, kings, and desperate men', and goes on to say 'death shall be no more! Death, thou shalt die!' By means of this the reader is more than usually involved in the thought and feelings of the poet. On a larger scale a paradox may be the awareness that a truth consists of two opposing elements. In 'Fern Hill' (p. 1) Thomas is expressing the paradox that as a young person is growing up he is moving closer to death. In 'The Tyger' (p. 85) Blake is exploring the paradox that innocence and daemonic energy both exist in a world created by God.

PARODY A satire on a literary style or a particular work of literature, which exaggerates its characteristic features, usually in dealing with an inappropriate subject. 'Hymn to Rover' (p. 182), for example, parodies inspirational poetry by applying its clichés to the death of a dog.

PASTORAL A highly conventionalized form of literary expression, usually in poetry, which deals with life in an idealized rural setting.

Whenever men find themselves living in a complicated or artificial society, particularly in a great, impersonal city, or even in the countryside, they exhibit what might be called the pastoral impulse – a longing for a gentle country setting in which they feel they could be more fully themselves. Feeling this, they may create the appropriate setting in pastoral literature. In fact, a coherent pastoral tradition extends from the poetry of Greece and Rome to that of the Renaissance and the seventeenth century.

In expressing the pastoral impulse, such classical poets as Theocritus and Vergil evolved a series of conventions. The Greek poets' favourite pastoral landscape was Arcadia, a name which has become synonymous with rural peace and contentment. The heroes were graceful shepherds (hence 'pastoral', from the Latin *pastor,* shepherd), with few problems beyond making themselves sufficiently amiable to their charming companions. They danced, indulged in singing matches, serenaded their lovers, and played at being rustics in a serene landscape, with the livestock grazing at a discreet distance. No one supposes that life in the country was ever like that; but the pastoral poet is not speaking of real life. He is concerned to conjure up the innocence and simple dignity we feel we should ideally possess.

Such English writers as Spenser and Sidney wrote consciously within this pastoral tradition; their poetry and prose remained as highly stylized as that of their classical predecessors. Colin and Rosalind, Thyrsis and Philidda continued to act out their graceful pageant against an idyllic background. By the eighteenth century, however, many of the conventions were being gradually abandoned. Alexander Pope, in his four *Pastorals* of 1709, was the last writer to adhere to the traditional conventions. Later poets, such as Wordsworth and Dylan Thomas, re-express the pastoral impulse, making the hero a child in an idealized country setting.

The elaborate artifice of the pastoral can be better understood by reference to a contemporary parallel. In North America, the highly conventionalized mythology of the Golden West has been perpetuated, offering entry into a world where nature is primitive but not unmanageable, and where a person's identity is secured by his having a definite role and a simple code of right and wrong.

The pastoral can be enjoyed for its own sake, as a graceful fantasy. It has also been the means of posing certain searching questions about life and human nature. It is interesting to notice, in a given poem, whether the hero stays in his pastoral world, and whether the poet continues to believe in it as an ideal way of life.

Spenser's *The Shepheardes Calender* (see p. 165) falls within the formal pastoral tradition; Wordsworth's 'There Was a Boy' (p. 5) and Thomas's 'Fern Hill' (p. 1) illustrate later developments. There has been a long debate among poets as to whether the pastoral longing is honourable and realistic, or merely escapist, or some combination of the two. A part of that debate may be traced in poems 12, 13, and 14 (pp. 21-24).

PENTAMETER A verse line of five feet. For a fuller discussion of metre, see RHYTHM (below).

PERSONA See question (b) to poems 74, 75, 76, 77, and 78 (p. 383).

PERSONIFICATION In the metaphorical figure of speech known as personification the poet attributes human characteristics to an abstract idea or an inanimate object, often by depicting it as engaged in some typically human action: 'Alone sat Freedom on the heights'; 'Death lays his icy hand on kings.'

PETRARCHAN SONNET See SONNET (p. 512).

PORTMANTEAU WORD A composite word made up of parts of real words, and intended to convey, by an elaborate pun, a blend of the meanings of all the words that can be recognized in it. The technique was developed to its limit in *Finnegan's Wake* (see p. 31).

PROSODY The technical principles of poetry, including metre and rhythm, rhyme and other effects of sound, and stanza forms.

PUN A play on words of similar sound, in which one word is used with two or more different meanings. At present the device is generally used for humorous or witty effects; Crabbe, in 'The Newspaper' (p. 44), puns in this way on the word 'herald'. A pun can also occur in a serious context, as when, in 'A Hymn to God the Father' (p. 256), John Donne uses the word 'done' in two senses.

PYRRHIC A rare foot of two unstressed syllables (e.g. ĭn thĕ). For a fuller discussion of metre, see RHYTHM (below).

QUANTITATIVE VERSE See RHYTHM (p. 510).

QUATRAIN A stanza of four lines.

RHYME See SOUND (p. 513).

RHYTHM The ordered succession in time of stronger and weaker elements. From one point of view, rhythm and pattern are the modes in which we apprehend our experiences.

In literature, although prose does achieve rhythmic effects, we think of rhythm chiefly in respect to poetry. There, rhythm is established in particular by the more or less regular patterns of emphasis given to words in succession. On a larger scale, the rhythm of poetry is established by the syntax, by the grouping of words, the line lengths, the stanza form, even the combination of stanzas.

Metrical verse is by far the commonest form of rhythm in English poetry, and depends upon the emphasis given to stressed and unstressed syllables following one another. For other forms of rhythm, see the notes on accentual verse (p. 509), and on quantitative verse (p. 510).

The Foot. The basic unit of metrical rhythm is the foot, a group of stressed and unstressed syllables which recurs in accordance with a recognizable pattern.

The following feet have two syllables:—

An *iambus* (or iamb) has one unaccented and one accented syllable, e.g., tŏ bé. This is the commonest foot in English poetry.

A *trochee* has one accented and one unaccented syllable, e.g., lázy̆. It creates a sing-song effect when used as a steady rhythm, and is used more frequently as a variant, particularly as a strong opening foot in an iambic line.

A *spondee* has two accented syllables, e.g., fát mén. It is used in English only as a variant in order to add emphasis or to slow the pace.

A *pyrrhic*, which is seldom used in English poetry, has two unaccented syllables, e.g. ĭn thĕ.

The following feet have three syllables:—

An *anapaest* has two unaccented and one accented syllable, e.g., ă sŭrpríse. The preponderance of unaccented syllables tends to lighten the line.

A *dactyl* has one accented and two unaccented syllables, e.g., lázĭly̆. This is generally used as a variant foot.

An *amphibrach* has one unaccented, one accented, and one unaccented syllable, e.g., stăccátŏ. Only a few poets have used this foot successfully other than as a variant.

The term *rising foot* is applied to a foot in which stress falls on the final syllable (tŏ bé) and the term *falling foot* to one in which the stress comes at the beginning (bé̆ing).

If the final foot of a line is rising, as in

The hills and leafless forests slow/lў yíeld,

the ending is termed *masculine*. An ending with an unstressed final syllable is termed *feminine*. The latter can be used to create an effect of hesitation, or of pensive brooding.

Metre. The metre of a line is determined by the number and nature of its feet. The following terms are used to indicate the number of feet in each line:

monometer – one foot	*tetrameter* – four feet
dimeter – two feet	*pentameter* – five feet
trimeter – three feet	*hexameter* – six feet

A second term is added to describe the basic foot in the line. Thus, a line of three trochees is a trochaic trimeter; a line of six iambs is an iambic hexameter. Successive lines are seldom completely regular, however; indeed the rhythm of a poem may be so varied that its metre is not immediately apparent.

Scansion. In scansion, which is the identification of the metre of a poem, the syllables which are stressed in speech are marked with an oblique stroke (ictus):

The hílls and léafless fórests slówly yíeld.

The remaining syllables are marked as unstressed or weak:

Thĕ hílls ănd léaflĕss fórĕsts slówlў yíeld.

The line is then marked off into its component feet. Normally a foot has as its nucleus one stressed syllable:

Thĕ hílls / ănd léaf/lĕss fór/ĕsts slów/lў yíeld.

As the line contains five iambs, it is in iambic pentameter. It is the predominant foot which establishes the metre of a line, although any other foot may be interposed as a variant.

It is fortunate that the attempt to write completely regular English verse will result in something deadly to read. Each line of such doggerel will jog along at the same pace. That a good poem can vary, within a single metre, from limpid grace to rushing energy, is due to two other essential features of the rhythm of natural speech: syncopation (sometimes known as counterpoint) and cadence.

Syncopation. Syncopation or *counterpoint* can be readily understood if we examine a well-known line from *Hamlet.* If the line were mechanically scanned as iambic pentameter, we would have this:

Tŏ bé/ ŏr nót/ tŏ bé/ thăt ís/ thĕ quést/iŏn

Speaking the line with these stresses we would hear:

To BE *or* NOT *to* BE *that* IS *the* QUEST*ion*

Obviously this makes nonsense of the line. While the precise intonation of the line might vary, we would probably speak it rather like this:

To BE *or* NOT *to be,* THAT *is the* QUESTION

Notice what has taken place. What would have been the fourth metrical iamb, 'thăt ís', is spoken as a trochee, 'THAT *is*'. In other words, a trochee in speech stress has been counterpointed or mounted upon an iambic metre. Similarly, in the third foot of the line a pyrrhic has been mounted upon the iambic metre. Other instances of syncopation might show an anapaest counterpointed upon a dactylic metre, or a spondee upon a trochaic metre. This need to pronounce the words in a poem in the same way as we do in conversation, even if this breaks the regularity of the metre, can be used by a skilful poet to create a pleasurable tension between the expected and actual speech stresses. The effect is like syncopation in music.

A second kind of syncopation can occur over an entire line or over a group of lines. The line from *Hamlet,* as iambic pentameter, would have been given five metrical stresses. As a spoken line, it receives only four speech stresses. (*'To* BE *or* NOT *to be,* THAT *is the* QUEST*ion'*). This tendency to set four speech stresses over a line in which five are expected is common in English poetry. It is difficult to account for, although many critics link it with the Anglo-Saxon verse line, which always contained four heavily-accented speech stresses.

Cadence. Another way to create interesting rhythms is by means of cadence. Cadence is the product of three elements: the natural grouping of words, the length and syntax of the sentence unit, and the speed of the line.

If we think again of Hamlet's speech, we find that yet another factor, the natural *grouping* of the words, affects our spoken version of it. As it stands, the line sounds approximately like this:

To BE *or* NOT *to be,* THAT *is the* QUEST*ion.*

But when Hamlet speaks the line he does not simply trundle the words out one after another. He pauses over some and clusters others together. He groups the words into their natural phrases. The line might sound like this:

To BE / *or* NOT *to be,* // THAT / *is the* QUEST*ion.*

The words in every piece of poetry can be grouped in this way. Skilful grouping by the poet will add dignity to the meaning of the words, give them lightness and crispness, even create an ironic effect by giving the opposite impression to what the words intend.

On a larger scale than the grouping of phrases, cadence is determined by the nature of each *sentence unit* in a poem. Consider a passage from *Paradise Lost,* in which Milton describes the fall of Satan from heaven:

Him the Almighty Power
Hurl'd headlong flaming from th' Ethereal Skie
With hideous ruin and combustion down
To bottomless perdition, there to dwell

In Adamantine Chains and penal Fire,
Who durst defie th' Omnipotent to Arms.

These six lines form a single sentence which flows on through normal line endings. The effect of thundering power is achieved not only by the length of the sentence, but also by the welding together of its syntactical parts: the six lines form an indivisible whole. The length and structure of such a mighty periodic sentence convey in themselves the grandeur of Milton's theme.

Here is an excerpt from 'A Field of Light' (p. 16) by Theodore Roethke.

The dirt left my hand, visitor.
I could feel the mare's nose.
A path went walking.
The sun glittered on a small rapids.
Some morning thing came, beating its wings.
The great elm filled with birds.

These six lines contain six sentences. Each is short, and each follows the simple sequence of subject, verb, object. The cadence, as a result, spurts forward, pauses, and then bursts ahead again; the effect is of breathless wonder. Roethke has shaped his sentence units as deliberately as Milton did. They are entirely different, however, because they have such a different function.

One of Alexander Pope's technical gifts was the ability to increase or retard the *speed* of a line at will. In the *Essay on Criticism,* for example, he declared that the speed of a line should reinforce the sense, and made his own lines demonstrate what he meant. To discover what Pope has done, read this passage aloud.

When Ajax strives some rock's vast weight to throw,
The line too labours, and the words move slow:
Not so, when swift Camilla scours the plain,
Flies o'er th'unbending corn, and skims along the main.

In comparing the first and second couplets, which move at such different rates of speed, notice these points: the relation between the last letter of one word and the first letter of the next; the predominant vowel sounds; the predominant foot; the placing of monosyllables and polysyllables. Notice also the additional problem Pope set himself in the fourth line, which is nevertheless the swiftest.

Another factor in the speed of a line is the position of the *caesura*, or pause. In the first two lines quoted, Pope has used caesuras to retard the movement.

Pauses also occur at the conclusion of every line in the passage, creating *end-stopped* lines. Most poets rely at times on *enjambement*, the continuation of the sense and cadence of one line into the next, so that the reader does not pause between the two lines. The result is termed a *run-on* line. The massively proportioned sentence from *Paradise Lost* (p. 507) owes much of its power to the four run-on lines which buttress it.

Accentual Verse. The only alternative to metrical rhythm which has been adopted to any extent in English poetry is accentual rhythm, the rhythm of Anglo-Saxon poetry. It is based on the number of stressed syllables in each line. The number of unstressed syllables and the proximity of the stressed syllables to each other may vary. Sometimes the rhythm is not readily apparent and the reader must study the effect contrived by the poet. Ezra Pound reinvigorated the tradition of accentual verse. In 'The Triumph of Bacchus' (p. 176), it is possible to give at least two different accentual readings to these lines:

Héavy víne on the óarshafts,
And, óut of nóthing, a bréathing,
hót bréath on my ánkles,
Béasts like shádows in gláss,
a fúrred táil upon nóthingness.

Héavy vine on the oarshafts,
And, óut of nothing, a breathing,

hót breath on my ankles,
Beásts like shadows in glass,
a fúrred tail upon nothingness.

Gerard Manley Hopkins developed a refinement of accentual rhythm which he termed *sprung rhythm*. The number of stresses in the line remains constant, and each foot begins with a stress; a foot may consist of a single stressed syllable or of a stressed syllable followed by one, two, or three unstressed syllables. The feet are thus monosyllabic, trochaic, dactylic, or are 'first paeons' (—⏑⏑⏑). (If the rhythm is considered to run on from the end of one line to the beginning of the next, the unstressed syllables at the beginning of a line complete the preceding foot.) Two strong stresses may be given the value of one, in which case they are marked by a symbol ⌐¬. Some unstressed syllables may be discounted; they are then called *hangers* or *out-riders* and are marked ‿. The symbol ″ indicates a 'great stress'. Here is the octave of 'Hurrahing in Harvest' (p. 163) showing Hopkins' own scansion[1] of the sprung rhythm:

Summer énds now; now, bá̋rbarous in beáuty, the stóoks aríse
Aróund: up abóve, what wínd-walks! what lóvely beháviour
Of sílk-sack clóuds! has wílder, wílful-wávier
Meál-drift móulded ever and mélted acróss skíes?
I wálk, I líft up, I lift úp heárt, éyes,
Down áll that glóry in the heávens to gleán our Sáviour;
And éyes, heárt, what lóoks, what líps yet gáve you a
Rá̋pturous love's gréeting of reáler, of róunder replíes?

Quantitative Verse. A second alternative to metrical rhythm is quantitative verse, derived from classical poetry. Quantitative

---

[1] As in W. H. Gardner, *Gerard Manley Hopkins*, II, pages 253-4. The words 'melted across skies' in the fourth line are marked *rallentando*.

rhythm is based on the length of time required to utter a syllable, long vowels and stressed syllables taking more time than short vowels and unstressed syllables. The various classical verse forms had a fixed arrangement of long and short syllables for each foot, but the English language, with its natural accentual stresses, does not lend itself to the set classical patterns.

Kingsley's 'Andromeda' is an example of quantitative verse:

Ōvĕr thĕ / sēa, pāst / Crēte, // ŏn thĕ / Sȳrĭăn / shōre tŏ thĕ / sōuthwārd,
Dwēlls ĭn thĕ / wēll-tīlled / lōwlănd, // ă / dārk-hāired / Āethĭŏp / pēoplĕ,
Skīlfŭl wĭth / nēedlĕ ănd / lōom, // ănd thĕ / ārts ŏf thĕ / dȳĕr ănd / cārvĕr,

RISING FOOT A foot, such as the iambus or the anapaest, which begins with an unaccented syllable and ends with an accented. For a fuller discussion of metre, see RHYTHM (p. 503).

RUN-ON LINE A line whose sense and cadence continue into the next without a pause. See RHYTHM (p. 509).

SATIRE Ridicule directed against a vice or folly in a contemporary person or institution offensive to the writer. It may range from gentle mockery to bitter attack. See 'The Unknown Citizen' (p. 40), and 'Zimri' (p. 98).

SCANSION See RHYTHM (p. 505).

SESTET That part of a sonnet composed of the final six lines. See SONNET (below).

SIMILE See IMAGERY (p. 485).

SLANT-RHYME See SOUND (p. 514).

SONNET In writing a sonnet, the poet sets himself the task of developing a theme or subject within a strict form, normally of fourteen iambic pentameter lines. Its concentration makes it ideal for meditations on love and death, for descriptions of nature and states of mind, for compliments, or for invective. The thought pattern of the sonnet follows the structure very closely, each division making its own distinct contribution. In the more formal sonnet, the end of a statement corresponds to the end of a division. Conceits and a reliance on metaphorical expression add richness to the content and style.

The *Italian* or *Petrarchan Sonnet.* In the fourteenth century, Petrarch, an Italian poet, made the form famous by writing a sequence of love sonnets. The Italian sonnet consists of an octave or octet (eight lines) which describes the subject or introduces a problem, and a sestet (six lines) which comments on or resolves it. Two quatrains, each rhyming *abba* constitute the octave. Ordinarily the first quatrain introduces the subject while the second one provides a more specific elaboration. Two tercets, rhyming in various ways, *cde cde* or *cdc dcd,* constitute the sestet. The first tercet is usually the link which provides a continuity within the form; the final tercet makes a climactic statement. The transition from octave to sestet is sometimes referred to as the *volta.*

The *Shakespearean, Elizabethan* or *English Sonnet.* English sonneteers contributed to the evolution of both theme and form. The Shakespearean sonnets, embracing a variety of moods and themes, were written exclusively in a form which consisted of three quatrains with independent rhymes, concluding with a rhyming couplet *(abab, cdcd, efef, gg).* The quatrains may provide three examples of the theme with the couplet providing a conclusion; or they may present three metaphorical statements of the theme with a couplet providing a final statement. The first quatrain may introduce the subject while the second and third both present a more detailed treatment. A pause before the couplet sets it off, to establish an epigrammatic quality or a touch of novelty. Later poets, such as Donne and Keats, used this version, although the Italian sonnet retained popularity. Donne extended the scope of the sonnet to include religious themes. The trend to greater freedom continued.

The *Spenserian Sonnet.* Spenser's *Amoretti,* a sequence of love sonnets, established an interlocking rhyme pattern of *abab, bcbc, cdcd, ee.* The Spenserian sonnet is a form midway between the restrictions of the Petrarchan and the greater liberty of the Shakespearean sonnets.

The *Miltonic Sonnet.* The Miltonic sonnet follows the basic Italian form, with one very important development: the thought of the octave often flows freely without pause into the sestet. Milton also made the sonnet powerful enough for passionate statements of political and moral opinion. Milton's 'On His Blindness' (p. 264) and Wordsworth's 'The World is too much with us' (p. 6) illustrate these developments.

Some poets have used the sonnet as a basis from which to develop a wide variety of structural patterns. In his 'Ode To The West Wind' (p. 26), for example, Shelley used fourteen-line units composed of four tercets and a final couplet. Keats, in his 'Ode On A Grecian Urn' (p. 189), used a stanza form which was a ten-line adaptation of the sonnet form – a quatrain followed by two tercets. Other poets may even substitute assonance for rhyme or dispense with rhyme completely.

SOUND A number of the more important techniques involving the use of sound in poetry are grouped below.

Rhyme (also *Rime*). Rhyme occurs when there is an identical sound in the monosyllables or final stressed syllables of two or more words, and in any unstressed syllables which may follow.

Shakespeare's sonnet 'Let me not to the marriage of true minds' (p. 191) contains the *masculine* rhyme 'mark – bark', in which the final syllables of the lines are stressed. 'Shaken – taken' is a *feminine* rhyme, in which both stressed and subsequent unstressed syllables have identical sounds. A *polysyllabic* rhyme can give a comic or lugubrious effect, as when in 'No Doctors Today, Thank You' (p. 281) Nash rhymes 'Wurlitzer – Berlitzer' and 'euphorian – Victorian'.

Internal Rhyme. Internal rhyme usually occurs between the final word of a line and an earlier word in the same line. In a wider usage, it may be said to occur between any two words in a line. The device is used by Poe:

Once upon a midnight dreary, as I pondered, weak and weary
The Raven

Assonance and Consonance. Assonance occurs when the vowels of two stressed syllables sound alike but not the consonants following these vowels, as 'seem – clear'. The term consonance is used when the vowels in the stressed syllables differ but the consonants (especially the final consonants) agree, as in 'dive – dove', 'find – fanned' and 'dog – gig'.

When modern poets use consonance at line endings it is called *near-* or *slant-rhyme.* Wilfred Owen in 'Strange Meeting' (p. 68) rhymes 'escaped – scooped', 'groaned – groined'; Dylan Thomas in 'And Death Shall Have No Dominion' (p. 302) uses the freer slant-rhyme 'moon–gone' and 'ears–seashores', which contains assonance between '*EA*rs' and 's*EA*', and partial consonance between 'ea*RS*' and 'seasho*RES*'.

Alliteration. Alliteration is the repetition of a word's first letter or sound at the beginning of a subsequent word or words. A wider use of the term includes alliteration between the first letters of stressed syllables, whether or not they occur at the beginning of a word. An example of the latter can be found in Hopkins' 'Hurrahing in Harvest' (p. 163):

Summer ends now; now, barbarous in beauty, the stooks arise.

Alliteration is often used when the poet wishes to create a strong association between words. The effect is both musical and unifying.

Onomatopoeia. Onomatopoeia occurs when the sound of a word suggests its meaning; e.g., 'hurly-burly', 'whisper', 'plop'.

Imitative Rhythm. Imitative rhythm is found in entire phrases or lines, where the cadence imitates the movement described.

> *I sprang to the stirrup, and Joris and he,*
> *I galloped, Dirk galloped, we galloped all three,*
>
> ROBERT BROWNING, How They Brought the Good News from Ghent to Aix

Imitative Harmony. Imitative harmony unites onomatopoeia and imitative rhythm so that sound and cadence together suggest the sense, as in Lawrence's 'Snake' (p. 12):

> *He reached down from a fissure in the earth-wall in the gloom*
> *And trailed his yellow-brown slackness soft-bellied down, over the edge of the stone trough*
> *And rested his throat upon the stone bottom,*
> *And where the water had dripped from the tap, in a small clearness,*
> *He sipped with his straight mouth,*
> *Softly drank through his straight gums, into his slack long body,*
> *Silently.*

SPEED See RHYTHM (p. 508).

SPENSERIAN SONNET See SONNET (p. 513).

SPONDEE A foot having two accented syllables (e.g., fát mén). For a fuller discussion of metre, see RHYTHM (p. 503).

SPRUNG RHYTHM See RHYTHM (p. 510).

STANZA A unit of verse lines with certain formal characteristics. The TERCET (p. 516) and the QUATRAIN (p. 503) are among the simpler stanza forms; the TRIOLET (p. 516) is one of the more complex.

SUBJECT See IMAGERY (p. 485).

SYLLABIC VERSE In syllabic verse each line contains a predetermined number of syllables; the rhythm is provided by the normal accentuation of speech. Corresponding lines in successive stanzas normally contain the same number of syllables. The form has been most fully developed by Marianne Moore.

SYMBOL See IMAGERY (p. 487).

SYNCOPATION See RHYTHM (p. 506).

SYNECHDOCHE See METONYMY (p. 495).

TERCET A stanza of three lines, usually rhyming.

TERZA RIMA A series of tercets, normally in iambic pentameter, with interlocking rhymes *aba, bcb, cdc....* The form lends itself to the development of a quickly moving series of little scenes. Dante uses it in *The Divine Comedy,* and Shelley in his 'Ode to the West Wind' (p. 26).

TETRAMETER A verse line of four feet. For a fuller discussion of meter, see RHYTHM (p. 503).

TRANSFERRED EPITHET An adjective or adverb which is transferred from the word it naturally modifies to another word, normally nearby:

> *And as I was* green *and carefree, famous among the barns*
> *About the* happy yard
>
> DYLAN THOMAS, Fern Hill

Here, the device conveys the child's happy confusion of sense impressions and subjective feelings. For the complete poem, see p. 1.

TRIMETER A verse line of three feet. For a fuller discussion of metre, see RHYTHM (p. 503).

TRIOLET A light, carefree poem of eight lines with two rhymes (rhyming *abaaabab*). The first line is repeated as the fourth and seventh, and the second is repeated as the eighth. See 'A Kiss' (p. 53) and 'Girl's-Eye View of Relatives' (p. 230).

TROCHEE A foot having one accented syllable and one unaccented (e.g. lázy̆). For a fuller discussion of metre, see RHYTHM (p. 503).

VERSE FORMS The forms which poems may take, in whole or in part. There are innumerable combinations of rhymes and line lengths, and varying lengths of stanza. Some of the best known verse forms are couplet, quatrain, sonnet, terza rima, triolet.

WIT The framing, in vivid and memorable language, of unexpected parallels, incongruous juxtapositions, and paradoxes. Wit relies, for its stylistic sparkle, upon balanced constructions, deft phrasing, and a knowing, often ironic, tone; it is frequently epigrammatic. Its tendency is less to reveal deep truths about a subject than to impress us with the play of an urbane and agile mind, one which is sometimes willing to be less than fair with the subject for the pleasure of setting it in an unexpected perspective. Varieties of wit can be appreciated in 'To His Coy Mistress' (p. 243), 'Zimri' (p. 98), and 'No Doctors Today, Thank You' (p. 281).

A Bibliography

CRITICISM

R. P. BLACKMUR: *Form and Value in Modern Poetry*; Doubleday and Company

*BROOKS & WARREN: *Understanding Poetry*; Holt, Rinehart and Winston.

GLAUCO CAMBON: *Recent American Poetry*; University of Minnesota Press.

*JOHN CIARDI: *How Does a Poem Mean?* part 3 of *Introduction to Literature*; Houghton Mifflin Company.

ELIZABETH DREW: *Poetry: A Modern Guide* and *Discovering Poetry*; W. W. Norton and Company.

*GILBERT HIGHET: *The Powers of Poetry*; Oxford University Press.

RANDALL JARRELL: *Poetry and the Age*; Vintage Books.

JACOB KORG: *An Introduction to Poetry*; Holt, Rinehart and Winston.

JOHN CLARK PRATT: *The Meaning of Modern Poetry*; Doubleday and Company.

JOHN PRESS: *The Chequer'd Shade*; Oxford University Press.

*JAMES M. REID and others: *Poetry: A Closer Look*; Harcourt, Brace and World.

*These books contain excellent analyses of individual poems.

GLOSSARIES

M. H. ABRAMS: *A Glossary of Literary Terms*; Holt, Rinehart and Winston.

SYLVAN BARNET and others: *A Dictionary of Literary Terms*; Little, Brown and Company.

BABETTE DEUTSCH: *Poetry Handbook: A Dictionary of Terms*; Grosset and Dunlap.

W. F. THRALL and others: *A Handbook to Literature*; Odyssey Press.

An Index of Subjects and Verse Forms

References are to the pages on which relevant poems appear; where more than one poem begins on the same page, the poem number is added in brackets. The listing is by no means exhaustive.

Chronological Index

The authors are arranged in the order of their dates of birth, and the references are to the pages on which their poems appear. Some anonymous pieces are included in roughly appropriate positions and indicated by means of their titles. See also the historical note on p. 495.

Index of Authors

THE POEM NUMBERS ARE GIVEN IN BRACKETS

INDEX OF AUTHORS

Index of Titles

Titles such as 'Sonnet' may be found under the first line of the poem. The poem numbers are given in brackets.

Index of First Lines

THE POEM NUMBERS ARE GIVEN IN BRACKETS